CL

D1078929

An inveterate traveller, **ALEXANDER STEWART** has hiked in many parts of the world. In the course of these trips he has authored or co-authored more than half a dozen guidebooks including Trailblazer's *New Zealand – The Great Walks*; *Inca Trail, Cusco and Machu Picchu* and *The Walker's Haute Route*. When he isn't escaping the city he lives in London and works for Stanfords, the renowned map and travel specialist, wondering where to go next. He's also a freelance travel writer and photographer, contributing articles and pictures to various newspapers and magazines.

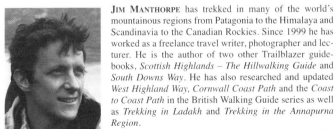

JIM MANTHORPE has trekked in many of the world's mountainous regions from Patagonia to the Himalaya and Scandinavia to the Canadian Rockies. Since 1999 he has worked as a freelance travel writer, photographer and lecturer. He is the author of two other Trailblazer guidebooks, *Scottish Highlands – The Hillwalking Guide* and *South Downs Way*. He has also researched and updated *West Highland Way, Cornwall Coast Path* and the *Coast to Coast Path* in the British Walking Guide series as well as *Trekking in Ladakh* and *Trekking in the Annapurna Region*.

Following stints at Stanfords in London and on *The Scotsman* newspaper in Edinburgh he is now living on the west coast of Scotland in Knoydart, accessible only by boat. When not writing, he works as a ranger. He can be contacted at 💻 www.jimmanthorpe.com.

Pembrokeshire Coast Path
First edition: 2004; this third edition: 2010

Publisher
Trailblazer Publications
The Old Manse, Tower Rd, Hindhead, Surrey, GU26 6SU, UK
Fax (+44) 01428-607571, info@trailblazer-guides.com
www.trailblazer-guides.com

British Library Cataloguing in Publication Data
A catalogue record for this book is available from the British Library

ISBN 978-1-905864-27-0

© **Trailblazer** 2004, 2007, 2010
Text and maps

Editor: Anna Jacomb-Hood
Proof-reading: Nicky Slade
Layout: Anna Jacomb-Hood
Illustrations: © Nick Hill (pp68-9); Rev CA Johns (p63)
Photographs (flora): C2 Row 1, middle, © Jane Thomas;
C3 Row 2, right, © Henry Stedman; all others © Bryn Thomas
All other photographs: © Alexander Stewart unless otherwise credited
Cartography: Nick Hill
Index: Anna Jacomb-Hood

The maps in this guide were prepared from out-of-Crown-
copyright Ordnance Survey maps amended and updated by Trailblazer.

Warning: coastal walking can be dangerous
Please read the notes on when to go (p24) and health and safety (pp54-7).
Every effort has been made by the author and publisher to ensure that the information
contained herein is as accurate and up to date as possible. However, they are unable
to accept responsibility for any inconvenience, loss or injury sustained by anyone
as a result of the advice and information given in this guide.

Printed on chlorine-free paper by
D2Print (☎ +65-6295 5598), Singapore

Pembrokeshire Coast Path

AMROTH TO CARDIGAN
planning, places to stay, places to eat,
includes 96 large-scale walking maps

JIM MANTHORPE

THIRD EDITION RESEARCHED AND UPDATED BY
ALEXANDER STEWART

TRAILBLAZER PUBLICATIONS

Acknowledgements

From Alex Stewart First off, thanks to the people along the Coast Path who assisted me with the research for this book. Particular mention goes to the Pembrokeshire Coast Path National Trail Officer, Dave MacLachlan, for his enduring passion for Pembrokeshire and his patience with my many queries. Thanks, too, go to Jim Manthorpe for producing such a great book to work on in the first place, and for hints and tips as to how best to enjoy the route. Thanks also to Katie for keeping me company along some of the stretches of the path, and for everything she does to support and encourage me closer to home – I am so very grateful. Thanks must also go to several readers, in particular to Arendo de Vries, Pauline Boekraad, Andrew Heath and Alan Groves for their emailed comments following the last edition. As ever I'm indebted to the team at Trailblazer: Anna Jacomb-Hood for her diligent and detailed editing to pull the book into shape as well as for indexing, Nick Hill for once again drawing the maps; also to Roderick Leslie for looking through the bird text. Lastly, a big thank you to Bryn Thomas for his continued support and for finally enabling me to explore what's on my own back doorstep, after years of heading further afield in search of adventure.

From Jim Manthorpe I'd like to thank Alex Stewart for such dedicated work on this edition of the Pembrokeshire Coast Path. Many thanks, as always, to Bryn Thomas for giving me so many wonderful opportunities to write and travel. Also at Trailblazer, many thanks to Anna Jacomb-Hood and Nick Hill for editing, mapping and indexing this edition. Finally, thank you to Mum, Dad, Sam, Amy and Jack for their unstinting encouragement and just for being there.

A request

The author and publisher have tried to ensure that this guide is as accurate and up to date as possible. However, things change even on these well-worn routes. If you notice any changes or omissions that should be included in the next edition of this guide, please email or write to Trailblazer (address on p2). You can also contact us via the Trailblazer website at 🖥 www.trailblazer-guides.com). Those persons making a significant contribution will be rewarded with a free copy of the next edition and an acknowledgement in the front of that edition.

Front co
long   h as this
en.

CONTENTS

Map key

♠	Where to stay	⊛	Internet	⊕	Bus station
○	Where to eat and drink	☂	Museum/gallery	☉	Bus stop
⚲	Campsite	✚	Church/cathedral	—☐—	Rail line & station
✉	Post Office	☎	Public telephone	⚓	Ferry
ⓔ	Bank/ATM	☒	Public toilet	⌷	Lighthouse/beacon
ⓘ	Tourist Information	☐	Building	P ⚑	Beach flags
▣	Library/bookstore	●	Other		Park
		CP	Car park	082	GPS waypoint

	Coast Path		Cattle grid		Cliff
	Other path		Bridge		Stream
	4x4 track		Hedge		River
	Tarmac road		Stone wall		Bog or marsh
	Steps		Water		Sand dunes
	Slope/steep slope		Sand/mudflats		Trees/woodland
	Stile and fence		Pebbly beach		Grassland
	Gate and fence		Cleft/small valley	62	Map continuation

INTRODUCTION

The Pembrokeshire coast is not generally well known, yet in its obscurity it is outstanding. More and more people, however, are discovering this magnificent coastline on the extreme western point of Wales. What better way to explore it than to pull on your boots and walk the cliff tops and beaches of this superb 186-mile (299km) route.

The Pembrokeshire Coast Path begins in the seaside village of Amroth and takes you across the contorted sandstone cliffs of south Pembrokeshire past the colourful houses set above Tenby Harbour and on to the dramatic limestone cliffs at Stackpole. Around every corner the cliffs surprise you with blowholes, sea caves and spectacular natural arches such as the famous Green Bridge of Wales (see p100).

Then it's on across the immaculate sands of Freshwater West and through the patchwork fields around the lazy waters of the Daugleddau estuary to the town of Pembroke with its Norman castle and ancient town walls. North of the estuary everything changes. The scenery is wilder and the walking tougher. The path leaves the Norman south and enters true Welsh country crossing spectacular beaches at Broad Haven and Newgale to reach the beautiful village of Solva, its busy little harbour tucked in a fold in the cliffs.

Next is St David's, the smallest city in Britain, where you can hear the bells of the cathedral echoing across the wooded valley while paying homage to the patron saint of Wales. Leading towards the most westerly point at St David's Head the path takes you past Ramsey Island, a haven for dolphins and seals, and up the rugged heathery coastline to the curious little fishing village of Porthgain. At Fishguard you can learn about the Last Invasion of Britain, or you can catch a ferry over to Ireland from Goodwick.

The final stretch takes you beneath the shadow of the Preseli Hills, bluestone country, the source of some of the raw material for Stonehenge. Continuing over the highest, most spectacular cliffs in West Wales brings you to the end of the path at St Dogmaels, near Cardigan. The Pembrokeshire coast has everything – from endless, sandy beaches and rugged cliffs festooned with wild flowers to lonely hills and sleepy waterways; a beautiful blend of sand, sea and scents.

About this book

This guidebook contains all the information you need. The hard work has been done for you so you can plan your trip from home without the usual pile of books, maps, guides and tourist brochures. It includes:

● All standards of accommodation from campsites to luxurious guesthouses
● Walking companies if you want an organised tour
● Suggested itineraries for all types of walkers
● Answers to all your questions: when to go, degree of difficulty, what to pack and how much will the whole walking holiday cost me?

When you're all packed and ready to go, there's comprehensive information to get you to and from the coast path and 96 detailed maps (1:20,000) and town plans to help you find your way along it. The route guide section includes:

● Walking times in both directions
● Reviews of campsites, bunkhouses, hostels, B&Bs and guesthouses
● Cafés, pubs, tea shops, takeaways, restaurants and shops for buying supplies
● Rail, bus and taxi information for all the villages and towns along the coast path
● Street maps of the main towns and villages: Kilgetty, Amroth, Saundersfoot, Tenby, Penally, Manorbier, Pembroke, Pembroke Dock, Milford Haven, Broad Haven & Little Haven, Lower Solva, St David's, Goodwick, Fishguard, Newport and Cardigan
● Historical, cultural and geographical background information

Minimum impact for maximum insight

Everybody needs a break; climb a mountain or jump in a lake.
Christy Moore, *Lisdoonvarna*

Why is walking in wild and solitary places so satisfying? Partly it is the sheer physical pleasure: sometimes pitting one's strength against the elements, sometimes relaxing on the springy turf or sand. The beauty and wonder of the natural world restore our sense of proportion, freeing us from the stresses and strains of everyday life.

All this the countryside gives us and the least we can do is to safeguard it by supporting rural economies, local businesses and environmentally sensitive forms of transport, and low-impact methods of farming and land use. In this book there is a detailed and illustrated chapter on the wildlife and conservation of Pembrokeshire and a chapter on minimum impact walking with ideas on how to tread lightly in this fragile environment. By following these principles we can help to preserve our natural heritage for future generations.

PART 1: PLANNING YOUR WALK

About the Pembrokeshire Coast Path

HISTORY

It was in 1952 that the Pembrokeshire coast received National Park status. At the same time naturalist Ronald Lockley proposed a long-distance footpath that would provide an uninterrupted walking route through the length of the park. But it was not until 1970 that the coast path was finally opened.

A number of problems arose when choosing the best route for the path, particularly around the, quite frankly, ugly industrial stretches among the power stations and oil refineries on either side of the Milford Haven estuary. It is hard to avoid these eyesores, but the path designers have done a good job in choosing a route that keeps the chimneys and towers out of sight for as long as possible. In many places trees and shrubs have been planted alongside the perimeter fences to act as a screen. At times it is only by looking at the map or sensing the acrid smell that you realise you are walking right next to a major refinery. Nevertheless many walkers quite justifiably choose to leave out this uninspiring section between Angle and Milford Haven. For the rest of its length the path hugs the coastline where possible but inland diversions are inevitable to avoid private land, geographical obstacles and the artillery range at Castlemartin.

The official length of the path has changed over the years. It presently stands at 186 miles (299km) but the distance that any one person walks really depends on how many detours or shortcuts they choose to take.

HOW DIFFICULT IS THE PEMBROKESHIRE COAST PATH?

This is not a technically difficult walk and most reasonably fit people should be able to tackle it without any problems. However, the distance should not be underestimated; although it is not a mountainous path there are many steep up-and-down sections. On completion you will have ascended more than the height of Everest.

The southern section is tamer than the northern stretch with its mighty cliffs where the sense of exposure is more marked and the distances between villages are greater. Always be aware of the ever-present danger of the cliff edge. Accidents often happen late in the day when fatigue sets in and people lose their footing. Be aware of your capabilities and limitations and plan each day accordingly. Don't try to do too much in one day: taking it slowly allows you to relax, see a lot more and you'll enjoy the walk without becoming exhausted or fed up.

Route finding

This should not be a problem since the path is well trodden and obvious. The entire length is waymarked with 'finger-posts' bearing an acorn symbol.

Waymarker
© Alex Stewart

For the most part the path hugs the coastline, although detours are sometimes necessary due to erosion of the cliff. Every year at least one large cliff section gives way but the park authorities are usually very quick to realign the path.

Check the tide times (see p56) to avoid lengthy detours around bays and estuaries. You will need to carefully plan crossing the river mouths at Sandy Haven and The Gann, just to the north of Dale, as they are flooded at high tide. If you time it right you will be able to cross them both on the same day (see box p136 for further details). One other area for confusion is the Castlemartin MoD range. When firing is taking place a detour must be taken along the road (see p100).

GPS

Whilst modern Wainwrights will scoff, more open-minded walkers will accept that GPS technology can be an inexpensive, well-established if non-essential, navigational aid. In no time at all a GPS receiver, given a clear view of the sky, will establish your position and altitude in a variety of formats, including the British OS grid system (see p38), to within a few metres. However, you must not treat a GPS unit as a replacement for a map and compass. Although modern units are robust and durable it takes only a flat battery to render them useless. GPS should be viewed as a navigational aid or back-up, to be used in tandem with more traditional tools. In almost all cases it is best used in conjunction with a paper map and traditional navigational techniques. What a GPS will do is prevent you from making exaggerated navigational errors and will reduce the time taken to correct them if you do stray off the path.

Using GPS with this book is an option. Without it you might find yourself ambling confidently along the wrong path. With it you can quickly establish your position or work out how far and in what direction is a known point on the trail.

Using GPS with this book

It is not expected that you will walk along checking off the GPS waypoints found throughout the book since the detailed maps and route descriptions are more than sufficient most of the time. Only when you are unsure of your position or need reassurance as to which way to go might you feel the need to reach for your GPS for confirmation.

Most of the maps throughout the book include numbered waypoints from Amroth to St Dogmaels. These correlate to the list on pp217-220 which gives the longitude/latitude position in a decimal minute format as well as a description. You'll find more waypoints where the path is indistinct or there are several options as to which way to go. Typically significant landmarks, cairns and other obvious features are also marked. Waypoints are less common in towns or villages but can still be found so as to pin down the path ahead or identify an unsigned alleyway.

You can manually key the nearest presumed waypoint from the list into your GPS as and when the need arises. Alternatively, with less room for error when inputting the co-ordinates, download the complete list for free as a GPS-readable file (that doesn't include the text descriptions) from the Trailblazer website. You'll need the correct cable and adequate memory in your unit (typically the ability to store 500 waypoints or more). The file as well as instructions on how to interpret an OS grid reference can be found on the Trailblazer website: 🖳 www.trailblazer-guides.com.

It's also possible to buy state-of-the-art digital mapping to import into your GPS unit, assuming you've sufficient memory capacity, but it's not the most reliable way of navigating and the small screen on your pocket-sized unit will invariably fail to put places into context or give you the 'big picture'. This is also a far more expensive option than buying the traditional OS paper maps which, whilst bulkier, are always preferable.

Bear in mind that the vast majority of people who tackle the Pembrokeshire Coast Path do so perfectly successfully without a GPS unit. Instead of rushing out to invest in one, consider putting the money towards good-quality waterproofs or footwear instead. That said, using a GPS unit may assist in the odd dicey decision, and if used correctly in tandem with this book's waypoints might just see you safely to the next pub or overnight stop that much more quickly.

HOW LONG DO YOU NEED?

This depends on your fitness and experience. Do not try to do too much in one day if you are new to long-distance walking. Most people find that two weeks is enough to complete the walk and still have time to look around the villages and enjoy the views along the way. Alternatively the entire path can be done in eleven days or less if you are fit enough.

If you're camping don't underestimate how much a heavy pack laden with camping gear will slow you down. It is also worth bearing in mind that those who take it easy on the path tend to see a lot more than those who sweat out long days and only ever see the path in front of them. When deciding how long you need remember to allow a few extra days for side trips or simply to rest. On pp30-2 there are some suggested itineraries covering different walking speeds.

If you have only a few days available concentrate on the best parts of the coast path; there is a list of recommended day and weekend walks on p33.

❏ **The Coast Path Challenge and certificate**
The Pembrokeshire Coast National Park Authority has teamed up with pubs at each end of the trail to offer a free certificate to those who have walked all 186 miles of the Coast Path, no matter how long it has taken. Visit 🖳 http://nt.pcnpa.org.uk/web site/Documents/cp_challenge_english.pdf and download a form (available in English and Welsh). As you make your way along the coast, sign and date the relevant section to record your progress. Take your completed form to one of the pubs in Amroth, at the southern end of the trail, or St Dogmaels, in the north, and claim your free certificate. Alternatively, send your form to Tenby National Park Centre, Ruabon House, South Parade, Tenby SA70 7DL. If you would like an embroidered badge commemorating your achievement as well include a cheque for £5 made payable to PCNPA.

Practical information for the walker

ACCOMMODATION

Most of the coast path is well served with accommodation for all budgets, from campsites to luxurious hotels. The route guide (Part 4) lists a selection of places to stay along the full length of the trail. It's advisable to book all accommodation in advance, particularly during the high season (Easter to August). The most barren area for accommodation is from Manorbier to Pembroke where pre-planning is even more crucial. Remember that the advantages of walking at less busy times are countered by the fact that many places are closed during the winter months.

Camping

Wild camping is not strictly allowed in the national park but a kind landowner may let you camp in a field (see p51). There are a number of official campsites with basic facilities such as toilets and the all-important showers with prices from as little as £2 to £12 per person making this the cheapest accommodation option.

In the summer there are usually plenty of places to camp along the length of the coast path, but if you are planning short days you may have to find alternative accommodation on two or three nights. This is particularly true around Bosherston and the Dale peninsula where you can stay in bed and breakfasts instead (see box p30). Those hardy souls who plan to walk in winter (November to Easter) will find many of the campsites closed, although a few remain open all year.

Camping is like being a snail; carrying your home on your back and travelling at a similar speed. However, there is great satisfaction to be had from spending not just the day but the night in the great outdoors, watching the stars and witnessing the sunset and sunrise. Those who shy away from tented travel because of its perceived disadvantages really miss out on an enlightening experience.

Hostels and bunkhouses

The **YHA hostels** (see box opposite) on the coast path are cheap (members pay £11.95-19.95/£7.50-11.95 adult/child under 18 per night) so enable you to travel on a budget without having to carry cumbersome camping equipment. Non members can stay in YHA hostels but pay an additional charge (£3/1.50 adult/child) per night.

YHA hostels vary greatly in style; St David's hostel, above Whitesands Bay, is an old farmhouse while the one at Manorbier is a converted NATO storage building. They are good places to meet fellow walkers and in many cases are just as comfortable as B&Bs. However, there is a problem. With the exception of Manorbier Hostel (Lydstep) there are no other hostels or bunkhouses for the first

❏ **The YHA (Youth Hostel Association)**
YHA hostels are, despite their name, for anyone of any age. You can join YHA England and Wales (☎ 01629-592700, 🖥 www.yha.org.uk) at any of the hostels, or over the phone or online, for £15.95 per year for an individual (£22.95 for two people living at the same address or a family, £9.95 for people under 26). There is a 10% discount if paying by direct debit. Children under age 18 travelling with either one or both of their parents are covered on their parents' membership card.

70 miles or so between Amroth and Marloes Sands. Depending on your speed, you will need to use B&Bs for the first 3-7 nights and again in St David's itself if you plan to stop there (see box p31).

On the positive side there are six YHA hostels conveniently spaced a day apart from Marloes Sands to the end of the coast path at St Dogmaels. All these provide bedding so there is no need to carry a sleeping bag. Increasingly YHA hostels have (en suite) rooms with locks as well as the traditional dorms. Additionally they all have self-catering kitchens; most on the route are self-catering only but a couple provide meals. All provide toilets and washing facilities, most have a sitting area and a drying room, some also have a games room/TV lounge. A few have a small shop for emergency groceries. Most YHA hostels will only save your booked bed until 6pm which puts you in an uncomfortable rush if you have a lot of walking to do. It's worth phoning ahead to let them know if you're going to arrive later.

If you are planning to walk in **winter** you should bear in mind that some or all of the YHA hostels may be closed, especially during the week. However, if there is enough demand they may open so it is always worth checking.

In addition to the YHA hostels there are **independent hostels** at Trefin and Fishguard. These have the welcome advantage of having few rules and no curfew. Otherwise they are similar to YHA hostels with accommodation in dormitories and/or single/twin/family rooms, bed linen is provided and they have fully equipped self-catering kitchens. Rates are similar also.

Finally you could try the only remaining **bunkhouse** on the coast path (at Cyffredin, near Abereiddy). Bunkhouses provide more basic accommodation but are generally full of character and eccentricity and are well worth visiting, if only for one night. The drawback is that you need your own sleeping bag.

By using hostels on the northern half of the walk and bed and breakfasts on the southern half you cut out the need to pack a sleeping bag altogether, thus significantly lightening your load.

Bed and breakfast

Anyone who has not stayed in a bed and breakfast (B&B) has missed out on something very British. They vary greatly in quality, style and price but usually consist of a bed in someone's house and a big cooked breakfast (see p15) in the morning. For visitors from outside Britain it can provide an interesting insight into the Welsh way of life as you often feel like a guest of the family.

PLANNING YOUR WALK

What to expect All the coastal walker wants is a warm bed and a hot bath. For this reason most B&Bs listed in this guide are recommended because of their usefulness to the walker and their proximity to the path.

Many B&Bs now offer rooms with **en suite** facilities. However, often this means a shower and toilet squeezed into a corner of the room. For a few pounds less you can usually get a standard room and it's rarely far to the **bathroom**; in some places you may have your own bathroom but even if you have to share access it may be preferable to be able to relax in a hot bath after a long day's walking, rather than having a shower.

Anyone walking alone may find it hard to find establishments with **single** rooms. **Twin** rooms and **double** rooms are often confused but a twin room usually comprises two single beds while a double room has one double bed. **Family** rooms are for three or more people; they often have a double bed and bunk beds but occasionally three single beds.

Tariffs B&Bs in this guide vary in price from £18.50 per person for the most basic accommodation to over £40 for the most luxurious en suite places. Most charge around £25-30 per person. Remember that many places do not have single rooms and usually charge a supplement of between £5 and £10 for single occupancy of a double or twin room.

Rates can be substantially lower during the winter months, or if you stay for a few nights, and if you are on a budget you could always ask to go without breakfast which will usually result in a lower price.

Guesthouses, hotels, pubs and inns

Guesthouses and hotels are usually more sophisticated than B&Bs offering evening meals and a lounge for guests. Pubs and inns offer bed and breakfast of a medium to high standard and have the added advantage of having a bar downstairs, so it's not far to stagger back to bed. However, the noise from tipsy punters might prove a nuisance if you want an early night. Rates usually range from £25 to £35 per person per night.

Hotels are usually aimed more at the motoring tourist than the muddy walker and the tariff (£40-75 per person) is likely to put off the budget traveller. A few hotels have been included in the trail guide for those feeling they deserve at least one night of luxury during their trip.

Holiday cottages

Self-catering cottages are ideal for small groups who want to base themselves in the same place for a week or more. This can be a good way to walk parts of the coast path using public transport (see pp43-7) to travel to and from each day's stage.

A good base for a week's walking in south Pembrokeshire would be the seaside town of Tenby which has good public transport links. If you prefer something quieter you could try Freshwater East which has lots of holiday cottages.

St David's, or somewhere close to Fishguard, would be a convenient place to base yourself for walks in north Pembrokeshire. Try the tiny holiday village of Cwm-yr-eglwys which has a good bathing beach.

❏ **Booking accommodation**

You should always book accommodation: in summer there can be stiff competition for beds and in winter there's the distinct possibility that the place could be closed. Bookings for any YHA hostel can be made through the centralised reservation service (☎ 01629-592700) but some can be booked online (🖳 www.yha.org.uk, or through 🖳 www.hihostels.com for instant confirmation). Many B&Bs and hotels can also now be booked via email or through a website, either their own or an agency's; however, phoning is probably best because you can check details more easily.

In most cases you will have to pay a **deposit** or the full charge at the time of booking. Always let the establishment know if you have to cancel your booking so they can offer the bed to someone else.

There is a ban on smoking in all public places in Wales but places to stay are able to designate rooms for smokers; do check this if it's important to you. See also box p19.

Many B&Bs and hotels ban dogs and young children so it is worth checking in advance if either or both of these is likely to be a problem.

If you don't want to book all your accommodation yourself some of the walking companies listed on pp21-2 might. Alternatively, all Visit Wales information centres (see p40) in Pembrokeshire offer a bed-booking service. They charge a £2 fee plus 10% of the total bill as a deposit; this is taken off the final bill paid to the proprietor. They can also do phone bookings but need payment by credit/debit card. However, they will provide you with free contact details of places to stay.

Prices for holiday cottages usually start at £120 per person for the week based on four to six people sharing. Cottages haven't been listed in this book; contact the tourist information centre (see box p40) in the area you want to go to for details. Alternatively, contact the Landmark Trust (🖳 www.landmark trust.org.uk) or the National Trust (🖳 www.nationaltrustcottages.co.uk), both of which have some properties in Pembrokeshire.

FOOD AND DRINK

Breakfast and lunch

If staying in a B&B or hotel you can be sure to enjoy a full Welsh cooked breakfast (similar to an English breakfast but with laverbread and Welsh produce) which may be more than you are used to. Ask for a lighter continental or vegetarian breakfast if you prefer.

Many B&Bs and hostels can also provide you with a packed lunch at an additional cost; if you want an early start or have had enough of cooked breakfasts it may be worth asking for a packed lunch instead of a cooked breakfast. Alternatively, breakfast and packed lunches can be bought and made yourself. There are some great cafés and bakeries along the way which can supply both eat-in or takeaway; many pubs also offer lunches. Remember that stretches of the walk are devoid of anywhere to eat so check the information in Part 4 to make sure you don't go hungry.

❏ Local food

As for food, it would be easy to walk the entire coast path surviving on a diet of fish and chips and junk food and, like the rest of Britain, West Wales seems to have claimed Indian food as its own. All the towns have at least one curry house, many of them of very high quality. Even the old traditional pubs have got in on the act with chicken tikka masala ever present on the menu.

But Welsh cuisine should not be overlooked, as it so often is. The coast path gives you the perfect opportunity to try it for yourself. Unsurprisingly seafood is a speciality with many restaurants and pubs serving local **cockles** and **mussels**, **sea trout** and **pints of prawns**. If this is not your thing there is always the famous **Welsh lamb**. Here are some other Welsh delicacies:

● **Laverbread** Has been described as Welsh caviar but equally as a seaweed pancake; take your pick. It is certainly seaweed based and is mixed with oatmeal and fried in fat. Even supermarkets stock it now.

● **Bara brith** A rich fruity bread made by soaking fruit in tea and then adding marmalade, spices and other ingredients.

● **Welsh cakes** Tasty cakes full of currants and sultanas; you can find them in supermarkets and in most tea shops and cafés.

● **Welsh rarebit** Melted cheese with a hint of mustard poured over buttered toast, though recipes vary.

● **Cawl cennin a phersli** (Leek and parsley broth) A soup made from root vegetables (such as parsnips, carrots, swede, potatoes) with leeks and parsley in a lamb stock.

● **Cawl mamgu Tregaron** (Tregaron granny's broth) Another soup full of vegetables with shin beef and bacon.

● **Stuffed leeks with cheese and mustard sauce** Leeks stuffed with sausagemeat and served with a cheese and mustard sauce.

● **Gorfoledd y glowyr** *(Miner's delight)* A rabbit casserole.

● **Oggy** The Welsh equivalent of the Cornish pasty containing Welsh beef, leeks, potato, onions and gravy in a thick pastry crust. It was originally the standard lunch for miners.

● **Preseli cheese** Goat's cheese, two soft cow cheeses and smoked cheese are all made at Pant Mawr Farm (🖳 www.pantmawrcheeses.co.uk), Rosebush, Clynderwen, in the Preseli Hills. All the cheeses carry the Pembrokeshire Produce seal of approval and are made from pasteurised milk with vegetarian rennets.

Evening meals

Hotels and guesthouses almost always offer evening meals; some B&Bs and YHA hostels may also but you will almost always need to book in advance and eat at a set time. Hostels always have self-catering kitchens so you can make your own meal. Most B&Bs are close enough to a pub or restaurant and if they are not, the owner may give you a lift to and from the nearest eating place.

The Pembrokeshire coast is blessed with some outstanding **pubs** and inns. There is nothing quite like the lure of a pint to get you through those last few miles of the day. Most pubs offer lunch and evening meals and usually have some vegetarian options. The standard varies from basic pub grub from the bar menu to à la carte restaurant food. Most walkers will be happy with whatever is put in front of them after working up an appetite.

There are some quality **restaurants** in most of the towns, with menus varying from Welsh, French and Italian to the ubiquitous seafood. Many places now try to source local produce and change their menus regularly.

Most towns and some of the larger villages are riddled with cheap **take-away** joints offering kebabs, pizzas, Chinese, Indian, and fish & chips. They can come in handy if you finish your walk late in the day since they usually stay open until at least 11pm.

Buying camping supplies

If you are camping, fuel for your stove, outdoor equipment and food supplies are important considerations. The best places for outdoor gear are the outdoor adventure shops in Tenby and St David's. In the summer many of the campsites have shops that sell fuel as do most of the general stores along the route but remember that in the winter months many of the smaller ones open for a shorter time or not at all. Check the services details in Part 4 for more information. Particularly barren areas for supplies of any kind are from Tenby to Pembroke and St David's to Fishguard.

Drinking water

Depending on the weather you will need to drink as much as two to four litres of water a day. If you're feeling lethargic it may well be that you haven't drunk

---

❏ Local beers

Many of the pubs promote **real ales**. There are plenty of the well-known brands from across the border but look out for the Welsh ales produced in some of the southern cities.

The Cardiff-based brewery **Brains**, which has been in business for more than 125 years, is synonymous with Wales and covers the south-east of the country. The rich, nutty, copper-coloured **Brains SA** is the staple drink for many people and one of the country's best-known beers; the initials stand for Special Ale but it is more colloquially and alarmingly known as Skull Attack. Their legendary **Dark** is a velvety smooth, treacle-coloured mild that has hints of liquorice and freshly ground coffee. The latest addition to their cask range is **SA Gold**, a full-flavoured, hoppy golden ale that's very refreshing. Brains also produces a range of seasonal ales including the **St David's Ale**, which is available February-March in honour of the patron saint, and **Iechyd Da!** (pronounced Yeh-keed-Dah!), which means Good Health, or Cheers in Welsh, and is available throughout the Christmas/New Year period. Brains has taken over **Crown Buckley** but continues to produce three Buckley's beers at their Cardiff brewery. The **Reverend James** bitter is the pick of the bunch. Named after one of the original owners of the Buckley Brewery, the recipe for the full-bodied, spicy, satisfying beer dates back to 1885.

The **Felinfoel** brewery, based in the town of the same name close to Llanelli, is an independent family business that distributes to almost all the southern half of the country. Look out in particular for their **Double Dragon** bitter, an aromatic, malty ale with a rich colour and a smooth balance. Also worth trying are their: **Felinfoel Stout**, which tastes of roast barley and has a thick creamy head; **Cambrian Bitter**, which is golden-coloured and aromatic; and their **Best Bitter**, a medium strength beer that's subtly hoppy and flavoursome.

PLANNING YOUR WALK

enough, even if you're not feeling particularly thirsty. Drinking directly from streams and rivers is tempting, but is not a good idea. Streams that cross the path tend to have flowed across farmland where you can be pretty sure any number of farm animals have relieved themselves. Combined with the probable presence of farm pesticides and other delights it is best to avoid drinking from these streams.

Drinking-water taps and fountains are marked in the trail guide. Where these are thin on the ground you can usually ask a friendly shopkeeper or pub barman to fill your bottle or pouch for you, from the tap of course.

❏ Information for foreign visitors

● **Currency** The British pound (£) comes in notes of £100, £50, £20, £10 and £5, and coins of £2 and £1. The pound is divided into 100 pence (usually referred to as 'p', pronounced 'pee') which comes in silver coins of 50p, 20p, 10p and 5p, and copper coins of 2p and 1p. The design of the pound coin is different in Wales, the Welsh coin carrying a leek. However, Welsh coins are legal tender in England and Scotland.

● **Rates of exchange** Up-to-date rates of exchange can be found on 🖳 www.xe .com/ucc, at some post offices, or at any bank or travel agent.

● **Business hours** Most **shops** and main **post offices** are open at least from Monday to Friday 9am-5pm and Saturday 9am-12.30pm but many choose longer hours and some open on Sunday as well. Occasionally, especially in rural areas, you'll come across a local shop that closes at midday during the week, usually a Wednesday or Thursday, a throwback to the days when all towns and villages had an 'early closing day'. Many **supermarkets** remain open 12 hours a day; the Spar chain usually displays '8 till late' on the door. **Banks** typically open Monday to Friday from 9.30am till 3.30pm or 4pm, but of course ATM machines are open all the time, except for those located in a shop. Be aware that some ATM machines may not accept foreign-issued debit cards. **Pub** hours are less predictable, and although generally they are open 11am-11pm, in rural areas opening hours are often 11am-3pm and 6-11pm Mon-Sat, opening an hour later on Sunday evenings.

● **National (bank) holidays** Most businesses in Wales are shut on 1 January, Good Friday (March/April), Easter Monday (March/April), first and last Monday in May, last Monday in August, 25 December and 26 December.

● **School holidays** State-school holidays in Wales (and England) are generally as follows: a one-week break late October, two weeks over Christmas and the New Year, a week mid-February, two weeks around Easter, one week at the end of May/early June (to coincide with the bank holiday at the end of May) and five to six weeks from late July to early September. Private-school holidays fall at the same time, but tend to be slightly longer.

● **EHICs and travel insurance** Although Britain's National Health Service (NHS) is free at the point of use, that is only the case for residents. All visitors to Britain should be properly insured, including comprehensive health coverage. The European Health Insurance Card (EHIC) entitles EU nationals (on production of the EHIC card so ensure you bring it with you) to necessary medical treatment under the NHS while on a temporary visit here. For details, contact your national social security institution. However, this is not a substitute for proper medical cover on your travel insurance for unforeseen bills and for getting you home should that be necessary. Also consider cover for loss and theft of personal belongings, especially if you are camping or

MONEY

On some sections of the coast path there is a distinct lack of banks. There are no banks along the 53-mile (85km) stretch between Tenby and Pembroke (though there is an ATM in the shop at Manorbier), for example, and there are only a couple of ATMs – one at Marloes, just off the path, and one in the post office/shop at Broad Haven – between Milford Haven and St David's, a distance of 47 miles (76km). Some Link ATMs are 'pay to use' though the charges are clearly displayed outside the machine and on the screen.

staying in hostels, as there will be times when you'll have to leave your luggage unattended.

● **Weights and measures** The European Commission is no longer attempting to ban the pint or the mile: so, in Britain, milk can be sold in pints (1 pint = 568ml), as can beer in pubs, though most other liquid including petrol (gasoline) and diesel is sold in litres. Distances on road and path signs will also continue to be given in miles (1 mile = 1.6km) rather than kilometres, and yards (1yd = 0.9m) rather than metres. The population remains split between those who still use inches (1 inch = 2.5cm), feet (1ft = 0.3m) and yards and those who are happy with millimetres, centimetres and metres; you'll often be told that 'it's only a hundred yards or so' to somewhere, rather than a hundred metres or so.

Most food is sold in metric weights (g and kg) but the imperial weights of pounds (lb: 1lb = 453g) and ounces (oz: 1oz = 28g) are often displayed too. The weather – a frequent topic of conversation – is also an issue: while most forecasts predict temperatures in centigrade (C), many people continue to think in terms of fahrenheit (F; see temperature chart on p25 for conversions).

● **Smoking** Smoking in public places in Wales is banned. The ban relates not only to pubs and restaurants, but also to B&Bs, hostels and hotels. These latter have the right to designate one or more bedrooms where the occupants can smoke, but the ban is in force in all enclosed areas open to the public – even if they are in a private home such as a B&B.

Should you be foolhardy enough to light up in a no-smoking area, which includes pretty well any indoor public place, you could be fined £50, but it's the owners of the premises who carry the can if they fail to stop you, with a potential fine of £2500.

● **Time** During the winter, the whole of Britain is on Greenwich Meantime (GMT). The clocks move one hour forward on the last Sunday in March, remaining on British Summer Time (BST) until the last Sunday in October.

● **Telephone** From outside Britain the international country access code for Britain is ☎ 44 followed by the area code minus the first 0, and then the number you require. Within Britain, to call a number with the same code as the phone you are calling from, the code can be omitted: dial the number only. It is cheaper to ring at weekends, and after 6pm and before 8am on weekdays.

If you're using a mobile phone that is registered overseas, consider buying a local SIM card to keep costs down. Be aware that public phone boxes often require a phone card rather than cash.

● **Emergency services** For police, ambulance, fire brigade and coastguard dial ☎ 999, or the EU standard number (☎ 112).

It is a good idea therefore to carry plenty of cash with you, maybe keeping it in a money belt for security. Small independent shops rarely accept payment by card and will require you to pay in cash or by cheque, as will most B&Bs, bunkhouses and campsites. Shops that do take cards, such as supermarkets, will sometimes advance cash against a card as long as you buy something at the same time, though you may have to spend a minimum of £5. Be aware that some supermarkets no longer accept cheques. **Travellers' cheques** can only be cashed at banks, foreign exchange offices and some large hotels.

See also p38 and the town and village facilities table, pp28-9.

Using the post office for banking   Several banks in Britain have agreements with the Post Office allowing customers to make cash withdrawals using a chip and pin debit card, or a chequebook and debit card, at post offices throughout the country. As there are plenty of post offices along the coast path this is a useful facility for the walker. For a full list of banks offering these facilities contact the Post Office (☎ 08457-223344, 🖳 www.postoffice.co.uk).

OTHER SERVICES

Most villages and all the towns have at least one public **telephone**, a small **shop** and a **post office**. Other than for withdrawing money (see above) post offices can be used for sending unnecessary clothes and equipment home which may be weighing you down.

In Part 4 special mention is given to services that may be of use to the walker such as the above as well as **banks**, **cash machines** (cashpoints), **outdoor equipment shops**, **launderettes**, **internet access**, **pharmacies**, and **tourist information centres** which can be used for finding and booking accommodation amongst other things.

WALKING COMPANIES

For walkers wanting to make their holiday as easy and trouble-free as possible there are several specialist companies offering a range of services from accommodation booking to fully guided group tours.

Expect to pay between £335 for a 5-day/6-night self-guided holiday and £920 for a 16-day/17-night fully guided tour. These prices are for two sharing a room; walkers on their own are likely to be charged an additional single supplement of £15-20 per night.

Baggage carriers
Some of the **taxi** firms listed in this guide (see Part 4) can provide a baggage-carrying service within a local area. B&Bs may also be willing to take your luggage to your next destination for a small charge. See also Self-guided holidays opposite.

Group/guided walking tours
Fully guided tours are ideal for individuals wanting to travel in the company of others and for groups of friends wanting to be guided. The packages usually

include meals, accommodation, transport arrangements, minibus back-up and baggage transfer, as well as a qualified guide. Companies' specialities differ widely with varying size of groups, standards of accommodation, age range of clients, distances walked and professionalism of guides. In the list of companies below we have indicated which offer a complete guided walking package.

Self-guided holidays
Self-guided holidays are all-in customised packages for walkers which usually include detailed advice and notes on itineraries and routes, maps, accommodation booking, daily baggage transfer and transport arrangements at the start and end of your walk. Some include meals but not all so consider this if comparing prices.

If you don't want the whole all-in package some companies may arrange the **accommodation booking** or **baggage-carrying** services on their own. The following companies provide self-guided holidays and, where specified, fully guided tours:

● **Celtic Trails** (☎ 0800-970 7585 or from overseas ☎ 01291-689774, 🖳 www .celtrail.com; PO Box 11, Chepstow, NP16 6ZD) Itineraries from 3 to 13 days covering either the southern, central or northern section or the full walk, Amroth to Poppit Sands/St Dogmaels. They can also tailor-make holidays.

● **Contours Walking Holidays** (☎ 017684-80451, 🖳 www.contours.co.uk; Gramyre, 3 Berrier Rd, Greystoke, CA11 0UB) Offers both the complete path, taking between 12 and 16 days (with optional rest days) and shorter trails covering either the northern (St Dogmaels to St David's; 66 miles), central (St David's to Milford Haven; 48 miles) or southern (Milford Haven to Amroth; 66 miles) sections of the path and taking 4 to 7 days to complete.

● **Footpath Holidays** (☎ 01985-840049; 🖳 www.footpath-holidays.com; 16 Norton Bavant, nr Warminster, Wilts BA12 7BB) Walkers are based in St David's (see p166). Self-guided holidays are available as short breaks or for stays of up to a week; note that single-centre fully guided tours are usually available but may not be in 2010.

● **Greenways Holidays** (☎ 01834-862109, 🖳 www.greenwaysholidays.com; The Old School, Station Rd, Narberth SA67 7DU) This company is managed by PLANED (Pembrokeshire Local Action Network for Enterprise and Development) so it supports locally owned facilities and uses sustainable means of transport, such as the coastal buses (see p45), on its Explorer breaks. They can also tailormake holidays and offer cycling holidays around the region.

● **HF Holidays** (☎ 0845-470 7558/020-8732 1250, 🖳 www.hfholidays.co.uk; Catalyst House, 720 Centennial Court, Centennial Park, Elstree, Hertfordshire WD6 3SY) Provides a self-guided (7 days/6 nights) holiday from Dale to St David's and a guided holiday from St Dogmaels to St David's (8 days/7 nights).

● **Explore Britain** (☎ 01740-650900, 🖳 www.xplorebritain.com; 6 George St, Ferryhill, Co Durham DL17 0DT) Self-guided treks along the coast path include a 6-night Dale to St David's trail and a 13-night St Dogmaels to Dale itinerary.

● **The Discerning Traveller** (☎ 01865-515618, 🖥 www.chycor.co.uk/holidays/ discerning-traveller/index.htm; 38 Canal St, Oxford OX2 6BQ) This company specialises in self-guided week-long tours – from Dale to St David's and from Newport to St David's.

● **Walkalongway.com** (☎ 01437-769344, 🖥 www.walkalongway.com; Bwthyn Clofer, Wiston, Haverfordwest, Pembrokeshire SA62 4PT) specialise in walks in Pembrokeshire and west Wales and offer guided walks for a day, or three-week group walks along the whole coastal path (north to south). From 2010 they are planning to let anyone booking the three-week walk spread it over 18 months if they are unable to do it in one go.

TAKING DOGS ALONG THE COAST PATH

The National Park trail officers have worked hard to make the path more dog friendly. Dog stiles, or doggy stiles as they are affectionately known, have been installed all along the path to prevent damage to the fences caused by dogs squeezing their way through. This acceptance shown towards the dog-walking fraternity is thanks in part to the responsible attitude that they have shown.

By law you must not allow your dog to disturb, chase or harass farm animals or wildlife. This includes all domestic livestock. Dogs should therefore always be kept on leads while on the footpath. Dog excrement should be cleaned up and not left to decorate the boots of other walkers.

Uncontrolled dogs can cause an animal stress, serious injury or even death. You should be particularly vigilant during the spring when young animals are being born and are least likely to be able to run away from an inquisitive dog.

Conversely, domestic livestock can potentially cause you and your dog harm if they become agitated. In rare but particularly serious cases, people have been trampled by cattle, when these typically docile creatures have become aggressive and charged in the course of defending their young. Usually the cattle are interested in the dog and not the walker, but can injure the person whilst attempting to get at the dog. Wherever possible avoid walking through fields of livestock when out with dogs. However, if this is unavoidable both the National Farmers Union and the Ramblers (Association) advise that walkers release dogs from their leads when passing through a field of cows but that they keep them under strict control nonetheless. The dog can then run away if charged, whilst the person is generally ignored.

Bear in mind that between 1 May and 30 September dogs are not allowed on certain parts of the following beaches: Amroth, Saundersfoot, Tenby South, Tenby Castle, Lydstep, Dale, Broad Haven, Newgale and Poppit Sands. Between the same dates complete bans exist on Tenby's North Beach, Tenby Harbour and at Whitesands Bay. However, these restrictions do not pose any great obstacle to coast-path walkers with dogs since the path only occasionally crosses a beach and where it does there is always an alternative route a short way inland.

Remember when planning and booking your accommodation you will need to phone ahead to check if your dog will be welcome. Not all places to stay accept dogs and of those that do, some charge extra (up to £10).

DISABLED ACCESS

Taking the coast path's undulating and rough terrain into account, it may come as a surprise to learn that sections of it are accessible by wheelchair. There is an ongoing programme to replace stiles with kissing gates which is also improving access.

The National Park Authority's website (see p40) lists a number of circular walks suitable for wheelchair access: click on Walking from the list of popular links and then click on Walks in the park and use the search engine to get a list of wheelchair-accessible walks for different areas. Alternatively, click on the Easy access guide for a map of Pembrokeshire showing 16 easy access walks. The walks are also published in a guide called *Walks for all* available through the national park authority or tourist information offices in Pembrokeshire. Some of these routes include: Tenby South beach to Penally (p89), St Govan's car park to Stack Rocks (p100), Abereiddy to The Blue Lagoon (p178-9) and Pwllgwaelod to Cwm-yr-eglwys (p198). The park authority also published *Easy Access Routes in the Pembrokeshire Coast National Park* (£2.95); this details 19 routes for wheelchair users ranging from 600m to 3km and may still be available in tourist information centres and local shops.

Buses on the Celtic Coaster and Coastal Cruiser services (see p45) are accessible for wheelchair users.

Budgeting

The amount of money you are likely to spend depends on your accommodation plans and how you're going to eat. If you camp and cook your own meals your expenses may stay very low but most people prefer to have at least some of their meals cooked for them and even the hardy camper may be tempted into the occasional B&B when the rain is falling.

CAMPING

You can survive on as little as £10 per person if you use the cheapest sites and cook all your own food from staple ingredients. Nevertheless, most people find that the best-laid plans to survive on the bare minimum fall flat after a couple of hard days' walking. Always budget for unforeseen expenses as well as for the end-of-day drink (a pint of beer costs around £2.50). Assuming such liquid treats and the occasional pub meal or takeaway a budget of £15-20 per day is more realistic.

HOSTELS AND BUNKHOUSES

Hostels (and the only bunkhouse) on the route charge between £12/8 and £20/12 per adult/child per night; most places have a self-catering kitchen allowing you to create your own meals from food bought at local shops or supermarkets. Some (YHA) hostels provide meals (breakfast costs £4.20/2.45 adult/child, a picnic lunch costs £4.80/3.80 and an evening meal costs £8.40/6.15).

Now and then you will need, or want, to eat out which adds to your daily costs. Around £30-35 per day should be enough to cover the cost of accommodation while still allowing for the occasional bar meal and end-of-day tipple. If you are planning on eating out most nights you should clearly increase your budget to around £40 per day.

B&Bs, INNS, GUESTHOUSES AND HOTELS

B&B prices can be as little as £18 per night but are usually nearer half as much again. This will almost always include breakfast. Add on the price of a packed lunch, pub evening meal, drink and other expenses and you can expect to need around £30-50 per day, and probably more if you are walking on your own. If staying in a guesthouse or hotel expect to pay £50-70 per day.

EXTRAS

Don't forget all those little things that inadvertently push up your daily costs: postcards, stamps, souvenirs, beer, camera film, buses here, buses there, more beer and getting to and from the trail in the first place; it all adds up!

When to go

SEASONS

Pembrokeshire is subjected to the full force of the weather sweeping in from the Atlantic so you can expect rain and strong winds at any time of year. Equally you can be blessed with blazing sunshine; the climate is unpredictable. The **main walking season** in Pembrokeshire is from Easter to the end of September.

Spring

Walking in Pembrokeshire from March to June has many rewards, the greatest of which is the chance to appreciate the spectacular wild flowers which come into bloom at this time.

Spring is also the time of year when you are most likely to have dry weather. Easter can be a busy time since it is the first major holiday of the year but at other times the path is relatively quiet.

Summer

Unsurprisingly, summer is when every man and his dog descend on the countryside with July and August, when the heather colours the hillsides purple, being the busiest months. At this time many of the beaches are packed and the coast path too. This isn't always a bad thing. Part of the enjoyment of walking is meeting like-minded people and there are plenty of them about. However, accommodation can be hard to come by, so do book well in advance.

Summer weather in west Wales is notoriously unpredictable. One day you can be sweating in the midday sun, the next day battling against the wind and rain. Remember to take clothes for any eventuality.

Autumn

Come September the tourists return home. Autumn can be wild with the first storms of winter arriving towards the end of September. Don't let this put you off. Although the likelihood of rain and wind increases as winter approaches, sunny days are still possible and the changing colours of the hillsides make the coastline spectacular.

Winter

There are a number of disadvantages to walking the coast path in winter: winter storms are common, the daylight hours are short and many of the places to stay are closed until spring. Experienced walkers who are not afraid of getting wet may appreciate the peace and quiet and may be rewarded with one of those beautifully crisp, clear winter days.

TEMPERATURE

The Welsh climate is temperate and even in winter the air temperature is relatively mild thanks to the warm Gulf Stream sea current. Consequently the temperature is usually quite comfortable at any time of year although on rare occasions in summer it can get a little too hot for walking.

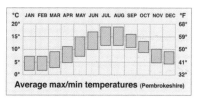

Average max/min temperatures (Pembrokeshire)

RAINFALL

Pembrokeshire bears the brunt of the violent weather systems that sweep in from the North Atlantic. As a result, the rainfall is usually higher here than in the more sheltered areas further east. The total annual rainfall for west Wales is 1000mm with most of it falling from late summer through into the winter with spring being the driest period.

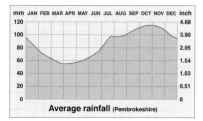

Average rainfall (Pembrokeshire)

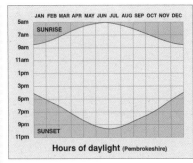

Hours of daylight (Pembrokeshire)

DAYLIGHT HOURS
If walking in autumn, winter or early spring, you must take account of how far you can walk in the available light. The sunrise and sunset times in the table are based on information for Milford Haven on the first of each month. This gives a rough picture for the rest of Pembrokeshire. Also bear in mind that you will get a further 30-45 minutes of usable light before sunrise and after sunset depending on the weather.

ANNUAL EVENTS AND FESTIVALS

The free national park newspaper *Coast to Coast* has a comprehensive 'What's On' page updated annually. Alternatively have a look at 🖥 www.visitpembroke shire.co.uk. Tourist information centres also have details and times of events in their area.

The National Park Authority organises events; see their website (🖥 www .pcnpa.org.uk) for details. Below is a taster of what can be found to distract you along the way.

January to March
● **New Year's Day Swim** An annual institution where people, often in fancy dress, plunge into the sea off Saundersfoot (🖥 www.saundersfootnyds.co.uk) at 11.30am, and at Whitesands Bay, whatever the weather!
● **Saundersfoot St David's Day Food and Craft Festival** (🖥 www.visit-saun dersfoot.com) During the last weekend in February or first weekend of March, two dozen stalls are set up alongside the harbour selling crafts and local produce; the celebrity-chef cookery demonstrations and Cawl Cooking Championship, where visitors are invited to taste and nominate the most delicious dish (see box p16), ensure you don't go hungry.

April to June
● **Fishguard Folk Festival** (🖥 www.pembrokeshire-folk-music.co.uk) The sound of fiddles and bodhrans (frame drums) fill the town in the last weekend of May. Concerts and workshops are also organised. The main venue is The Royal Oak Inn in Market Sq.
● **St David's Cathedral Festival** (🖥 www.stdavidscathedral.org.uk) Nine days of classical music in the wonderful St David's Cathedral, beginning the last weekend of May; widely considered to be one of the best music festivals in Wales.
● **Pembrokeshire Fish Week** (🖥 www.pembrokeshire.gov.uk/fishweek) Events take place throughout Pembrokeshire in late June-early July celebrating not just the county's fresh fish and shellfish, but also its beautiful coast and beaches. More than 200 events including gourmet seafood evenings, lobster

lunches, barbecues backed by bands playing shanty tunes, seafood cookery masterclasses, river boat trips, sea fishing and kayaking expeditions along the coast ensure there's something for everyone.

July to August

● **Pembrokeshire Coast Triathlon** (🖥 www.pembrokeshire-tri.org.uk) An annual triathlon involving a 1500m swim, 43km bike ride and 10.2km run, which takes place around Broad Haven in July.

● **Fishguard International Music Festival** (☎ 01348-891345; box office June-Aug ☎ 01348-875538, 🖥 www.fishguardmusicfestival.co.uk) A series of largely classical music concerts and performances held in Goodwick, Fishguard and St David's Cathedral at the end of July.

● **Pembrokeshire Jazz and Blues Festival** (🖥 www.aberjazz.com) Takes place over the August Bank Holiday, mainly in Fishguard, and includes live music events as well as workshops.

September to December

● **Really Wild Food and Countryside Festival** (🖥 www.reallywildfestival .co.uk) This celebration of food and countryside crafts originating from the wild takes place in St David's at the start of September. Competitions include axe throwing and wellie-wanging, whilst local chefs showcase their talents and discuss how best to use local produce.

● **Pembrokeshire Half Marathon** (🖥 www.pembrokeshire-tri.org.uk) Annual half marathon taking place mid-September. Starts and finishes in Dale having run round St Ann's Head.

● **Tenby Arts Festival** (🖥 www.tenbyartsfest.co.uk) Exhibitions in various venues around town in the last week of September. Dance workshops, kite-flying competitions, sand sculptures, music and drama.

● **Tenby Blues Festival** (🖥 www.tenbyblues.co.uk) Takes place in November in venues around town, where you can catch bands and performers or join in at the open mic sessions.

● **Tenby Winter Carnival Festival** Takes place in December. Craft fairs, carnival parades, choir performances and band gigs demonstrate that the town can be as much fun in winter as during the height of summer.

● **New Year's Eve** Extensive celebrations organised annually in Saundersfoot, Tenby and Fishguard to see in the New Year.

Itineraries

This guidebook has not been divided up into rigid daily stages. Instead, it's structured to make it easy for you to plan your own itinerary. The Pembrokeshire Coast Path can be tackled in any number of ways, the most challenging of which is to do it all in one go. This does require around two weeks, time which some people just don't have. *(cont'd on p30)*

				VILLAGE AND
Place name (places in brackets are a short walk off the path)	Distance from previous place approx miles/km	ATM/ Bank	Post Office	Tourist Information Centre/Point National Park Centre
(Kilgetty)		ATM only	✔	
Amroth	3/5			
Wiseman's Bridge	2/3			
Saundersfoot	1/1.5	✔	✔	TIC
Tenby	4/6.5	✔	✔	TIC
Penally	2.5/4		✔	
Lydstep	4/6.5			
Manorbier	4/6.5	ATM only		
Freshwater East	4/6.5			
Bosherston	6.5/10.5			
Merrion	8.5/13.5			
Angle	12/19.5			
Hundleton	9/14.5			
Pembroke	2.5/4	✔	✔	TIC
Pembroke Dock	3/5	✔	✔	TIP
Neyland & Hazelbeach	4/6.5		✔	
Milford Haven	5.5/9	✔		TIC
Sandy Haven (& Herbrandston)	4/6.5		✔	
(St Ishmael's)	2.5/4		✔	
Dale	3/5		✔	
Marloes Sands (& Marloes)	8/13		✔	
Little Haven	12/19.5			
Broad Haven	0.5/1	ATM only	✔	
Nolton Haven	3.5/5.5			
Newgale	3.5/5.5			
Solva	5/8		✔	
Caerfai Bay	4/6.5			
(St David's)	(1)/(1/5)	✔	✔	NPC/TIC
Porthclais	1.5/2.3			(NT kiosk)
St Justinian's & Porthselau	5/8			
Whitesands Bay	2/3.2			
Abereiddy	7.5/12			
Porthgain	2/3			
Trefin	2/3		✔	
Pwll Deri & Strumble Head	9.5/15.5			
Goodwick & Fishguard	10.5/17	✔	✔	TIC
Pwllgwaelod (& Dinas Cross)	4.5/7		✔	
Parrog & Newport	7/11	✔	✔	NPC/TIC
Ceibwr Bay (for Moylgrove)	9/14.5			
Poppit Sands	5/8			
St Dogmaels	2/3		✔	
(Cardigan)	(1)/(1.5)	✔	✔	TIC
TOTAL DISTANCE	186 miles (299km)			

TOWN FACILITIES

Eating Place ✔=one; ✔✔=two; ✔✔✔=three +	Food Store	Campsite or area where can camp	Hostels YHA =YHA Hostel; H = Ind hostel B = Bunkhouse	B&B-style accommodation ✔=one ✔✔=two; ✔✔✔=three +	Place name (places in brackets are a short walk off the path)
✔✔✔	✔	✔			(Kilgetty)
✔✔✔	(✔)			✔✔	Amroth
✔		✔		✔	Wiseman's Bridge
✔✔✔	✔	✔		✔✔✔	Saundersfoot
✔✔✔	✔	✔		✔✔✔	Tenby
✔✔	✔	✔		✔✔✔	Penally
✔		✔	YHA	✔✔	Lydstep
✔✔	✔	✔		✔✔	Manorbier
✔		✔		✔✔	Freshwater East
✔✔	(✔)			✔✔	Bosherston
		✔		✔✔	Merrion
✔✔	✔	✔		✔✔	Angle
✔				✔✔	Hundleton
✔✔✔	✔	✔		✔✔✔	Pembroke
✔✔✔	✔			✔✔✔	Pembroke Dock
✔	✔			✔	Neyland & Hazelbeach
✔✔✔	✔			✔✔	Milford Haven
✔	✔	✔		✔✔✔	Sandy Haven (& Herbrandston)
✔					(St Ishmael's)
✔✔	✔			✔✔	Dale
✔✔	✔	✔	YHA	✔✔	Marloes Sands (& Marloes)
✔✔✔		✔		✔✔✔	Little Haven
✔✔✔	✔		YHA	✔✔	Broad Haven
✔				✔	Nolton Haven
✔		✔		✔✔	Newgale
✔✔✔	✔	✔		✔✔✔	Solva
	(✔)	✔			Caerfai Bay
✔✔✔	✔			✔✔✔	(St David's)
		✔			Porthclais
		✔			St Justinian's & Porthselau
(✔)		✔	YHA		Whitesands Bay
(✔)		✔	B	✔✔	Abereiddy
✔✔				✔	Porthgain
✔✔		✔	H	✔✔	Trefin
		✔	YHA		Pwll Deri & Strumble Head
✔✔✔	✔	✔	H	✔✔✔	Goodwick & Fishguard
✔✔✔	✔			✔	Pwllgwaelod (& Dinas Cross)
✔✔✔	✔	✔	YHA	✔✔✔	Parrog & Newport
(✔)				✔	Ceibwr Bay (for Moylgrove)
		✔	YHA	✔	Poppit Sands
✔✔✔	✔				St Dogmaels
✔✔✔	✔			✔✔✔	(Cardigan)

PLANNING YOUR WALK

(cont'd from p27) Most people do the walk over a series of short breaks coming back year after year to do a bit more. Others just walk the best bits, avoiding the ugly industrial stretches around the Milford Haven estuary and others use the path for linear day-walks taking public transport there and back.

To help you plan your walk see the **planning map** (opposite the inside back cover) and the **table of village/town facilities** on pp28-9; the latter gives a run down on the essential information you will need regarding accommodation possibilities and services.

The **suggested itineraries** in the boxes below, opposite and on p32 may also be useful; they are based on different accommodation types – camping, hostels and B&Bs – with each one divided into three alternatives depending on

CAMPING

Night	Relaxed pace Place	Approx Distance miles/km	Medium pace Place	Approx Distance miles/km	Fast pace Place	Approx Distance miles/km
0	Amroth		Amroth		Amroth	
1	Penally	9.5/15	Penally (nr Manorbier)	9.5/15	Swanlake Bay	20/32
2	Swanlake Bay (nr Manorbier)	10.5/17	Swanlake Bay (nr Manorbier)	10.5/17	Merrion	16.5/26.5
3	Bosherston*	8/13	Merrion	16.5/26.5	Hundleton*	21/33.5
4	Merrion	8.5/13.5	Angle	12/19.5	Sandy Haven	19/31
5	Angle	12/19.5	Pembroke	11.5/19	Martin's Haven (nr Marloes)	16/26
6	Pembroke	11.5/19	Sandy Haven (nr Marloes Sands)	16.5/27	Newgale	17/27
7	Sandy Haven	16.5/27	Martin's Haven (nr Marloes)	16/26	Whitesands Bay (nr Marloes Sands)	17.5/28
8	Dale*	5.5/9	Newgale	17/27	Strumble Head	23.5/38
9	Martin's Haven (nr Marloes)	10.5/17	Whitesands Bay	17.5/28	Newport	19.5/3
10	Little Haven	9.5/15	Trefin	11.5/18	Poppit Sands	14/23
11	Newgale	7.5/12	Strumble Head	12/19	St Dogmaels*	2/3
12	Caerfai Bay	9/14	Fishguard Bay (nr Fishguard)	10/16		
13	Whitesands Bay	8.5/14	Newport	9.5/15		
14	Trefin	11.5/18	Poppit Sands	14/23		
15	Strumble Head	12/19	St Dogmaels*	2/3		
16	Fishguard Bay (nr Fishguard)	10/16				
17	Newport	9.5/15				
18	Poppit Sands	14/23				
19	St Dogmaels*	2/3				

* There are no campsites at places marked with an asterisk but alternative accommodation is available

STAYING IN HOSTELS/BUNKHOUSES

Relaxed pace		Medium pace		Fast pace	
Place	**Approx Distance**	**Place**	**Approx Distance**	**Place**	**Approx Distance**
Night	miles/km		miles/km		miles/km
0 Amroth		Amroth		Amroth	
1 Lydstep	13.5/22	Lydstep	13.5/22	Lydstep	13/22
2 Freshwater East*	8/13	Bosherston*	14.5/23	Merrion*	23/37
3 Bosherston*	6.5/10	Merrion*	8.5/13.5	Pembroke*	23.5/37.5
4 Merrion*	8.5/13.5	Angle*	12/19.5	Sandy Haven*	16.5/27
5 Angle*	12/19.5	Pembroke*	11.5/19	Marloes Sands	13.5/22
6 Pembroke*	11.5/19	Milford Haven*	12.5/20	Newgale*	19.5/31
7 Milford Haven*	12.5/20	Marloes Sands	17.5/28	Whitesands	17.5/28
8 Dale*	9.5/15	Broad Haven	12.5/20	Pwll Deri	21/34
9 Marloes Sands	8/13	Newgale*	7/11	Newport	22/35
10 Broad Haven	12.5/20	Whitesands Bay	17.5/28	Poppit Sands	14/23
11 Newgale*	7/11	Trefin	11.5/18	St Dogmaels*	2/3
12 St David's*	9/14	Fishguard	20/32		
13 Whitesands Bay	8.5/14	Newport	11.5/18		
14 Trefin	11.5/18	Poppit Sands	14/23		
15 Pwll Deri	9.5/15	St Dogmaels*	2/3		
16 Fishguard	10.5/17				
17 Newport	11.5/18				
18 Poppit Sands	14/23				
19 St Dogmaels*	2/3				

*No bunkhouses or hostels but alternative accommodation is available

your walking speed. They are only suggestions, feel free to adapt them to your needs. **Don't forget** to add your travelling time before and after the walk.

There is also a list of recommended linear day and weekend walks on p33; these cover the best stretches of the coast and those which are well served by public transport. The **public transport map and table** are on pp44-7.

Once you have an idea of your approach turn to **Part 4** for detailed information on accommodation, places to eat and other services in each village and town on the route. Also in Part 4 you will find summaries of the route to accompany the detailed trail maps.

WHICH DIRECTION?

There are a number of advantages in tackling the path in a south to north direction. An important consideration is the prevailing south-westerly wind which will, more often than not, be behind you, helping rather than hindering you.

On a more aesthetic note the scenery is tamer in the south, while more dramatic and wild to the north, so there is a real sense of leaving the best until last.

STAYING IN B&B-STYLE ACCOMMODATION

	Relaxed pace		Medium pace		Fast pace	
Night	**Place**	**Approx Distance** miles/km	**Place**	**Approx Distance** miles/km	**Place**	**Approx Distance** miles/km
0	Amroth		Amroth		Amroth	
1	Tenby	7/11	Penally	9.5/15	Manorbier	17.5/28
2	Manorbier	10.5/17	Freshwater East	12/19	Merrion	19/30.5
3	Bosherston	10.5/17	Merrion	15/24	Pembroke	23.5/37.5
4	Merrion	8.5/13.5	Angle	12/19.5	Herbrandston	16.5/27
5	Angle	12/19.5	Pembroke	11.5/19	Marloes	13.5/22
6	Pembroke	11.5/19	Milford Haven	12.5/20	Solva	24.5/39
7	Milford Haven	12.5/20	Marloes	17.5/28	Trefin	24/39
8	Dale	9.5/15	Broad Haven	12.5/20	Fishguard	20/32
9	Marloes	8/13	Solva	12/19	Newport	11.5/18
10	Broad Haven	12.5/20	Whitesands Bay	12.5/20	St Dogmaels*	16/26
11	Solva	12/19	Trefin	11.5/18		
12	St David's	4/6	Fishguard	20/32		
13	Whitesands Bay	8.5/14	Newport	11.5/18		
14	Trefin	11.5/18	St Dogmaels*	16/26		
15	Pwll Deri	9.5/15				
16	Fishguard	10.5/17				
17	Newport	11.5/18				
18	Poppit Sands	14/23				
19	St Dogmaels*	2/3				

* There is no B&B-style accommodation at St Dogmaels but there is plenty a mile away in Cardigan

In addition a south to north direction allows you to get used to the walking on easier ground before confronting the more strenuous terrain further north.

Some may choose to walk in the opposite direction, perhaps preferring to get the hard stuff out of the way at the beginning. The maps in Part 4 give timings for both directions so the guide can easily be used back to front, or for day trips.

SIDE TRIPS

The coast path gives a fairly thorough impression of what the national park has to offer. However, there are some other hidden gems to be discovered both inland and off-shore for those with some time to spare.

One of the wildest and most beautiful places is the Preseli Hills (see pp203-5) rising above Newport offering extensive views over the whole peninsula with gentle walks in the Cwm Gwaun valley. Closer to Tenby are the Bosherston Lily Ponds (see p101) for short woodland walks; a great place to spot otters. Over on the islands of Skomer, Skokholm and Grassholm (see box p144) and Ramsey

❏ Day and weekend walks

If you don't have the time to walk the whole trail the following day and weekend walks highlight the best of the coast path and most are well served by public transport (see pp43-7); details of some services are given below. For the more experienced walker many of the weekend walks suggested here can be completed in a day.

Day walks

● **Amroth to Tenby** 7 miles/11km (see pp79-88) An easy day passing through beautiful coastal woodland culminating in one of the prettiest seaside towns in Wales. Bus services to Amroth are limited but bus/rail connections from Tenby are good.

● **Freshwater East to Bosherston** 6½ miles/10km (see pp95-101) A short day, passing from a twisting sandstone coastline to spectacular limestone cliffs ending at the banks of the wooded lily ponds at Bosherston. Coastal Cruiser services call at Freshwater East and Bosherston.

● **Freshwater West to Angle** 8 miles/13km (see pp104-112) Starting at a wonderful beach this is one of the quietest stretches of the coast path. Both ends are stops on the Coastal Cruiser routes.

● **Dale to Marloes Sands (Marloes)** 8 miles/13km (see pp142-8) Varied scenery around the Dale peninsula, beginning with gentle wooded slopes leading to wild scenery around the vast sands of Marloes. On the Puffin Shuttle route.

● **Musselwick Sands (Marloes) to Little Haven** 8 miles/13km (see pp148-52) An easy start but a strenuous finale over high wooded cliffs with spectacular views over St Bride's Bay. Marloes and Little Haven are stops on the Puffin Shuttle route.

● **Nolton Haven to Solva** 8½ miles/14km (see pp156-63) A short day, taking in the fantastic Newgale Sands, passing through spectacular coastal scenery and finishing at the prettiest village on the coast. On the Puffin Shuttle route.

● **Circular walk from St David's via Caerfai Bay and St Justinian's** 6½ miles/10km (see pp165-72) Wild scenery and wildlife on this short stretch with views of Ramsey Island, starting and finishing in the tiny cathedral city of St David's. On the Celtic Coaster bus route.

● **St Justinian's to Abereiddy** 9½ miles/15km (see pp172-9) A beautiful stretch around the wild St David's peninsula passing Whitesands Bay and St David's Head. Both ends are stops on the Strumble Shuttle.

● **Newport to Poppit Sands** 14 miles/23km (see pp200-12) The toughest and most spectacular stretch of the coast path with the highest cliffs. On the Poppit Rocket route.

Weekend walks

● **Amroth to Freshwater East** 21½ miles/35km (see pp79-97) Easy walking passing through woodland with tiny hidden beaches and pretty villages in the coves. Bus services to both Amroth and Freshwater East are limited.

● **Freshwater East to Angle** 27 miles/43km (see pp95-112) A long stretch which takes in the spectacular limestone scenery around St Govan's and Castlemartin and the wonderful beach at Freshwater West. On the Coastal Cruiser routes.

● **Dale to Broad Haven** 20½ miles/33km (see pp142-54) Fantastic beaches and cliffs with the potential to include a trip over to Skomer Island to see the puffins. Both stops are on the Puffin Shuttle route.

● **Newgale to Trefin** 29 miles/47km (see pp156-80) Wild and rugged scenery around the St David's peninsula with a useful halfway point at the tiny cathedral city of St David's. Newgale is on the Puffin Shuttle route and Trefin on the Strumble Shuttle route.

● **Trefin to Fishguard** 20 miles/32km (see pp180-94). Pwll Deri and its jaw-dropping cliff scenery make a good halfway point on this beautiful stretch that takes in the rugged coast around Strumble Head. Both are stops on the Strumble Shuttle route.

(see box p163) gannets, gulls and puffins festoon the cliffs while the lazy creeks of the Daugleddau estuary (see pp121-3) make a relaxing change from the seething Atlantic surf. It is worth planning a few extra days on your trip to take in one or two, if not all, of these side trips. A boat trip to one of the islands makes for a good day off since it is not too strenuous.

The Pembrokeshire Coast National Park website (🖳 www.pcnpa.org.uk) lists over 200 circular walks in the National Park many of which are based around the coast path.

Day trips to Rosslare (by ferry) are perfectly feasible for anyone who fancies a break from the coast path. Contact **Irish Ferries** (☎ 08717-300400, 🖳 www.irishferries.com) for services from Pembroke Dock or **Stena Line** (☎ 08705-707070, 🖳 www.stenaline.co.uk) for services from Fishguard.

EXTENDING YOUR WALK

If you want to extend the Pembrokeshire Coast Path, there are options at either end. In the south, parts of the Carmarthen Bay Coast Path are accessible – the seven-mile section between Pendine and Amroth is particularly fine. In the north there is now a 60-mile stretch of graded path from Cardigan to Borth, north of Aberystwyth. However, neither is part of the official National Trail and they are in fact maintained by Carmarthen and Ceredigion County Councils respectively.

More adventurously, the Welsh Assembly government is currently working on creating a new coast path that, when connected to Offa's Dyke National Trail, will enable a walk right around Wales. The route in its entirety, all 800 miles of it, ought to be ready by 2013. Although most people will choose to simply tackle short sections, there are doubtless some brave souls who will undertake the whole thing.

What to take

Deciding how much to take with you can be difficult. Experienced walkers know that you should take only the bare essentials but at the same time you must ensure you have all the equipment necessary to make the trip safe and comfortable.

KEEP IT LIGHT

Carrying a heavy rucksack really can ruin your enjoyment of a good walk and can also slow you down, turning an easy seven-mile day into an interminable slog. Be ruthless when you pack and leave behind all those little home comforts that you tell yourself don't weigh that much really. This advice is even more pertinent to campers who have added weight to carry.

HOW TO CARRY IT

The size of your **rucksack** depends on where you plan to stay and how you plan to eat. If you are camping and cooking you will probably need a 65- to 75-litre rucksack which can hold the tent, sleeping bag, cooking equipment and food.

Make sure your rucksack has a stiffened back and can be adjusted to fit your own back comfortably. This will make carrying the weight much easier. When packing the rucksack make sure you have all the things you are likely to need during the day near the top or in the side pockets, especially if you don't have a bum bag or daypack (see below). This includes water bottle, packed lunch, waterproofs and this guidebook (of course). Make sure the hip belt and chest strap (if there is one) are fastened tightly as this helps distribute the weight with most of it being carried on the hips.

Rucksacks are decorated with seemingly pointless straps but if you adjust them correctly it can make a big difference to your personal comfort while walking.

Consider taking a small **bum bag** or **daypack** for your camera, guidebook and other essentials for when you go sightseeing or for a day walk.

Hostellers should find a 40- to 60-litre rucksack sufficient. If you have gone for the B&B option you will find a 30- to 40-litre day pack is more than enough to carry your lunch, warm and wet weather clothes, camera and guidebook.

A good habit to get into is always to put things in the same place in your rucksack and memorise where they are. There is nothing more annoying than having to pull everything out of your pack to find that lost banana when you're starving, or your camera when there is a seal basking on a rock ten feet away from you.

It's also a good idea to keep everything in **canoe bags**, **waterproof rucksack liners** or strong plastic bags. If you don't it's bound to rain.

FOOTWEAR

Boots

Your boots are the single most important item of gear that can affect the enjoyment of your trek.

In summer you could get by with a light pair of trail shoes if you're only carrying a small pack, although this is an invitation for wet, cold feet if there is any rain and they don't offer much support for your ankles. Some of the terrain can be quite rough so a good pair of walking boots is a safer bet. They must fit well and be properly broken in. It is no good discovering that your boots are slowly murdering your feet three days into a two-week trek. See p56 for more blister-avoidance advice.

Socks

The traditional wearing of a thin liner sock under a thicker wool sock is no longer necessary if you choose a high-quality sock specially designed for walking. A high proportion of natural fibres makes them much more comfortable. Three pairs are ample.

Extra footwear

Some walkers have a second pair of shoes to wear when they are not on the trail. Trainers, sport sandals or flip flops are all suitable as long as they are light.

CLOTHES

Experienced walkers will know the importance of wearing the right clothes. Don't underestimate the weather: Pembrokeshire pokes its nose into a wet and windy Atlantic so it's important to protect yourself from the elements. The weather can be quite hot in the summer but spectacularly bad at any time of the year. Modern hi-tec outdoor clothes can seem baffling but it basically comes down to a base layer to transport sweat from your skin; a mid-layer or two to keep you warm; and an outer layer or 'shell' to protect you from the wind and rain.

Base layer

Cotton absorbs sweat, trapping it next to the skin and chilling you rapidly when you stop exercising. A thin lightweight **thermal top** of a synthetic material is better as it draws moisture away keeping you dry. It will be cool if worn on its own in hot weather and warm when worn under other clothes in the cold. A spare would be sensible. You may also like to bring a **shirt** for wearing in the evening.

Mid-layers

In the summer a woollen jumper or mid-weight polyester **fleece** will suffice. For the rest of the year you will need an extra layer to keep you warm. Both wool and fleece, unlike cotton, have the ability to stay reasonably warm when wet.

Outer layer

A **waterproof jacket** is essential year-round and will be much more comfortable (but also more expensive) if it's also 'breathable' to prevent the build up of condensation on the inside. This layer can also be worn to keep the wind off.

Leg wear

Whatever you wear on your legs it should be light, quick-drying and not restricting. Many British walkers find polyester tracksuit bottoms comfortable. Poly-cotton or microfibre trousers are excellent. Denim jeans should never be worn; if they get wet they become heavy and cold, and bind to your legs. A pair of **shorts** is nice to have on sunny days. Thermal **longjohns** or thick tights are cosy if you're camping but are probably unnecessary even in winter. **Waterproof trousers** are necessary most of the year. In summer a pair of windproof and quick-drying trousers is useful in showery weather. **Gaiters** are not really necessary but may come in useful in wet weather when the vegetation around your legs is dripping wet.

Underwear

Three changes of what you normally wear is fine. Women may find a **sports bra** more comfortable because pack straps can cause bra straps to dig painfully into your shoulders.

Other clothes

A **warm hat** and **gloves** should always be kept in your rucksack; you never know when you might need them. In summer you should also carry a **sun hat** with you, preferably one which covers the back of your neck. Another useful piece of summer equipment is a **swimsuit**; some of the beaches are irresistible on a hot day. Also consider a small **towel**, especially if you are camping or staying in hostels.

TOILETRIES

Only take the minimum: a small bar of **soap** in a plastic container (unless staying in B&Bs) which can also be used instead of shaving cream and for washing clothes; a tiny tube of **toothpaste** and a **toothbrush**; and one roll of **loo paper** in a plastic bag. If you are planning to defecate outdoors you will also need a lightweight **trowel** for burying the evidence (see pp50-1 for further tips). In addition a **razor**; **deodorant**; **tampons/sanitary towels** and a high-factor **sun screen** should cover all your needs.

FIRST-AID KIT

Medical facilities in Britain are excellent so you only need a small kit to cover common problems and emergencies; pack it in a waterproof container. A basic kit should contain: **aspirin** or **paracetamol** for treating mild to moderate pain and fever; **plasters/Band Aids** for minor cuts; **Moleskin**, **Compeed**, or **Second Skin** for blisters; a **bandage** for holding dressings, splints or limbs in place and for supporting a sprained ankle; elastic knee support (tubigrip) for a weak knee; a small selection of different-sized **sterile dressings** for wounds; **porous adhesive tape**; **antiseptic wipes**; **antiseptic cream**; **safety pins**; **tweezers** and **scissors**.

GENERAL ITEMS

Essential

The following should be in everyone's rucksack: a one-litre **water bottle or pouch**; a **torch** (flashlight) with spare bulb and batteries in case you end up walking after dark; **emergency food** which your body can quickly convert into energy; a **penknife**; a **watch** with an alarm; and a **plastic bag** for packing out any rubbish you accumulate. A **whistle** is also worth taking; although you are very unlikely to need it you may be grateful of it in the unlikely event of an emergency (see p54).

Useful

Many would list a **camera** as essential but it can be liberating to travel without one once in a while; a **notebook** can be a more accurate way of recording your impressions. Other things you may find useful include a **book** to pass the time on train and bus journeys; a pair of **sunglasses**, particularly in summer; **binoculars** for observing wildlife; a **mobile phone** or a **phone card** to use in public phone boxes; a **walking stick** or pole to take the shock off your knees and a

vacuum flask for carrying hot drinks. Although the path is easy to follow a 'Silva' type **compass** and the knowledge of how to use it is a good idea in case the sea mist comes in or for any side trips in the Preseli Hills.

SLEEPING BAG

A sleeping bag is only necessary if you are camping or staying in one of the bunkhouses on the route. Campers should find that a two- to three-season bag will suffice but obviously in winter a warmer bag is a good idea.

CAMPING GEAR

Campers will need a decent **tent** (or bivvy bag if you enjoy travelling light) able to withstand wet and windy weather; a **sleeping mat**; a **stove** and **fuel** (there is special mention in Part 4 of which shops stock fuel); a **pan** with a lid that can double as a frying pan/plate is fine for two people; a **pan handle**; a **mug**; a **spoon**; and a wire/plastic **scrubber** for washing up.

MONEY

There are not many banks or cash machines along the coast path so you will have to carry most of your money as **cash**. A **debit card** is the easiest way to withdraw money from banks or cash machines and a **credit card** can be used to pay in larger shops, restaurants and hotels. A **cheque book** is very useful for walkers with accounts in British banks as a cheque will often be accepted where a card is not, though some supermarkets no longer accept cheques.

MAPS

The hand-drawn maps in this book cover the trail at a scale of 1:20,000; plenty of detail and information to keep you on the right track. For side trips to the Preseli Hills, the Daugleddau estuary, or anywhere else in the national park you will need an Ordnance Survey map (☎ 08456-050505, 🖳 www.ordnancesur vey.co.uk, or for the online map shop 🖳 http://leisure.ordnancesurvey.co.uk). There are two excellent maps of the National Park: OS Explorer (OL) Maps (with an orange cover) Nos 35 and 36 for North and South Pembrokeshire at a scale of 1:25,000. Laminated, waterproof Active Map editions are also available.

Enthusiastic map buyers can reduce the often-considerable expense of purchasing them: members of the **Backpackers' Club** (see box p40) can purchase maps at a significant discount through their map service. Alternatively, members of the **Ramblers** (Association, see box p40) can borrow up to 10 maps from their library for a period of four weeks at 50p per map (£1 for weatherproof maps) plus post and packing.

RECOMMENDED READING

Most of the following books can be found in the tourist information centres in Pembrokeshire as well as good bookshops in the rest of Britain.

General guidebooks

The Rough Guide series includes the comprehensive *Wales: The Rough Guide* by Mike Parker. Lonely Planet also produce a guide to the country. *Cool Camping Wales* by Punk Publishing selects some of the finest places to pitch your tent and includes a number of sites relevant to the coast path.

Walking guidebooks

A couple of books cover day walks away from the coast path that explore the hidden corners of Pembrokeshire. The National Park Authority used to publish a guide to *Walking in the Preseli Hills* which you may still find lurking in one of the local bookshops, and Abercastle Publications have a *Short Guide to the Best Walks in Pembrokeshire* by A Roberts for just £2.10. Those who like to round off the day with a pint may appreciate *Pub Walks in Pembrokeshire* published by Sigma with a cover price of £6.95.

Of course, if you are a seasoned long-distance walker or even if you are new to the game and like what you see, check out the other titles in the Trailblazer series; see pp223-4.

General reading

I never knew that about Wales by Christopher Winn (Ebury) is full of fascinating facts and quirky vignettes for all 13 counties of Wales. John Davies's *History*

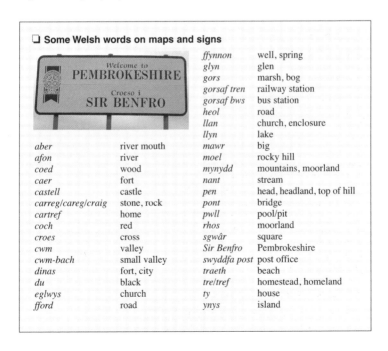

❏ **Some Welsh words on maps and signs**

Welsh	English		Welsh	English
			ffynnon	well, spring
			glyn	glen
			gors	marsh, bog
			gorsaf tren	railway station
			gorsaf bws	bus station
			heol	road
			llan	church, enclosure
			llyn	lake
aber	river mouth		*mawr*	big
afon	river		*moel*	rocky hill
coed	wood		*mynydd*	mountains, moorland
caer	fort		*nant*	stream
castell	castle		*pen*	head, headland, top of hill
carreg/careg/craig	stone, rock		*pont*	bridge
cartref	home		*pwll*	pool/pit
coch	red		*rhos*	moorland
croes	cross		*sgwâr*	square
cwm	valley		*Sir Benfro*	Pembrokeshire
cwm-bach	small valley		*swyddfa post*	post office
dinas	fort, city		*traeth*	beach
du	black		*tre/tref*	homestead, homeland
eglwys	church		*ty*	house
fford	road		*ynys*	island

of Wales, published by Penguin, looks at the political, cultural and social development of the lands now known as Wales from the Ice Age to the modern day. Jan Morris's *Wales*, published by Viking, is the master travel writer's introduction to the country, its literature, folklore, buildings and landscapes.

❏ SOURCES OF FURTHER INFORMATION

Trail information
● **Pembrokeshire Coast National Park Authority** (☎ 0845-345 7275, 🖥 www.pcnpa.org.uk) The park authority provides a wealth of useful information about the area from specific information about the coast path and outdoor activities to wildlife and beaches. The website is very informative and has a detailed section on the coast path.

Tourist information
● **Tourist information centres (TICs)** TICs are based in towns throughout Britain and provide all manner of locally specific information and an accommodation-booking service (see box p15). The centres relevant to the coast path, with the national park information centres at St David's and Newport doubling up as TICs, are in: **Saundersfoot** (p80), **Tenby** (p84), **Pembroke** (p116), **Milford Haven** (p130), **St David's** (p167), **Goodwick** (p190), **Fishguard** (p192), **Newport** (p200) and **Cardigan** (p214). **Pembroke Dock** (p123) is now an information point ie there are only leaflets. For further information see 🖥 www.visitpembrokeshire.co.uk.
● **Wales Tourist Board** (☎ 0870-830 0306, 🖥 www.visitwales.co.uk) The tourist board oversees all the local tourist information centres. It's a good place to find general information about the country and information on outdoor activities and local events. They can also help with arranging holidays and accommodation.

Organisations for walkers
● **Friends of Pembrokeshire National Park** (🖥 www.fpnp.org.uk; FPNP) Besides arranging walks on which the members are the guides this organisation also gives you the opportunity to give something back to the park. They arrange projects which involve repairing footbridges and dry stone walls and clearing overgrown paths. You do not have to be from the local area to join. There's a minimum 'donation' of £10 to join.
● **Backpackers' Club** (🖥 www.backpackersclub.co.uk) A club aimed at people who are involved or interested in lightweight camping through walking, cycling, skiing, canoeing, etc. They produce a quarterly magazine, provide members with a comprehensive advisory and information service on all aspects of backpacking, organise weekend trips and also publish a farm-pitch directory. Membership is £12/15/7 per year for an individual/family/anyone under 18 or over 65.
● **Long Distance Walkers' Association** (🖥 www.ldwa.org.uk) An association of people with a common interest in long-distance walking. Membership includes a thrice-yearly magazine, *Strider*, giving details of challenge events and local group walks as well as articles on the subject. Information on hundreds of long-distance paths is presented in their newly revised *UK Trailwalkers' Handbook*. Individual membership is £13 per year whilst family membership for two adults and all children under 18 is £19.50 per year.
● **Ramblers** (formerly Ramblers' Association: ☎ 020-7339 8500, 🖥 www.ramblers.org.uk; Welsh branch: ☎ 029-2064 4308, 🖥 www.ramblers.org.uk/wales) Looks after the interests of walkers throughout Britain. They publish a quarterly *Walk* magazine (£3.40 to non-members) and *Walk Britain's Great Views* (£14.99), a guide to Britain's top 50 viewpoints. Membership costs £29.50/39.50 individual/joint.

Flora and fauna field guides

The National Park Authority published a small booklet highlighting the more common species along the coastline called *The Birds of the Pembrokeshire Coast* by Peter Knights; it's out of print now but you may be able to find a copy on the trail. Dyfed Wildlife Trust's *Birds of Pembrokeshire* by Donovan and Rees at £17.95 is an expensive yet useful guide but some might prefer a book which is also of use when travelling elsewhere. The AA's *Birds of Britain and Europe* at £9.99 is one of many excellent bird guides that can fit inside a rucksack pocket. *Where to watch birds – Wales* by David Saunders (Helm) has a comprehensive chapter on the best birding sites in Pembrokeshire.

Pembrokeshire is famous for its wild flowers so a guidebook on these may come in handy. At just £3.99 Andrew Branson's *Wild Flowers of Britain and Europe*, published by Bounty Books, is an excellent pocket-sized guide that categorises flowers according to habitat.

Welsh publisher Graffeg produce an attractive, illustrated introduction to *Skomer*.

Getting to and from the Coast Path

A glance at any map of Britain gives the impression that Pembrokeshire is a long way from anywhere and hard to get to. In reality road and rail links with the coast path are excellent with Kilgetty, close to the start of the coast path, lying on both the national rail network and the National Express coach network. Travelling to the start of the coast path by public transport makes sense. There's no need to worry about the safety of your abandoned vehicle while walking, there are no logistical headaches about how to return to your car when you've finished the walk and it's obviously one of the biggest steps you can take towards minimising your ecological footprint. Quite apart from that, you'll simply feel your holiday has begun the moment you step out of your front door, rather than having to wait until you've slammed the car door behind you. However, the end of the coast path is not so well served with no rail or National Express coach service to/from Cardigan. The best option is Richards Brothers Nos 460/461 (see box p47) service from Cardigan to Carmarthen; Carmarthen has good rail links (see below) to the rest of the UK. Alternatively, Eurolines (see box p42) operates one service a day from Fishguard (Goodwick).

NATIONAL TRANSPORT

By rail

For those walking the whole path the nearest train stations are Kilgetty (3 miles/ 5km from the start of the path at Amroth) and Carmarthen (an 85-minute bus ride from Cardigan) or Fishguard Harbour (at Goodwick; a 50-minute bus ride from the end of the coast path near Cardigan). There are frequent services to

Kilgetty and Carmarthen from both Cardiff and Swansea which in turn are served by trains from all over the country. However, services to Fishguard Harbour are limited (see box p47).

Other points of the path can also be reached by train; there are stations at Tenby, Penally, Pembroke, Pembroke Dock and Milford Haven.

Arriva Trains Wales (🖳 www.arrivatrainswales.co.uk) operates most services within Wales, First Great Western (🖳 www.firstgreatwestern.co.uk) has services to Cardiff and Swansea from London Paddington, and Cross Country Trains (🖳 www.crosscountrytrains.co.uk) from Scotland and central England to Cardiff.

All timetable and fare information can be found at **National Rail Enquiries** (☎ 08457-484950, 24hrs; 🖳 www.nationalrail.co.uk). Tickets can be booked online direct through the companies mentioned above, or through 🖳 www .thetrainline.com and 🖳 www.qjump.co.uk.

If you think you may want to book a taxi when you arrive visit 🖳 www .traintaxi.co.uk or phone ☎ 01733-237037 for details of taxi companies operating at rail stations throughout England.

❑ **Getting to Britain**

● **By air**　Most international airlines serve London Heathrow and London Gatwick. In addition a number of budget airlines fly from many of Europe's major cities to the other London terminals at Stansted and Luton and increasingly to Cardiff (🖳 www .tbicardiffairport.com), the nearest airport with international services to the coast path, and to Bristol airport as well.

From London (Paddington) it is 5-6 hours by train to Kilgetty via Swansea; from Bristol or Cardiff it is about $2^{1}/_{2}$-3 hours.

● **From Europe by train (with or without a car)**　Eurostar (🖳 www .eurostar.com) operates a high-speed passenger service via the Channel Tunnel between Paris and London, and Brussels and London. Trains arrive at and depart from St Pancras International station, which also has good underground links to Paddington and other railway stations in London. For more information about rail services between Europe and Britain contact your national rail operator or Railteam (🖳 www.railteam.eu).

Eurotunnel (🖳 www.eurotunnel.com) operates a shuttle train service for vehicles via the Channel Tunnel between Calais and Folkestone, taking 35 minutes.

● **From Europe by coach**　Eurolines (🖳 www.eurolines.com) have a huge network of services connecting over 500 cities in 25 European countries to London. From Cork there is one service (IS890) daily to Fishguard (Goodwick); the service continues to London.

● **From Europe by ferry (with or without a car)**　Numerous ferry companies operate routes between the major North Sea and Channel ports of mainland Europe and the ports on Britain's eastern and southern coasts. A useful website for further information is 🖳 www.directferries.com.

Visitors from the Republic of Ireland have the choice of two ferry services direct to Pembrokeshire; both operate daily. Irish Ferries (🖳 www.irishferries.com) operates from Rosslare to Pembroke Dock, and Stena Line (🖳 www.stenaline.ie/ferry) from Rosslare to Fishguard (Goodwick).

By coach

National Express (☎ 0871-781 8181, lines open 8am-8pm daily; ▭ www
.nationalexpress.com) is the principal coach (long-distance bus) operator in
Britain. Coach travel is generally cheaper but takes longer than travel by train.
Tickets booked over the phone are now subject to a £2 charge.

Kilgetty, which is just three miles (5km) from Amroth and the start of the
coast path, is a stop on the twice-daily (one overnight) NX508 service from
London to Haverfordwest via Tenby, Pembroke, Pembroke Dock and Milford
Haven. The NX528 service operates daily from Birmingham to Haverfordwest
via Swansea, Kilgetty, Tenby, Pembroke, Pembroke Dock and Milford Haven.
National Express doesn't operate any services to/from Cardigan (near the end
of the walk) but Eurolines (see box opposite) has one a day from Fishguard
(Goodwick) to London.

By car

Pembrokeshire has good links to the national road network with the M4 motor-
way stretching as far as Swansea. From here Kilgetty can be reached by following the A48 to Carmarthen, A40 to St Clears and finally the A477. From
Kilgetty it is a short drive down the lane to Amroth and the start of the path. The
National Park Authority has a (free) car park, indicated by a blue 'P' sign, just
off the seafront road near the Amroth Arms pub.

The end of the coast path and the northern half of the coast are reached by
following the A484 from Carmarthen to Cardigan. The best place to park your
car is at the National Park supervised car park at Poppit Sands which is opposite the lifeboat station.

LOCAL TRANSPORT

Pembrokeshire has an excellent public transport system reaching some of the
smallest, most out-of-the-way villages. This is great news for anyone hoping
to do any linear day or weekend walks. Of particular interest are the coastal
shuttle bus services (see p45) that are designed especially for coast-path walkers, serving all the villages along the coast between Milford Haven and St
David's.

The public transport map on p44 shows the most useful bus and train routes
and the box on pp45-7 gives details of the frequency of services and whom you
should contact for detailed timetable information.

The whole county is covered in the *Pembrokeshire Bus Timetable*, published each year. It can be picked up for free at any of the tourist information
centres. Alternatively, copies of that and the Coastal Buses timetable, as well as
train information, are available from Pembrokeshire County Council Transport
Unit (☎ 01437-764551, ▭ www.pembrokeshire.gov.uk).

For information on how best to access the countryside by sustainable modes
of transport check out ▭ www.pembrokeshiregreenways.co.uk, a site dedicated to promoting public transport and walks or cycle routes that can be accessed
via it.

There's also a useful travel information line and website for Wales: ☎ 0871-200 2233, 🖳 www.traveline-cymru.info. Up-to-date information can also be found at both St David's National Park Information Centre (see p167) and Newport National Park Information Centre (see p200).

Summer services operate from early May until late September; winter services operate from late September to early May. Sunday services also often operate on Bank Holiday Mondays as well.

Public transport around the coast

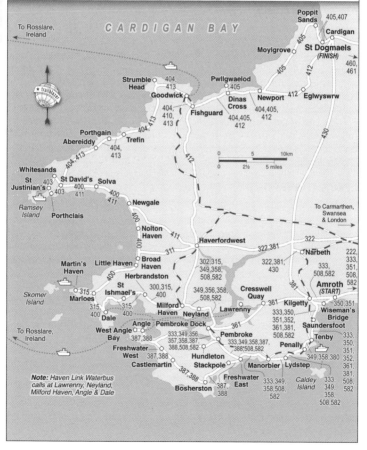

Coastal bus services

The five excellent services (Coastal Cruiser 1 & 2, Puffin Shuttle, Strumble Shuttle, Poppit Rocket and Celtic Coaster 1 & 2; four are powered by eco-friendly recycled vegetable oil sourced from the county's civic amenity sites and local catering businesses), aimed directly at weary coast-path walkers, cover most of the path; see the public transport map (opposite) and table below and pp46-7 for full details. Most operate year-round but services in the winter months are limited. All operate on a Hail and Ride basis in rural areas, as long as you are standing in a safe place for the bus to stop. Buses on the Celtic Coaster and Coastal Cruiser services are accessible for wheelchair users. For more information on the coastal buses and to see an up-to-date timetable visit 🖳 www.pembrokeshire.gov.uk/coastbuses.

Haven Link Waterbus

Although its future is uncertain, the Haven Link Waterbus runs along the Milford Haven waterway and Lower Cleddau Estuary, connecting the towns and villages along the estuary and providing a shortcut from Angle to Dale. Piloted in 2008 the service, operated by Rudders Boatyard (see p47), runs from late June until late September. Starting at Lawrenny, one boat travels down the river via stops at Burton, Hobbs Point, Neyland, Hazelbeach, Milford Haven, Angle and Dale. A second vessel operates in the reverse direction. Bear in mind that owing to tidal restrictions it is not always possible to call at some points.

For walkers who wish to cut out the industrialised section around Milford Haven, there is the option of catching the waterbus from Angle (see p110) to Dale (see p142). For an up-to-date timetable, fares or to book your passage (advisable in the high season) contact Rudders Boatyard or Pembrokeshire Greenways (☎ 01437-776313, 🖳 www.pembrokeshiregreenways.co.uk).

❏ PUBLIC TRANSPORT SERVICES

The following list is not completely comprehensive but does cover the most important services. Unless specified otherwise services operate year-round.

Buses
Silcox Coaches (Pembroke Dock ☎ 01646-683143, Tenby ☎ 01834-842189; 🖳 www.silcoxcoaches.co.uk)

222	Amroth to Carmarthen via Pendine, Sun 3/day (services connect with the 350, see below)
300	Milford Haven town service including Herbrandston, Mon-Sat 2/day
311	Haverfordwest to Broad Haven, Mon-Sat 5-7/day
322	Haverfordwest bus station to Carmarthen via Narberth, Mon-Sat 3/day
333	Pembroke Dock to Carmarthen via Manorbier, Tenby, Saundersfoot & Kilgetty, Wed & Fri 1/day
350	Tenby to Amroth via Saundersfoot, Kilgetty & Wiseman's Bridge, summer Sun 4/day (connects with the 222, see above)
351	Pendine to Tenby via Amroth, Saundersfoot, Wiseman's Bridge & Kilgetty, Mon-Sat 6-7/day plus 1/day Amroth to Tenby
352	Tenby to Kilgetty via Saundersfoot, Mon-Sat 8-12/day *(cont'd overleaf)*

❑ PUBLIC TRANSPORT SERVICES *(cont'd from p45)*

Buses

Silcox Coaches *(cont'd)*

356   Milford Haven to Monkton via Hazelbeach, Neyland, Pembroke Dock & Pembroke, Mon-Sat approx 1/hr

357   Monkton to Pembroke Dock via Pembroke, Mon-Sat 5/day

358   Pembroke Dock to Tenby via Pembroke, Manorbier, Lydstep & Penally, Fri & Sat 1/night

361   Pembroke Dock to Tenby via Cresswell Quay, Kilgetty & Saundersfoot, Mon-Sat 3/day

380   Tenby town service including Penally, Mon-Sat 8/day

381   Tenby to Haverfordwest via Saundersfoot, Kilgetty & Narberth, Mon-Sat 9-10/day

387   **Coastal Cruiser 1**: circular route to/from Pembroke Dock via Pembroke, Hundleton, West Angle Bay, Angle, Freshwater West, Castlemartin, Bosherston, Stackpole, Stackpole Quay, Freshwater East & Pembroke, early May to late Sep daily 3/day, late Sep to early May Mon, Thur & Sat 2/day

388   **Coastal Cruiser 2**: circular route to/from Pembroke Dock – route as above but in reverse, early May to late Sep daily 3/day, late Sep to early May Mon, Thur & Sat 1/day

First (general enquiries only ☎ 01437-763284; 🖳 www.firstgroup.com/ukbus/wales/swwales/home)

302   Haverfordwest to Hubberston via Milford Haven, Mon-Sat 2/hr, Sun 7/day

349   Haverfordwest to Tenby via Neyland, Pembroke Dock, Pembroke, Manorbier, Lydstep & Penally, Mon-Sat 1/hr, summer Sun 4/day plus 1/day Haverfordwest to Pembroke, winter Sun 2/day plus 1/day Haverfordwest to Pembroke

Acorn Travel (☎ 01348-874728; 🖳 www.acorntravel.co.uk)

315   **Puffin Shuttle** Haverfordwest to Marloes via Milford Haven, Herbrandston, St Ishmael's, Dale & Martin's Haven; daily 3/day.
This service connects with Richards Brothers 400 service (see below).

412   Cardigan to Haverfordwest via Eglwyswrw, Newport, Dinas Cross & Fishguard, Sun 3/day plus 2/day Fishguard to Haverfordwest (see Richards Brothers for Mon-Sat service)

Richards Brothers (☎ 01239-613756; 🖳 www.gobybus.net)

400   **Puffin Shuttle** Marloes to St David's via Martin's Haven, Little Haven, Broad Haven, Haroldston West, Druidstone Haven, Nolton Haven, Newgale & Solva, early May to late Sep daily 3/day, late Sep to early May Mon, Thur & Sat 2/day plus one service to Milford Haven via Dale & Herbrandston (but only for the St David's to Marloes service). The 400 connects with Acorn Travel's 315 service (see above).

404   **Strumble Shuttle** Fishguard to St David's via Goodwick, Strumble Head, Abercastle, Trefin, Porthgain & Abereiddy, early May to late Sep daily 2/day plus 1/day to/from Newport via Dinas Cross; late Sep to early May Mon, Thur & Sat 2/day

Richards Brothers *(cont'd)*
405 **Poppit Rocket** Cardigan to Fishguard via St Dogmaels, Poppit Sands,
  Moylgrove, Newport, Dinas Cross & Pwllgwaelod early May to late Sep daily
  3/day; late Sep to early May Cardigan to Newport only Mon, Thur, Sat 3/day
407 Poppit Sands to Cardigan via St Dogmaels, Mon-Sat 6/day plus 8/day from
  Glanteifion/The Moorings (after Poppit Sands)
410 Fishguard town service including Goodwick & Fishguard Harbour,
  Mon-Sat roughly 2/hr
411 Haverfordwest (bus and rail stations) to St David's via Newgale & Solva,
  Mon-Sat 11/day (for Sun service see Summerdale Coaches No 411)
412 Cardigan to Haverfordwest via Eglwyswrw, Newport, Dinas Cross &
  Fishguard, Mon-Sat 1/hr (see Acorn re Sunday service)
413 Fishguard to St David's via Goodwick & Trefin, Mon-Sat 5-7/day
430 Narberth to Cardigan, Mon-Sat 3/day
460/461 Cardigan to Carmarthen via Newcastle Emlyn & Llandysul,
  Mon-Sat 1/hr, Sun 3/day

Summerdale Coaches (☎ 01348-870270)
411 Haverfordwest (bus and rail stations) to St David's via Newgale & Solva,
  Sun 4/day plus 1/day to/from Fishguard (see Richards Brothers for Mon-Sat
  services)

Alun Phillips (☎ 01348-840539)
403 **Celtic Coaster 1** St David's (Peninsula Shuttle Service, circular route) via
  Porthclais, St Justinian & Whitesands, early Apr to late Sep daily 1/hr
403 **Celtic Coaster 2** St David's (Peninsula Shuttle Service, circular route) via
  Porthclais, St Justinian & Whitesands, late May to late Aug daily 1/hr.
  Between mid July and late Aug an additional shuttle service operates from
  St David's to St Justinian's daily 2/hr.

Waterbus
  Rudders Boatyard (☎ 01646-602681, 🖥 www.ruddersboatyard.co.uk)
  Haven Link Waterbus Lawrenny to Dale via Burton, Hobbs Point, Neyland,
  Hazelbeach, Milford Haven, Angle & Dale, Fri, Sat & Sun late June to late
  Sep, 2/day in each direction. (Note: At the time of writing funding had not
  been confirmed so it's not certain that the service will continue in 2010.)

Trains
Arriva Trains Wales (🖥 **www.arrivatrainswales.co.uk**)
● Swansea to Pembroke Dock via Narberth, Kilgetty, Saundersfoot, Tenby, Penally,
Manorbier & Pembroke, Mon-Sat 8-9/day, Sun 2-3/day (late afternoon/evening only)

● Cardiff Central to Milford Haven via Haverfordwest Mon-Sat 8/day, Swansea to
Milford Haven Sun 4/day

● Cardiff/Swansea to Fishguard Harbour (Goodwick), Mon-Sat 1/day linked to the
departure (and arrival) of the Stenalink ferry service.

PART 2: MINIMUM IMPACT & OUTDOOR SAFETY

Minimum impact walking

In this chaotic world in which people live their lives at an increasingly frenetic pace, many of us living in overcrowded cities and working in jobs that offer little free-time, the great outdoors is becoming an essential means of escape. Walking in the countryside is a wonderful means of relaxation and gives people the time to think and rediscover themselves.

Of course, as the popularity of the countryside increases so do the problems that this pressure brings. It is important for visitors to remember that the countryside is the home and workplace of many others. Walkers in particular should be aware of their responsibilities. Indeed a walker who respects and understands the countryside will get far more enjoyment from their trip.

By following a few simple guidelines while walking the coast path you can have a positive impact, not just on your own well-being but also on local communities and the environment, thereby becoming part of the solution.

ECONOMIC IMPACT

Rural businesses and communities in Britain have been hit hard in recent years by a seemingly endless series of crises. Most people are aware of the Countryside Code (see box p53); not dropping litter and closing the gate behind you are still as pertinent as ever, but in light of the economic pressures that local countryside businesses are under there is something else you can do: buy local.

Buy local

Look and ask for local produce (see box p16) to buy and eat. Not only does this cut down on the amount of pollution and congestion that the transportation of food creates (the so-called 'food miles'), but also ensures that you are supporting local farmers and producers; the very people who have moulded the countryside you have come to see and who are in the best position to protect it. If you can find local food which is also organic so much the better.

Support local businesses

It's a fact of life that money spent at local level – perhaps in a market, or at the greengrocer, or in an independent pub – has a far greater impact for good on that community than the equivalent spent in a branch of a national chain store or

---

(Opposite) There's more geological variety to be seen in Pembrokeshire than in any other part of Britain. Even if you don't have an interest in geology you can't fail to be impressed by some of the rock formations, such as these cliffs between Lydstep and Manorbier Bay.

restaurant. While no-one would advocate that walkers should boycott the larger supermarkets, which after all do provide local employment, it's worth remembering that businesses in rural communities rely heavily on visitors for their very existence. If we want to keep these shops and post offices, we need to use them. The more money that circulates locally and is spent on local labour and materials, the greater the impact on the local economy and the more power the community has to effect the change it wants to see.

Encourage local cultural traditions and skills

No part of the countryside looks the same. Buildings, food, skills, and language evolve out of the landscape and are moulded over hundreds of years to suit the locality. Discovering these cultural differences is part of the pleasure of walking in new places. Visitors' enthusiasm for local traditions and skills brings awareness and pride, nurturing a sense of place; an increasingly important role in a world where economic globalisation continues to undermine the very things that provide security and a feeling of belonging.

ENVIRONMENTAL IMPACT

A walking holiday in itself is an environmentally friendly approach to tourism. The following are some ideas on how you can go a few steps further in helping to minimise your impact on the natural environment while walking the Pembrokeshire Coast Path.

Use public transport whenever possible

Public transport in Pembrokeshire is excellent and in many cases specifically geared towards the coast-path walker. By using the local bus you will help to keep the standard high. Public transport is always preferable to using private cars as it benefits everyone: visitors, locals and the environment.

Never leave litter

Leaving litter shows a total disrespect for the natural world and others coming after you. As well as being unsightly litter kills wildlife, pollutes the environment and can be dangerous to farm animals. **Please** carry a degradable plastic bag so you can dispose of your rubbish in a bin in the next village. It would be very helpful if you could pick up litter left by other people too.

● **Is it OK if it's biodegradable?** Not really. Apple cores, banana skins, orange peel and the like are unsightly, encourage flies, ants and wasps and ruin a picnic spot for others. Using the excuse that they are natural and biodegradable just doesn't cut any ice. When was the last time you saw a banana tree in Wales?

● **The lasting impact of litter** A piece of orange peel left on the ground takes six months to decompose; silver foil 18 months; a plastic bag 10 years; clothes 15 years; and an aluminium can 85 years.

MINIMUM IMPACT & OUTDOOR SAFETY

(Opposite) Popular with surfers, Freshwater West (see p108) is one of the best beaches in Pembrokeshire. (Photo © Jim Manthorpe).

❏ **Maintaining the Pembrokeshire Coast Path**

Maintenance of the path is carried out by the National Trail officer and is funded largely by the Countryside Council for Wales (who contribute 75%) and 25% by the National Park Authority. Teams of rangers, wardens and volunteers undertake various tasks throughout the year. In summer, for example, there is the constant battle to cut back vigorous growth which would engulf the path if left alone and repairs need to be carried out on some of the footbridges, stiles and kissing gates. Many of the stiles have been replaced by kissing gates to make access easier for the less able and the project is still ongoing.

Where erosion of the path becomes a problem wooden causeways or steps are constructed and particularly boggy areas are drained by digging ditches. Occasionally the authorities will re-route the path where erosion has become so severe as to be a danger to the walker. In the winter some sections of the path slip into the sea necessitating the realignment of the path, often involving the instalment of new stiles or kissing gates in order to run the path through a field.

Take these potential route changes into account when using the maps in Part 4. They usually cover a very short distance but have the potential to cause a little confusion.

Erosion

● **Stay on the main trail** The effect of your footsteps may seem minuscule but when they are multiplied by several thousand walkers each year they become rather more significant. Avoid taking shortcuts, widening the trail or taking more than one path; your boots will be followed by many others.

● **Consider walking out of season** The maximum disturbance by walkers coincides with the time of year when nature wants to do most of its growth and repair. In high-use areas, such as many parts of the coast path, the trail never recovers. Walking at less busy times eases this pressure while also generating year-round income for the local economy. Not only that, but it may make the walk a more relaxing experience with fewer people on the path and less competition for accommodation.

Respect all wildlife

Care for all wildlife you come across along the coast path; it has as much right to be there as you. Tempting as it may be to pick wild flowers leave them so the next people who pass can enjoy them too. Don't break branches off or damage trees in any way. If you come across wildlife keep your distance and don't watch for too long. Your presence can cause considerable stress, particularly if the adults are with young, or in winter when the weather is harsh and food is scarce. Young animals are rarely abandoned. If you come across young birds keep away so that their mother can return. Anyone considering a spot of climbing on the sea cliffs should bear in mind that there are restrictions in certain areas due to the presence of nesting birds. Check with the local tourist information office.

The code of the outdoor loo

'Going' in the outdoors is a lost art worth re-learning, for your sake and everyone else's. As more and more people discover the joys of the outdoors this is becoming an important issue. In some parts of the world where visitor pressure is higher than in Britain walkers and climbers are required to pack out their excrement. This may one day be necessary here. Human excrement is not only offensive to our senses but, more importantly, can infect water sources.

● **Where to go** Wherever possible **use a toilet**. Public toilets are marked on the trail maps in this guide and you will also find facilities in pubs, cafés and campsites along the coast path.

If you do have to go outdoors choose a site at least **30 metres away from running water**. Carry a small trowel and **dig a small hole** about 15cm (6") deep to bury your excrement in. It decomposes quicker when in contact with the top layer of soil or leaf mould. Use a stick to stir loose soil into your deposit as well as this speeds up decomposition even more. Do not squash it under rocks as this slows down the composting process. If you have to use rocks to cover it make sure they are not in contact with your faeces.

Make sure you do not dig any holes on ground that is, or could be, of historic or archaeological interest.

● **Toilet paper and tampons** Toilet paper takes a long time to decompose whether buried or not. It is easily dug up by animals and may then blow into water sources or onto the path. The best method for dealing with it is to **pack it out**. Put the used paper inside a paper bag which you then place inside a plastic bag (or two). Then simply empty the contents of the paper bag at the next toilet you come across and throw the bag away. You should also pack out **tampons** and **sanitary towels** in a similar way; they take years to decompose and may also be dug up and scattered about by animals.

Wild camping

Unfortunately, wild camping is not encouraged within the national park. In any case there are few places where it is a viable option. This is a shame since wild camping is an altogether more fulfilling experience than camping on a designated site. Living in the outdoors without any facilities provides a valuable lesson in simple, sustainable living where the results of all your actions, from going to the loo to washing your plates, can be seen.

If you do insist on wild camping **always** ask the landowner for permission. Anyone contemplating camping on a beach should be very aware of the times and heights of the tide. Follow these suggestions for minimising your impact and encourage others to do likewise.

● **Be discreet** Camp alone or in small groups, spend only one night in each place and pitch your tent late and move off early.

● **Never light a fire** The deep burn caused by camp fires, no matter how small, damages the turf which can take years to recover. Cook on a camp stove instead.

● **Don't use soap or detergent** There is no need to use soap; even biodegradable soaps and detergents pollute streams. You won't be away from a shower for more than a day or so. Wash up without detergent; use a plastic or metal scourer, or failing that, a handful of fine pebbles from the beach or some bracken or grass.

● **Leave no trace** Learn the skill of moving on without leaving any sign of having been there: no moved boulders, ripped up vegetation or dug drainage ditches.

Make a final check of your campsite before departing; pick up any litter that you or anyone else has left, so leaving the place in a better state than you found it.

ACCESS

Britain is a crowded cluster of islands with few places where you can wander as you please. Most of the land is a patchwork of fields and agricultural land and the Pembrokeshire Coast National Park is no different. However, there are countless public rights of way, in addition to the coast path, that criss-cross the land. This is fine, but what happens if you feel a little more adventurous and want to explore the beaches, dunes, moorland, woodland and hills that can also be found within the national park boundaries?

Right to roam

The Countryside & Rights of Way Act 2000, or 'Right to Roam' as dubbed by walkers, was passed by parliament after a long campaign to allow greater public access to areas of countryside in England and Wales deemed to be uncultivated open country. This essentially means moorland, heathland, downland and upland areas. In the case of the Pembrokeshire Coast National Park this implies the Preseli Hills and the wild country around the St David's peninsula. It does not mean free access to wander over farmland, woodland or private gardens. The legislation came into effect in October 2005.

Some land is covered by restrictions (ie high-impact activities such as driving a vehicle, cycling, horse-riding are not permitted) and some land is excluded (such as gardens, parks and cultivated land). If the urge takes you and you feel like tramping the Preseli Hills or getting lost among the sand dunes check with the Countryside Council for Wales (🖥 www.ccw.gov.uk) first.

With more freedom in the countryside comes a need for more responsibility from the walker. Remember that wild open country is still the workplace of farmers and home to all sorts of wildlife. Have respect for both and avoid disturbing domestic and wild animals.

Lambing

Around 80% of the coast path passes through private farmland much of which is pasture for sheep. Lambing takes place from mid-March to mid-May when dogs should not be taken along the path. Even a dog secured on a lead is liable

---

❏ **National Trails**

The Pembrokeshire Coast Path is one of 15 National Trails (🖥 www.national trail.co.uk) in England and Wales. These are Britain's flagship long-distance paths which grew out of the post-war desire to protect the country's special places, a movement which also gave birth to national parks and AONBs (see p59-60).

National Trails in Wales are designated and largely funded by the Countryside Council for Wales and are managed on the ground by a National Trail Officer. They co-ordinate the maintenance work undertaken by the local highway authority and landowners to ensure that the trail is kept to nationally agreed standards.

to disturb a pregnant ewe. If you should see a lamb or ewe that appears to be in distress contact the nearest farmer. For further details about taking a dog along the coast path see p22.

The Countryside Code

The aim of the code (see box) is to help everyone **respect**, **protect** and **enjoy** the countryside. The country-side is a fragile place which every vis-

> ❑ **The Countryside Code**
> ● Be safe – plan ahead and follow any signs (see pp54-7)
> ● Leave gates and property as you find them
> ● Protect plants and animals and take your litter home
> ● Keep dogs under close control
> ● Consider other people

itor should respect. The countryside code seems like common sense but sadly some people still seem to have no understanding of how to treat the countryside they walk in. Everyone visiting the countryside has a responsibility to minimise the impact of their visit so that other people can enjoy the same peaceful land-scapes. It does not take much effort; it really is common sense. Below is an expanded version of the Countryside Code:

● **Enjoy the countryside and respect its life and work** Access to the coun-tryside depends on being sensitive to the needs and wishes of those who live and work there. Being courteous and friendly to those you meet will ensure a healthy future for all based on partnership and co-operation.

● **Guard against all risk of fire** Accidental fire is a great fear of farmers and foresters. Never make a camp fire and take matches and cigarette butts out with you to dispose of safely.

● **Keep your dog under close control** The only place you can safely allow your dog off the lead is along the beaches but there are restrictions in the summer (see p22). Across farmland dogs should be kept on a short lead at all times but must be kept on one between 1 March and 31 July on most areas of open country and common land. If a farm animal starts to chase you/your dog let your dog off the lead. Also take care that your dog does not disturb birds that nest on the ground, or other wildlife. During lambing time they should not be taken with you at all (see opposite).

Don't disturb farm animals

Farmers are permitted to destroy any dog that injures or worries their ani-mals. For further information call the CCW enquiry line (☎ 0845-130 6229).

● **Keep to paths across farmland** Stick to the official coast path across arable or pasture land. Minimise erosion by not cutting corners or widening the path.

● **Use gates and stiles to cross fences**, **hedges and walls** The coast path is well supplied with gates where it crosses field boundaries. On some of the side trips you may find the paths less accommodating. If you do have to climb over a gate which you can't open always do so at the hinged end.

● **Leave livestock**, **crops and machinery alone** Help farmers by not interfering with their means of livelihood.

● **Take your litter home** 'Pack it in, pack it out'. Litter is not only ugly but can be harmful to wildlife. Small mammals often become trapped in discarded cans and bottles. Many walkers think that orange peel and banana skins do not count as litter. Even biodegradable foodstuffs attract common scavenging species such as crows and gulls to the detriment of less dominant species. Carry a plastic bag to put yours and other people's litter and food scraps in and take it home or find a bin. See also p49.

● **Help keep all water clean** Leaving litter and going to the toilet near a water source can pollute people's water supplies. For information on going to the toilet in the outdoors see pp50-1.

● **Protect wildlife**, **plants and trees** Care for and respect all wildlife you come across along the coast path. Don't pick plants, break trees or scare wild animals. If you come across young birds that appear to have been abandoned leave them alone. If you visit any of the islands always stick to the designated paths to avoid disturbing nesting seabirds.

● **Take special care on country roads** Cars travel dangerously fast on narrow winding lanes. To be safe walk facing the oncoming traffic and carry a torch or wear highly visible clothing when it's getting dark.

● **Make no unnecessary noise** Enjoy the peace and solitude of the outdoors by staying in small groups and acting unobtrusively.

Outdoor safety

AVOIDANCE OF HAZARDS

With good planning and preparation most hazards can be avoided. This information is just as important for those out on a day walk as for those walking the entire coast path.

Ensure you have suitable **clothes** to keep you warm and dry, whatever the conditions (see p56) and a spare change of inner clothes. A compass, whistle, torch and first-aid kit should be carried and are discussed on pp37. The **emergency signal** is six blasts on the whistle or six flashes with a torch. A **mobile phone** may also be useful.

Take plenty of **food** with you for the day and at least one litre of **water** although more would be better, especially on the long northern stretches. It is a good idea to fill up your bottle/pouch whenever you pass through a village since stream water cannot be relied upon. You will eat far more walking than you do normally so make sure you have enough for the day, as well as some high-energy snacks (chocolate, dried fruit, biscuits) in the bottom of your pack for an emergency.

Stay alert and know exactly where you are throughout the day. The easiest way to do this is to **regularly check your position** on the map. If visibility suddenly decreases with mist and cloud, or there is an accident, you will be able to make a sensible decision about what action to take based on your location.

If you choose to walk alone you must appreciate and be prepared for the increased risk. It's a good idea to leave word with someone about where you are going and remember to contact them when you have arrived safely.

Safety on the cliff top

Sadly every year people are either injured or killed walking the coast path. Along the full length of the path you will see warning signs urging you to keep well away from the cliff edge. They are there for a reason. Cliffs are very dangerous. In many places it is difficult to see just where the edge is since it is often well hidden by vegetation. Added to this is the fact that, in places, the path is extremely close to the edge. Always err on the side of over-caution and think twice about walking if you are tired or feeling ill. This is when most accidents happen. To ensure you have a safe walk it is well worth following this advice:

● Keep to the path – avoid cliff edges and overhangs
● Avoid walking in windy weather – cliff tops are particularly dangerous in such conditions
● Be aware of the increased possibility of slipping over in wet or icy weather.
● Wear strong sturdy boots with good ankle support and a good grip rather than trainers or sandals
● Be extra vigilant with children
● Keep dogs under close control
● Wear or carry warm and waterproof clothing
● In an emergency dial ☎ 999 and ask for the coastguard

Take note of signs warning of dangerous cliffs

Safety on the beach

Pembrokeshire's beaches are spectacular in any weather but it's when the sun is shining that the sweaty walker gets the urge to take a dip. The sea can be a dangerous environment and care should be taken if you do go for a swim and even if you're just walking along the beach. Follow this common-sense advice:

● If tempted to take a shortcut across a beach be aware of the tides to avoid being cut off or stranded
● Do not sit directly below cliffs and do not climb them unless you are an experienced climber with the right equipment, or with someone who has experience
● Don't swim immediately after eating, or after drinking alcohol; swimming in itself can be dangerous
● Be aware of local tides and currents – don't assume it is safe just because other people are swimming there; if in doubt consult the tide tables (see below) or check with the nearest tourist information centre
● Be extra vigilant with children
● In an emergency dial ☎ 999 and ask for the coastguard.

TIDE TABLES

Tide tables are available from newsagents in the area. Between Easter and the end of October they are also published in the free newspaper, *Coast to Coast*, which you can get from tourist information centres.

WEATHER FORECASTS

The Pembrokeshire coast is exposed to whatever the churning Atlantic can throw at it. Even when it's sunny sea breezes usually develop during the course of the day so it's worth taking weather forecasts with a pinch of salt. A warm day can feel bitterly cold when you stop for lunch on a cliff top being battered by the wind. Try to get the local weather forecast from either a newspaper, TV or radio, online (⌨ www.metoffice.gov.uk/weather/uk or ⌨ http://news.bbc.co.uk/weather) or a telephone forecast (see below) before you set off. Alter your plans for the day accordingly.

Telephone forecasts

Weather call (☎ 09068-500414; ⌨ www.weathercall.co.uk) provides frequently updated and generally reliable weather forecasts. However, calls are charged at the expensive premium rate. To get the most relevant forecast and to save money and time, when prompted input the four-digit area code: 1406 for Tenby, 1405 for Pembroke and 1404 for Fishguard.

BLISTERS

It is important to break in new boots before embarking on a long walk. Make sure the boots are comfortable and try to avoid getting them wet on the inside. Air your feet at lunchtime, keep them clean and change your socks regularly. If you feel any hot spots stop immediately and apply a few strips of zinc oxide tape and leave them on until it is pain-free or the tape starts to come off.

If you have left it too late and a blister has developed you should surround it with 'moleskin' or any other blister kit to protect it from abrasion. Popping it can lead to infection. If the skin is broken keep the area clean with antiseptic and cover with a non-adhesive dressing material held in place with tape.

HYPOTHERMIA

Also known as exposure, this occurs when the body can't generate enough heat to maintain its normal temperature, usually as a result of being wet, cold, unprotected from the wind, tired and hungry. It is usually more of a problem in upland areas. However, even on the Pembrokeshire coast in bad weather the body can be exposed to strong winds and driving rain making the risk a real one. The northern stretches of the path are particularly exposed and there are fewer villages making it difficult to get help should it be needed.

Hypothermia is easily avoided by wearing suitable clothing, carrying and eating enough food and drink, being aware of the weather conditions and checking the morale of your companions. Early signs to watch for are feeling cold and tired with involuntary shivering. Find some shelter as soon as possible and warm the victim up with a hot drink and some chocolate or other high-energy food. If possible give them another warm layer of clothing and allow them to rest until feeling better.

If allowed to worsen, strange behaviour, slurring of speech and poor co-ordination will become apparent and the victim can quickly progress into unconsciousness, followed by coma and death. Quickly get the victim out of wind and rain, improvising a shelter if necessary. Rapid restoration of bodily warmth is essential and best achieved by bare-skin contact: someone should get into the same sleeping bag as the patient, both having stripped to their underwear, any spare clothing under or over them to build up heat. Send urgently for help.

HYPERTHERMIA

Heat exhaustion is often caused by water depletion and is a serious condition that could eventually lead to death. Symptoms include thirst, fatigue, giddiness, a rapid pulse, raised body temperature, low urine output and later on, delirium and coma. The only remedy is to re-establish water balance. If the victim is suffering severe muscle cramps it may be due to salt depletion.

Heat stroke is caused by failure of the body's temperature-regulating system and is extremely serious. It is associated with a very high body temperature and an absence of sweating. Early symptoms can be similar to those of hypothermia, such as aggressive behaviour, lack of co-ordination and so on. Later the victim goes into a coma or convulsions and death will follow if effective treatment is not given. To treat heat stroke sponge the victim down or cover with wet towels and vigorously fan them. Get help immediately.

SUNBURN

Even on overcast days the sun still has the power to burn. Sunburn can be avoided by regularly applying sunscreen. Don't forget your lips and those areas affected by reflected light off the ground; under the nose, ears and chin. You may find that you quickly sweat sunscreen off, so consider wearing a sun hat. If you have particularly fair skin wear a light, long-sleeved top and trousers.

DEALING WITH AN ACCIDENT

- Use basic first aid to treat the injury to the best of your ability.
- Work out exactly where you are. If possible leave someone with the casualty while others go to get help. If there are only two people, you have a dilemma. If you decide to get help leave all spare clothing and food with the casualty.
- Telephone ☎ 999 and ask for the coastguard. They will assist in both offshore and onshore incidents.

MINIMUM IMPACT & OUTDOOR SAFETY

PART 3: THE ENVIRONMENT & NATURE

The Pembrokeshire coast is not just about beaches and the sea. The coast path takes you through all manner of habitats from woodland and grassland to heathland and dunes providing habitats for a distinct array of species. This book is not designed to be a comprehensive guide to all the wildlife that you may encounter, but serves as an introduction to the animals and plants that the walker is likely to find within the boundaries of the national park.

Making that special effort to look out for wildlife and appreciating what you are seeing enhances your enjoyment of the walk. To take it a step further is to understand a little more about the species you may encounter, appreciating how they interact with each other and learning a little about the conservation issues that are so essential today. At a time when man seems ever more detached from the natural world it is important to remember that we continue to be a part of this complex web and this brings a responsibility to limit our negative influences.

Conserving Pembrokeshire

Like much of the British Isles, the Welsh countryside has had to cope with a great deal of pressure from the activities of an increasingly industrialised world. It must have been a fascinating place when the broadleaved forests, home to wolves and wild boar, stretched as far as the eye could see. Today the surviving pockets of forest and heathland are still under threat but, thankfully, there is a greater understanding of the value of the natural environment and with it a number of organisations who are actively helping to safeguard what remains of Wales's natural heritage.

As beautiful as the modern-day countryside may be it is sad to note that almost every acre of land has been altered in some way by man. What we have today are fragments of semi-natural woodland and hedgerows stretched across farmland. Aside from the tops of the highest Welsh mountains the only truly untouched land is found on the coast; the cliffs, islands and beaches.

This plundering of the countryside has had a major effect on its biodiversity. To the loss of the wolf and wild boar add a number of other species lost and yet more severely depleted in number and one begins to appreciate the influence that man has had over the years.

There is good news, however. In these enlightened times when environmental issues are quite rightly given more precedence, many endangered species, such as the otter, have increased in number thanks to the active work of voluntary conservation bodies. One such success story is the red kite, a beautiful bird of prey which was all but extinct in Britain some ten years ago when just 50 pairs remained in the hills of Mid-Wales. Since then their range has increased to cover greater parts of Wales as well as Scotland and England thanks to an on-going release programme that covers the country.

There is reason to be optimistic. The environment is no longer the least important issue in party politics and this reflects the opinions of everyday people who are concerned about conservation on both a global and local scale. In Wales there are organisations, both voluntary and government based, dedicated to conserving their local heritage; everything from Norman castles to puffins.

GOVERNMENT AGENCIES AND SCHEMES

The **Countryside Council for Wales** (CCW) is the government body responsible for conservation and landscape protection in Wales. The CCW and other agencies (see box below) aim to give protection from modern development and to maintain the countryside in its present state. An effective plan until the government decides a new road or housing estate needs to be built, ignoring their own legislation.

The CCW oversees the **Pembrokeshire Coast National Park Authority** (PCNPA), whose role is to conserve and manage the national park; its wardens and conservation officers work with landowners, encouraging traditional farming and land-use techniques. The aim is to safeguard the environment and features that make the landscape of Pembrokeshire what it is. The stone walls and cliff-top heathland can only survive through careful grazing methods. The CCW also manages a number of **National Nature Reserves** (NNR) within the national park including the limestone cliffs of Stackpole estate on the south coast and the **Marine Nature Reserve** (MNR) around Skomer Island.

It is also responsible for the active protection of endemic species and habitats, as well as geological features, within the national park. If necessary this may involve access restrictions and designating and maintaining specific areas as **Sites of Special Scientific Interest** (SSSI). These range in size from tiny patches set aside for an endangered plant or nesting site, to larger expanses of dunes,

❏ **Government agencies and schemes**
● **Countryside Council for Wales** (CCW ☎ 0845-130 6229, 🖳 www.ccw.gov.uk)
● **Pembrokeshire Coast National Park Authority** (PCNPA: ☎ 0845-345 7275, 🖳 www.pcnpa.org.uk); **The Welsh Association for National Park Authorities** (WANPA; ☎ 029-2049 9966, 🖳 www.nationalparks.gov.uk/wanpa.htm or 🖳 www .nationalparks.gov.uk) works with the other national park authorities in Wales to promote their purposes and interests and to provide a place where they can share information and experiences.
● **Pembrokeshire County Council** (☎ 01437-764551, 🖳 www.pembrokeshire.gov.uk).

THE ENVIRONMENT & NATURE

saltmarsh, woodland and heathland. However, promoting public access and appreciation of Pembrokeshire's natural heritage is also of importance, as is educating locals and visitors about the significance of the local environment.

However, Pembrokeshire is not just about the national park. Outside its boundaries the CCW has an array of designations for land of special interest. Being an **Area of Outstanding Natural Beauty** (AONB; 🖳 www.aonb.org.uk) gives some protection to land, though less than that enjoyed by the national parks. In addition, 500km of the Welsh coast, much of it in Pembrokeshire, has been defined as **Heritage Coast**.

There is no doubt that the Countryside Council plays a vital role in safeguarding Pembrokeshire for future generations. But the very fact that we rely on national parks and other such designations for protecting limited areas begs the question: what are we doing to the vast majority of land that remains relatively unprotected? Surely we should be aiming to protect the natural environment outside national parks just as much as within them.

CAMPAIGNING AND CONSERVATION ORGANISATIONS

The **Royal Society for the Protection of Birds** (RSPB) was the pioneer of voluntary conservation bodies. It began over a hundred years ago when concern was raised about the use of feathers in ladies' hats. Since then voluntary conservation and environmental organisations have flourished both on a local and global scale. They play a vital role in education, conservation and campaigning and many of the local organisations in Wales are also some of the most signifi-

---

❏ **Campaigning and conservation organisations**
- **Butterfly Conservation Wales** (🖳 www.southwales-butterflies.org.uk or 🖳 www .butterfly-conservation.org)
- **Campaign for the Protection of Rural Wales** (☎ 01938-552525, 🖳 www.cprw .org.uk)
- **Friends of the Pembrokeshire National Park** (🖳 www.fpnp.org.uk)
- **Marine Conservation Society** (☎ 01989-566017, 🖳 www.mcsuk.org)
- **National Trust in Wales** (☎ 01492-860123, 🖳 www.nationaltrust.org.uk)
- **Royal Society for the Protection of Birds (RSPB)** (Wales headquarters ☎ 029-2035 3000, 🖳 www.rspb.org.uk/wales)
- **The Wildlife Trust of South & West Wales** (☎ 01656-724100, 🖳 www.welsh wildlife.org) For details about staying on Skomer call ☎ 01239-621600.
- **Woodland Trust** (Welsh office ☎ 08452-935860, 🖳 www.woodland-trust.org.uk) Restores woodland throughout Britain for its amenity, wildlife and landscape value.
- **World Wide Fund for Nature (WWF**; 🖳 www.wwf.org.uk, Welsh office ☎ 029-2045 4970, 🖳 http://wales.wwf.org.uk). Welsh branch of one of the world's largest conservation and campaigning organisations.
- **Friends of the Earth** (Welsh office ☎ 029-2022 9577, 🖳 www.foe.co.uk/cymru) International network of environmental groups campaigning for a better environment. Also appreciates the value of local environmental issues.

THE ENVIRONMENT & NATURE

cant landowners in the national park. The RSPB manage a number of nature reserves including the islands of Ramsey (see box p163) and Grassholm (see box p144).

The **Wildlife Trust of South and West Wales** manages 92 nature reserves and actively promotes and protects the area's wildlife as well as organising marine and coastal wildlife-watching events. It manages Skokholm Island and Skomer Island (see box p144 for details of both islands) on behalf of the Countryside Council for Wales.

The **National Trust** owns and protects countryside and historic buildings such as Tudor Merchant's House (see p84), Tenby, as well as many stretches of the mainland coast including the Stackpole Estate, St David's peninsula, the Solva coast and Abereiddy to Abermawr.

Butterfly Conservation was formed in 1968 by some naturalists who were alarmed at the decline in the number of butterflies, and moths, and who aim to reverse the situation. They now have 31 branches throughout the British Isles and operate 33 nature reserves and also sites where butterflies are likely to be found.

Friends of the Pembrokeshire National Park is a conservation charity dedicated to protecting, conserving and enhancing the national park. **Campaign for the Protection of Rural Wales** campaigns on a number of local issues from sustainable development to conservation of landscape, historic sites and local traditions. The **Marine Conservation Society** aims to protect Britain's marine environment and its wildlife and promote global marine conservation. They organise lots of voluntary projects such as beach cleans and species surveys.

BEYOND CONSERVATION

Pressures on the countryside grow year on year. Western society, whether directly or indirectly, makes constant demands for more oil, more roads, more houses, more cars. At the same time awareness of environmental issues increases, as does the knowledge that our unsustainable approach to life cannot continue. Some governments appear more willing to adopt sustainable ideals, others less so.

Yet even the most environmentally positive of governments are some way off perfect. It's all very well to classify parts of the countryside as national parks and Areas of Outstanding Natural Beauty but it will be of little use if we continue to pollute the wider environment; the seas and skies. For a brighter future we need to adopt that sustainable approach to life. It would not be difficult and the rewards would be great.

The individual can play his or her part. Walkers in particular appreciate the value of wild areas and should take this attitude back home with them. This is not just about recycling the odd green bottle or two and walking to the corner shop rather than driving, but about lobbying for more environmentally sensitive policies in local and national government. The first step to a sustainable way of living is in appreciating and respecting this beautiful complex world we live in and realising that every one of us plays an important role within the great web.

THE ENVIRONMENT & NATURE

The natural world is not a separate entity. We are all part of it and should strive to safeguard it rather than work against it. So many of us live in a way that does seem far removed from the real world, cocooned in centrally heated houses and upholstered cars. Rediscovering our place within the natural world is both uplifting on a personal level and important regarding our outlook and approach to life.

Walkers are in a great position to appreciate this, yet some people still find it difficult to shake off the chaos of modern life even when they are in the countryside. When you are out on the coast path don't just look at the view. Slow down and use all your senses. Listen, smell and touch everything you see.

Flora and fauna

TREES

Before man and his axe got to work there were forests covering 80% of what is now the national park. Sadly this woodland cover has dropped to just 6%, some of which is coniferous plantation.

From an ecological perspective the most important forest cover is the ancient semi-natural woodland which covers a mere 1% of the national park area. Twenty of these ancient broadleaved woodlands are designated sites of special scientific interest (SSSI; see p59).

On the Pembrokeshire Coast Path most of the woodland is encountered along the southern section from Amroth to Tenby and on the southern side of the Milford Haven estuary. The windswept northern stretches are more barren although many of the small valleys are wooded.

Another good place to find ancient broadleaved woodland is the Cwm Gwaun valley in the Preseli Hills. Look out for lichen on the tree trunks as this is a classic indicator of clean air. Over 300 species of lichen can be found in many of the forests.

None of the woodland in Pembrokeshire can be described as completely natural as it has all been managed or altered in some way by man. In the past rural communities coppiced the trees and used the wood from hazel for fencing and thatching. Evidence of charcoal burning is also present and oak was grown along sheltered bays and estuaries to provide wood for shipbuilding.

These practices began to die out at the end of the 19th century when cheap coal started to replace coppiced wood and charcoal as fuel. However, there has been a small revival in recent years by aficionados of traditional countryside ways and conservationists who recognise the benefits of coppicing for a number of species, including the endangered dormouse. In Pembrokeshire coppicing can be seen in several places and is a method of woodland management that has been used by the National Park Authority itself.

Hazel (with flowers)

Ash (with seeds)

Predominant tree species

The dominant species in semi-natural broadleaved woodland is the **sessile oak** (*Quercus petraea*) with good examples around the Daugleddau estuary. The sessile oak differs from the English common oak in a number of ways; most notably in having brighter, more shapely leaves. The name 'sessile' means 'without stalks' referring to the acorns which grow directly from thin branches.

Oak woodland is a diverse habitat and is also home to **downy birch** (*Betula pubescens*), **holly** (*Ilex aquifolium*) and **hazel** (*Corylus avellana*) which has traditionally been used for coppicing.

The **common ash** (*Fraxinus excelsior*) is well adapted to cope with the salt-laden sea winds and can be found on the limestone-rich soils in the south of the county, around the Bosherston lily ponds for example. The **common alder** (*Alnus glutinosa*) is often found alone growing by streams. Perhaps surprisingly the mighty **beech** (*Fagus sylvatica*) is not native to this part of the country but has established itself wherever there is well-drained soil and is surely one of the most beautiful of the broadleaved trees. Other species to look out for include the **aspen** (*Populus tremula*), **hawthorn** (*Crataegus monogyna*) and **rowan** or mountain ash (*Sorbus aucuparia*) with its slender leaves and red berries.

FLOWERS

The coast path is renowned for its wild flowers. Spring is the time to come and see the spectacular displays of colour on the cliff tops while in late summer the heather on the northern slopes turns a vibrant purple.

Alder (with flowers)

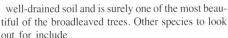

The coast and cliff-top meadows

The coastline is a harsh environment subjected to strong winds, wind-blown salt and tides. Plants that colonise this niche are hardy and well adapted to the

THE ENVIRONMENT & NATURE

conditions. Many of the cliff-top species such as the pink flowering **thrift** (*Armeria maritima*) and white **sea campion** (*Silene maritima*) turn the cliff tops into a blaze of colour from May to September.

On shingle beaches and dunes you might see the **yellow-horned poppy** (*Glaucium flavum*), but don't think about eating it, it's poisonous. On the cliff top and track sides you might encounter the straggly stems of **fennel** (*Foeniculum vulgare*), a member of the carrot family which grows to over a metre high.

Other plants to look for are **spring squill** (*Scilla verna*) and **scurvygrass** (*Cochlearia officilanis*), and in saltmarshes and estuaries **sea-lavender** (*Limonium vulgare*) and **sea aster** (*Aster tripolium*).

Woodland and hedgerows

The **wood anemone** (*Anemone nemorosa*), the **bluebell** (*Hyacinthoides nonscripta*) and the yellow **primrose** (*Primula vulgaris*) flower early in spring, with the bluebell and wood anenome covering woodland floors in a carpet of blue and white. The bluebell and primrose are also common on open cliff tops. **Red campion** (*Silene dioica*), which flowers from late April, can be found in hedgebanks along with **rosebay willowherb** (*Epilobium augustifolium*) which also has the name fireweed owing to its habit of colonising burnt areas.

In scrubland and on woodland edges you will find **bramble** (*Rubus fruticosus*), a common vigorous shrub, responsible for many a ripped jacket thanks to its sharp thorns and prickles. The blackberry fruits ripen from late summer to autumn. Fairly common in scrubland and on woodland edges is the **dog rose** (*Rosa canina*) which has a large pink flower, the fruits of which are used to make rose-hip syrup.

Other flowering plants to look for in wooded areas and in hedgerows include the tall **foxglove** (*Digitalis purpurea*) with its trumpet-like flowers, **forget-me-not** (*Myosotis arvensis*) with tiny, delicate blue flowers and **cow parsley** (*Anthriscus sylvestris*), a tall member of the carrot family with a large globe of white flowers which often covers roadside verges and hedgebanks.

Heathland and scrubland

Some of the cliff tops, particularly in the north of the region, are carpeted in heather resulting in a spectacular purple display when it comes into flower in late summer. Heathland is an important habitat for butterflies, snakes and lizards. There are good examples of it on the west side of the Dale peninsula, east of Marloes Sands, on the high slopes north of Newport Sands and most notably on the St David's peninsula.

There are three species of heather. The dominant one is **ling** (*Calluna vulgaris*) which has tiny flowers on delicate upright stems. The other two species are **bell heather** (*Erica cinera*), with deep purple bell-shaped flowers, and **cross-leaved heath** (*Erica tetralix*) with similarly shaped flowers of a lighter pink, almost white colour. Cross-leaved heath prefers wet and boggy ground. As a consequence, it usually grows away from bell heather which prefers well-drained soils.

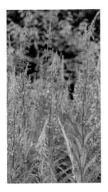

Rosebay Willowherb
Epilobium angustifolium

Common Fumitory
Fumaria officinalis

Thrift (Sea Pink)
Armeria maritima

Lousewort
Pedicularis sylvatica

Bell Heather
Erica cinerea

Heather (Ling)
Calluna vulgaris

Foxglove
Digitalis purpurea

Common Centaury
Centaurium erythraea

Red Campion
Silene dioica

Spear Thistle
Cirsium vulgare

Sea Holly
Eryngium maritimum

Sea Campion
Silene maritima

Herb-Robert
Geranium robertianum

St John's Wort
Hypericum perforatum

Scarlet Pimpernel
Anagallis arvensis

Cornflower
Centaurea cyanus

Bluebell
Endymion non-scriptus

Rowan (tree)
Sorbus aucuparia

Honeysuckle
Lonicera periclymemum

Common Ragwort
Senecio jacobaea

Gorse
Ulex europaeus

Tormentil
Potentilla erecta

Primrose
Primula vulgaris

Evening Primrose
Oenothera erythrosepala

Ransoms (Wild Garlic)
Allium ursinum

Hogweed
Heracleum sphondylium

Yarrow
Achillea millefolium

Common Vetch
Vicia sativa

Old Man's Beard
Clematis vitalba

Germander Speedwell
Veronica chamaedrys

Silverweed
Potentilla anserina

Self-heal
Prunella vulgaris

Violet
Viola riviniana

Meadow Buttercup
Ranunculis acris

Birdsfoot-trefoil
Lotus corniculatus

Cowslip
Primula veris

Dog Rose
Rosa canina

Common Hawthorn
Crataegus monogyna

Ox-eye Daisy
Leucanthemum vulgare

Heathland is also the stronghold of **gorse** (*Ulex europeous*), a dark green bush of sharp thorns with spectacular displays of yellow flowers from February through to June. Not a flower but worthy of mention is the less attractive species **bracken** (*Pteridium aquilinum*), a vigorous non-native fern that has invaded many heathland areas to the detriment of native species.

In more overgrown areas where the heath has reverted to scrubland you invariably find **broom** (*Cytisus scoparius*), a big bushy plant with dark green stalk-like leaves and bright yellow flowers. As its name suggests it looks like a big upturned broom and was indeed used for this purpose. It was also believed to have magical powers and was used as a diuretic. On hot days you can hear the seed pods cracking open, spreading the seeds about.

REPTILES

The only poisonous snake in Wales is the **adder** (*Vipera berus*) which can be identified by its dark colouring, the zigzagging down its back and a diamond shape on the back of its head. Common on heathland, it can be seen basking in the sun on rocks or on the path during warm spring and summer days. If you see one consider yourself lucky and don't frighten it. Despite their reputation adders are not as fearsome as you might think. Their venom is designed to kill small mammals, not humans and they bite only if provoked. However, in the unlikely event of a bite, stay still and send someone else to get medical attention. Deaths in humans are extremely rare but the bite is unpleasant and can be dangerous to children, the elderly and pets.

The **grass snake** (*Natrix natrix*) is an adept swimmer and is a much longer, slimmer snake with a yellow collar around the neck. It's non-venomous but does emit a foul stench should you attempt to pick one up. It's much better for you and the snake to leave it in peace.

The **common lizard** (*Lacerta vivipara*) is a harmless creature often seen basking in the sun on rocks and stone walls.

MAMMALS

The Pembrokeshire coast is a stronghold for marine mammals and no trip to the region is complete without spotting a **grey seal** (*Halichoerus grypus*). From late August to October the downy white pups can be seen in the breeding colonies hauled up on the rocks. The best places to spot them are around the Skomer Marine Nature Reserve (see box p144) and in Ramsey Sound (see p163) and your chances of a sighting increase should you take a boat trip to one of the islands. Look out too for schools of **common porpoise** (*Phocoena phocoena*), a small slate-grey dolphin which can be seen breaking the surface as they head up Ramsey Sound, and the **bottle-nosed dolphin** (*Tursiops truncatus*) which can be found in Cardigan Bay.

Further inland in woodland and on farmland, particularly around the Preseli Hills, are a number of common but shy mammals. One of the most difficult to see is the **badger** (*Meles meles*), a sociable animal with a distinctive black-and-

THE ENVIRONMENT & NATURE

white-striped muzzle. Badgers live in family groups in large underground setts coming out to root for worms on the pastureland after sunset. Unfortunately the most common way of seeing them is as a bloody mess on the road: they are one of the most frequent animal road casualties.

The much maligned **fox** (*Vulpes vulpes*) inhabits similar country to the badger. Despite relentless persecution it is a born survivor, even having adapted to life in cities where they are quite tolerant of human presence. In Pembrokeshire the fox is far more wary and any sightings are likely to be brief. Keep an eye out for one crossing fields or even scavenging on the beach. They are not exclusively nocturnal. In fact where they are least disturbed they are more likely to be active during the day.

The cliff tops are home to the **rabbit** (*Oryctolagus cuniculus*) where their warrens can prove to be quite a safety hazard to the careless walker. They come out both during the day and at night.

The **otter** (*Lutra lutra*) is a rare native species which is slowly increasing in numbers thanks to long-running conservation efforts. It's at home both in salt and fresh water, although here in Pembrokeshire they are more likely to inhabit rivers and lakes. The otter is a good indicator of a healthy unpolluted environment and it's encouraging to see their numbers increasing not only in Wales but across the British Isles. A good place to see an otter is at the Bosherston lily ponds (see Map 11 p98 and Map 12 p99), where a walk at dawn or dusk may reward the patient and quiet watcher with a sighting. If you are serious about otter watching take binoculars and choose a good vantage point above the lake, making sure the wind is blowing into your face. A calm evening or morning is best as it is easier to spot the wake of a swimming otter on a still lake surface than a choppy one.

The **grey squirrel** (*Sciurus carolinensis*) was introduced from North America at the turn of the 20th century. Its outstanding success in colonising Britain is very much to the detriment of other native species including songbirds and, most famously, the red squirrel. Greys are bigger and stockier than reds and to many people the reds, with their tufted ears, bushy tails and small beady eyes are the far more attractive of the two.

The **roe deer** (*Capreolus capreolus*) is a small native species of deer that tends to hide in woodland. They can sometimes be seen alone or in pairs on field edges or clearings in the forest but you are more likely to hear its sharp dog-like bark when it smells you coming.

On Ramsey Island there is a famous herd of **red deer** (*Cervus elaphus*), the largest land mammal in Britain. They have adapted successfully to open country due to the loss of their natural habitat of deciduous woodland and can be spotted quite easily on Ramsey's windswept slopes.

At dusk **bats** can be seen hunting for moths and flying insects along hedgerows, over rivers and around street lamps. Bats have had a bad press thanks to Dracula and countless other horror stories but anyone who has seen one up close knows them to be harmless and delightful little creatures. As for their blood-sucking fame, the matchbox-sized species of Britain would not even

❏ **The Skomer vole**
The island of Skomer (see box p144) is famous for its puffins and shearwaters but is also home to a diminutive character perhaps deserving of a little more attention. The Skomer vole (*Clethrionomys glaeolus skomerensis*) is a sub-species of the bank vole. An estimated 20,000 of the little rodents inhabit the island, playing an important role in the diet of the resident short-eared owls. Unique to the island, the Skomer vole is larger than its mainland cousin and is a perfect example of Darwin's evolutionary theory, evolving differing characteristics from its mainland cousin due to its geographic isolation.

be able to break your skin with their teeth let alone suck your blood. Their reputation is improving all the time thanks to the work of the many bat conservation groups around the country and all fourteen species in Britain are protected by law. The commonest species in Britain, and likewise in Pembrokeshire, is the **pipistrelle** (*Pipistrellus pipistrellus*).

Some other small but fairly common species which can be found in the scrubland and grassland on the cliff tops include the carnivorous **stoat** (*Mustela erminea*), its smaller cousin the **weasel** (*Mustela nivalis*), the **hedgehog** (*Erinaceus europaeus*) and a number of species of **voles**, **mice** and **shrews**.

BIRDS

Without doubt Pembrokeshire is a hot spot for ornithologists. The cliffs, and more especially the islands, are important breeding grounds for a number of species such as the razorbill (see p68) which has been adopted as the symbol of the national park authority. Away from the rolling waves other species, adapted to completely different habitats, can be spotted in the woodland, farmland and heathland that covers the cliff tops and valleys. Sightings of **red kites** (*Milvus milvus*) are becoming more common; they can be seen almost anywhere on the coast path and at any time of the year.

Islands and cliffs

The islands of Skomer and Skokholm are home to the **manx shearwater** (*Puffinus puffinus*), an auk which lives in huge colonies of thousands, breeding in burrows along the cliff top. They can be identified by their dark upperside and paler underside with slender pointed wings and a fast swerving flight across the surface of the sea. Boat trips (see box p144) at dusk can be taken to watch the spectacular displays as the birds leave their burrows to look for food.

Grassholm Island is one of the world's most important breeding sites for the **gannet** (*Morus bassanus*), a large bird with a wing span of 175cm. They are easily identified by their size and white plumage, with a yellow head and black wing tips. In winter they spend most of their time over the open sea, returning in summer to breed in huge colonies on offshore rocky outcrops such as Grassholm. They catch fish by folding their wings back and diving spectacularly into the water.

THE ENVIRONMENT & NATURE

A prehistoric-looking bird, the **cormorant** (*Phalacrocorax carbo*) can often be seen perched on rocks, its wings outstretched. Unlike other birds their feathers are not oily and water resistant so this is the only way of drying out. Dark in appearance, often with a white patch around the stocky bill, it swims with an outstretched neck and frequently dives underwater with a little jump as it bobs on the surface. It is commonly seen in estuaries and on more sheltered stretches of water. From the same family as the cormorant is the **shag** (*Phalacrocorax aristotelis*).

The **razorbill** (*Alca torda*) is an auk that breeds on the cliff tops. It is black with a white belly and has a distinctive white stripe across the bill to the eye. Similar in appearance to the razorbill but with a much more slender bill is the **guillemot** (*Uria aalge*). It stands more upright than the razorbill and is less stocky. They nest in huge colonies on cliff-face ledges and are often seen in small groups flying close over the surface of the sea with very fast wing beats.

The **storm petrel** (*Hydrobates pelagicus*) spends most of the time over the open sea. It has an erratic flight pattern often just skimming the surface. It can be identified by the square tail, white rump and a white band on the underside of the wings which contrasts with the dark body. They also have strange tube-like nasal implements on a hooked beak.

Looking something like a medium-sized gull, the **fulmar** (*Fulmarus glacialis*) can also be seen far out to sea but nests on ledges on the cliff face. They vary in appearance from a buff grey to white and can be distinguished from gulls by their gliding flight pattern and occasional, slow, stiff wing beats.

The **kittiwake** (*Rissa tridactyla*) spends the winter out at sea where large flocks follow the fishing boats. In the summer they breed in large colonies on the coastal cliffs. It is a small gull with a short

Cormorant

It's not difficult to tell cormorants and shags apart. The **cormorant** is larger than the shag and has a bigger bill and head. In the breeding season the cormorant has a white patch on its flank. The **shag** is slimmer, has a more uniform dark plumage with a green glossy sheen. It also has a more slender bill and a pronounced tuft on the top of the head. Shags are often seen in flocks on the coast or out to sea, whereas cormorants are usually found in river estuaries and in pairs or alone except when in nesting colonies.

Shag

THE ENVIRONMENT & NATURE

yellow bill and short black legs. It has a white plumage except for the light grey wings with black tips. The tail is distinctively square when in flight.

The **common tern** (*Sterna hirundo*) is gull-like but smaller. It is generally white but with grey wings and a black crown. Its short legs are red as is its short, pointed bill which usually has a black tip.

The third and most popular species of auk in Pembrokeshire has to be the **puffin** (*Fratercula arctica*) with its lavishly coloured square bill. Like the manx shearwater, puffins breed in burrows or under boulders. They can often be seen with a bill full of fish on their way back to their burrows. Skomer Island is Puffin Central but remember that they come to the island only during the breeding season (April to early August), spending the winter out at sea. You are far less likely to spot a puffin on the mainland.

Puffin

The **chough** (*Pyrrhocorax pyrrhocorax*), pronounced 'chuff', is one of the more attractive members of the crow family; slender and elegant in appearance with a deep red curved and pointed bill and legs of the same colour. Choughs are often found in mountainous areas, but in Pembrokeshire they breed on the coast where they can be seen flying acrobatically around the cliffs.

The **peregrine falcon** (*Falco peregrinus*) is a beautiful raptor that can be found nesting on some of the sea cliffs. It is a lean and efficient hunter with slate grey plumage and a white underside with thin black barring. It kills its prey with a spectacular dive known as stooping, in which the bird closes its wings and plummets from the sky like a small missile, stunning its prey on impact. It's a fantastic sight.

Of the numerous gulls the most common include the **herring gull** (*Larus argentatus*), a large white gull with grey wings tipped with black, a bright yellow bill with a red spot at the end and yellow eyes. It is not a shy bird and can often be seen around harbours where it is something of a scavenger. Some other gulls which you may spot include the **great black-backed gull** (*Larus marinus*), similar to the herring

Herring gull

Great black-backed gull

The **Herring gull** (above) is the most frequently-seen member of the gull family. It has pink legs and feet and a grey upper body. Largest of the gulls is the **great black-backed gull** (left) which has, as the name implies, a black back. It also has pink legs and feet which distinguish it from the **lesser black-backed gull**, which has yellow legs.

THE ENVIRONMENT & NATURE

gull but with black wings and the **lesser black-backed gull** (*Larus fuscus*) which is, not surprisingly, smaller.

The **black-headed gull** (*Larus ridibundus*) spends a lot of time feeding in large flocks on farmland close to the coast. It is a slender gull with a distinctive black head and black wing tips.

Beaches and mudflats

A distinctive bird that can often be seen running along the shingle and sandy beaches is the **ringed plover** (*Charadrius hiaticula*). This stocky little bird, the size of a thrush, has a white belly and brown upper-parts with a pair of characteristic black bands across its face and throat. The legs and bill are both orange.

Similar in size is the **common sandpiper** (*Actitis hypoleucos*), a small bird that can be found on rocky shores. It has white under-parts with a light brown breast and upper-parts. White bars can be seen on the wings when it is in flight.

Also to be found on the beach and often feeding on inland fields is the **oystercatcher** (*Haematopus ostralegus*). It is quite common and easily identified by the distinctive black upper-parts and white belly. It has a sharp stabbing orange bill used for probing the ground when feeding and a distinctive shrill call.

The **lapwing** (*Vanellus vanellus*) with its long legs, short bill and distinctive long head crest also feeds on arable farmland. Sadly, this attractive bird is declining in numbers. The name comes from its lilting flight, frequently changing direction with its large rounded wings. It is also identified by a white belly, black and white head, black throat patch and distinctive dark green wings.

Inhabiting the sand dunes, moors and bogs is the **curlew** (*Numenius arquata*), a brown mottled bird with a very long slender bill which curves downwards. It has an evocative far-reaching call that reflects its name: 'Kooor-lee'. In the winter it groups in large flocks on open ground such as fields and mudflats.

Scrubland and grassland

On open ground you may be lucky enough to see the **short-eared owl** (*Asio flammeus*) which, unlike other owls, often hunts during the day. Skomer is a good place to look out for it. It is quite large with fairly uniform dark streaks and bars over an otherwise golden-brown plumage. The pale face is a typical round owl's face with golden eyes ringed by black eye patches.

A more common sight is the **stonechat** (*Saxicola torquata*), a colourful little bird with a deep orange breast and a black head. Its name comes from its call which sounds like the chink of two stones being knocked together. During the summer months you will see it along the coast path flitting from the top of one gorse bush to another.

The **yellowhammer** (*Emberiza citrinella*), a bunting, is not seen quite so much as the stonechat though it has the same habit of singing atop gorse bushes. It has a distinctive call said to sound like 'a little bit of bread and no cheese' according to those with vivid imaginations, although it's certainly no mynah bird. Less striking in appearance is the **meadow pipit** (*Anthus pratensis*), a rather drab-looking small brown bird. It can be identified by white flashes on the edge of its tail as it flies away. Another small brown bird spotted above grassland is the **skylark** (*Alauda arvensis*). It has a distinctive flight pattern rising directly upwards ever higher singing constantly as it goes. It climbs so high that the relentless twittering can be heard while the bird is nowhere to be seen.

Woodland

The **raven** (*Corvus corax*) is so big that it is often mistaken for a buzzard. They have lifelong breeding partners and nest on rocky ledges along the coast and further inland high in the tree tops. The raven has all-black plumage, a thick stocky bill and a deep guttural croaking call.

A common raptor that is often heard before being seen is the **buzzard** (*Buteo buteo*), a large broad-winged bird of prey which looks much like a small eagle. It is dark brown in appearance and slightly paler on the underside of its wings. It has a distinctive mewing call and can be spotted soaring ever higher on the air thermals, or sometimes perched on the top of telegraph poles.

Much smaller than the buzzard is the **kestrel** (*Falco tinnunculus*), a small falcon and the most commonly seen bird of prey. It hovers expertly in a fixed spot, even in the strongest of winds, above grassland and road side-verges hunting for mice and voles.

BUTTERFLIES

The Pembrokeshire Coast is also a good place to spot British butterflies, with a number of species common throughout the summer and a couple of others, such as skippers, found here but almost nowhere else in the British Isles. To get a comprehensive overview of the butterflies found in the region visit Butterfly Conservation's website (see box p60), where you can download a photo guide to the most commonly-spotted species.

Whilst on the coast path keep an eye out in particular for the distinctive **red admiral** (*Vanessa atalanta*), which has brown/black wings with red bands and white spots near the tips, and **peacock** (*Inachis io*), which has red wings with black markings and startling eyespots, both of whose arresting colour and pattern combinations make them easy to find in the shelter of sunny woodland clearings or the fringes of forests.

The **small tortoiseshell** (*Aglais urticae*) is amongst the most well known and widespread of butterflies in Britain, and its striking pattern makes it easy to spot in a variety of grassy habitats.

Grassy habitats are also home to the **common blue** (*Polyommatus icarus*), which may be seen on coastal dunes as well. The **orange-tip** (*Anthocharis cardamines*), which has orange-tipped white wings, also thrives in grassy areas such as meadows or along the banks of a river.

The attractive **clouded yellow** (*Colias croceus*), which has greenish yellow underwings with silvery spots, is found in flower-filled areas. Flower rich grasslands, scrubby dunes and coastal grasslands are also home to the **dark green fritillary** (*Argynnis aglaja*), a large orange and black butterfly. The more diminutive **small pearl-bordered fritillary** (*Boloria selene*) has black markings and silvery patches on the underside of its orange wings. The **grayling** (*Hipparchia semele*) also prefers coastal dunes and clifftops but is harder to spot as its mottled colouring provides excellent camouflage when resting. In flight orange-yellow bands are more of a giveaway. Look out along dunes and under-cliffs for the **small copper** (*Lycaena phlaeas*), whose bright copper-coloured wings have brown spots and a brown margin.

Amongst tall grasses, particularly under hedgerows or clumped around fence or gateposts, you might see the **gatekeeper** (*Pyronia tithonus*), an orange and brown butterfly with a black eyespot on its forewing. It's also known as the hedge brown. Similar in size and colour is the **wall brown** (*Lasiommata megera*) which can be seen basking on walls, stones and bare ground including rocky foreshores. The bright orange-brown wings of the **small skipper** (*Thymelicus sylvestris*) can also often be spotted amidst tall grasses, as the butterfly darts from flower to flower, whilst the dark brown **ringlet** (*Aphantopus hyperantus*), whose underwing boasts distinctive eyespots, prefers damper, shadier woodland areas. The ragged, scalloped edges of the **comma**'s (*Polygonia c-album*) orange and brown mottled wings help to distinguish this species.

Around fields of oil seed rape look out for the **small white** (*Pieris rapae*) and **large white** (*Pieris brassicae*), both of which boast brilliant white wings with black tips. **Painted ladies** (*Vanessa cardui*), which have orange-brown wings with black and white spots, tend to congregate in open areas with plenty of thistles.

Whilst most of the above species are widespread and common, the **grizzled skipper** (*Pyrgus malvae*), which has black or brown wings with a mass of white spots and the smaller, slightly duller **dingy skipper** (*Erynnis tages*) are becoming increasingly rare. They can still occasionally be spotted in sunny habitats such as coastal dunes, though.

THE ENVIRONMENT & NATURE

PART 4: ROUTE GUIDE & MAPS

Using this guide

The trail guide and maps have not been divided into rigid daily stages since people walk at different speeds and have different interests. The **route summaries** below describe the trail between significant places and are written as if walking the path from south to north.

To enable you to plan your own itinerary **practical information** is presented clearly on the trail maps. This includes walking times for both directions, all places to stay, camp and eat, as well as shops where you can buy supplies. Further service details are given in the text under the entry for each settlement. For an overview of this information see Itineraries, pp30-2.

TRAIL MAPS   [for map key see p6]

Scale and walking times
The trail maps are to a scale of 1:20,000 (1cm = 200m; 3¹/8 inches = one mile). Walking times are given along the side of each map and the arrow shows the direction to which the time refers. Black triangles indicate the points between which the times have been taken. **See note below on walking times.**

The time-bars are a tool and are not there to judge your walking ability. There are so many variables that affect walking speed, from the weather conditions to how many beers you drank the previous evening. After the first hour or two of walking you will be able to see how your speed relates to the timings on the maps.

Up or down?
The trail is shown as a dotted line. An arrow across the trail indicates the slope; two arrows show that it is steep. Note that the arrow points towards the higher part of the trail. If, for example, you are walking from A (at 80m) to B (at 200m) and the trail between the two is short and steep it would be shown thus: A— — — >> — — – B. Reversed arrow heads indicate a downward gradient.

GPS waypoints
The numbered GPS waypoints refer to the list on pp217-20.

❏ **Important note – walking times**
Unless otherwise specified, **all times in this book refer only to the time spent walking**. You will need to add 20-30% to allow for rests, photography, checking the map, drinking water etc. When planning the day's hike count on 5-7 hours' actual walking.

Accommodation

Apart from in large towns where some selection of places has been necessary, almost every place to stay that is within easy reach of the trail is marked. Details of each place are given in the accompanying text. Unless otherwise specified **B&B rates are summer high-season prices per person (/pp)**, or **per room**, assuming two people are sharing. Single occupancy rates are also given. The number and type of rooms are given after each entry: S = single room, T = twin room, D = double room, F = family room (sleeps at least three people).

Other features

Features are marked on the map when pertinent to navigation. In order to avoid cluttering the maps and making them unusable not all features have been marked each time they occur.

The Pembrokeshire Coast Path

KILGETTY (CILGETI)   MAP 1

If you are coming by train or coach Kilgetty is the closest stop to the start of the coast path at Amroth three miles (5km) away. Kilgetty is pleasant enough but there is not much to keep you here so it would be best to head straight to the start of the trail proper.

Services

Everything of importance can be found by turning left out of the train station and walking down the main street.

The Co-op **supermarket** (Mon-Sat 8am-10pm, Sun 10am-4pm) is a good place to get some last-minute supplies, as is the smaller **Bridge Stores** which is closer to the railway station.

There is a **cash machine** (note: there is no bank or ATM at Amroth) at the Co-op and a **post office** (☎ 01834-812239; Mon-Fri 9am-1pm & 2-5.30pm, Sat 9am-12.30pm). If you are already worried about blisters you should head for the **chemist** near The White Horse.

Transport

Bear in mind that Kilgetty is a request stop so trains only stop at the **railway station** if you let the driver know before you get on, otherwise you will end up in Tenby, missing the first seven miles (11km) and that's just cheating.

Silcox Coaches' **bus** services (No 333 Pembroke Dock to Tenby, No 350 Tenby to Amroth; No 351 Pendine to Tenby; No 352 to Tenby; No 361 Pembroke Dock to Carmarthen and No 381 Tenby to Haverfordwest) stop near the post office. The **bus stop** for the National Express coach (see p43) is at the far western end of the village. If you have come by car (see box p43), or have a return bus or train ticket from Kilgetty, you could make your way to Cardigan (Silcox's No 381 service to Narberth and then Richards Bros' No 412) and do the entire coast path in reverse so that you end up back here at the end of the walk. For full details see the public transport map and table, pp44-7.

Where to stay

The only accommodation options here are campsites so it's likely most people will go straight to Amroth.

Campers should aim for *Ryelands Park Campsite* (☎ 01834-812369; Apr-Oct; £10-12.50 per tent, solo campers £5) which is about half a mile up Ryelands Lane to the north of the village. The site has washing and shower facilities as well as water points.

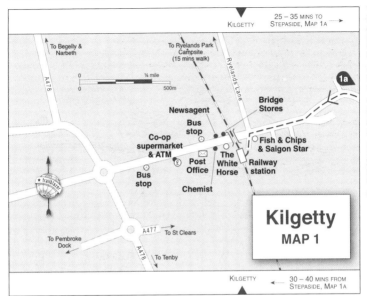

Mill House Camping and Caravan Park (see Map 1a; ☎ 01834-812069, 🖳 www.millhousecaravan.co.uk; Mar-Oct), in **Stepaside**, is geared more towards caravans and those big tents that are the size of bungalows but they should be able to squeeze in a smaller one. Prices are £9.75-14.50 a pitch. Book well in advance in the summer; in the summer school holidays bookings are only accepted for full weeks. Mill House is on the way towards the start of the coast path about a mile east of Kilgetty.

Where to eat and drink
Next to the exit from the train station is a **fish and chip** shop (☎ 01834-812024; Mon-Thu 9am-2pm & 4-10pm, Fri/Sat 9am-10pm) and *Saigon Star* (☎ 01834-814100; Wed-Mon 5.30-11pm), a Vietnamese takeaway. On the other side of the bridge, *The White Horse* by the railway bridge now does food (Tue-Sun noon-2.30pm & 6-8.30pm), including their popular curry nights on Wednesday.

KILGETTY TO AMROTH   MAPS 1, 1a & 1b

These **three miles (5km, 1-1½hrs)** provide a pleasant walk to the coast and the start of the path at Amroth but if you are feeling lazy you can catch Silcox's No 350 or 351 bus (see p45). The bus drops you at Amroth Castle (see p76, Map 1b, p77), close to the start of the coast path at New Inn.

If you want to limber up for the big trek ahead you may as well walk to the start of the path by following the lane to **Stepaside**. Take care crossing the main road, the A477. Stepaside received its quirky name thanks, it is said, to Oliver Cromwell who in 1648, while marching to Pembroke, stopped here and told his men to step aside and take their victuals. At Stepaside you should join the little

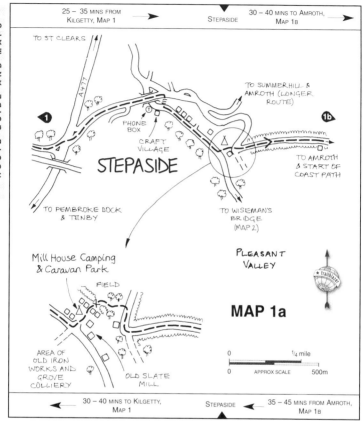

TO ST CLEARS

A477

1

PHONE BOX

CRAFT VILLAGE

STEPASIDE

TO SUMMERHILL & AMROTH (LONGER ROUTE)

1b

TO PEMBROKE DOCK & TENBY

TO AMROTH & START OF COAST PATH

TO WISEMAN'S BRIDGE (MAP 2)

Mill House Camping & Caravan Park

FIELD

PLEASANT VALLEY

★ trailblazer

MAP 1a

0   ¼ mile
0   APPROX SCALE   500m

AREA OF OLD IRON WORKS AND GROVE COLLIERY

OLD SLATE MILL

lane through Pleasant Valley to Mill House Camping and Caravan Park (see p75) where you can see the **old slate mill** and the **iron works**, both dating from the mid-19th century. A path takes you through the caravan park and then you join the lane through **Summerhill** to **Amroth**. You are now on the coast path but unfortunately it officially begins at the northern end of the village, at New Inn. If you want to say you have done the whole path you will have to walk to the start and then return the way you have just come.

AMROTH   MAP 1b & MAP p78

Amroth is stretched out along a single road facing a pretty beach with forested slopes at either end. It's not a big place but being a popular holiday spot there are a few eating places and B&Bs. At the southern end of the village, where the coast path leaves the road, there is a **toilet** block and a **phone box**. Amroth Castle (☎ 01834-813217, 💻 www .amrothcastle.com) is now a holiday park with static caravans and self-catering

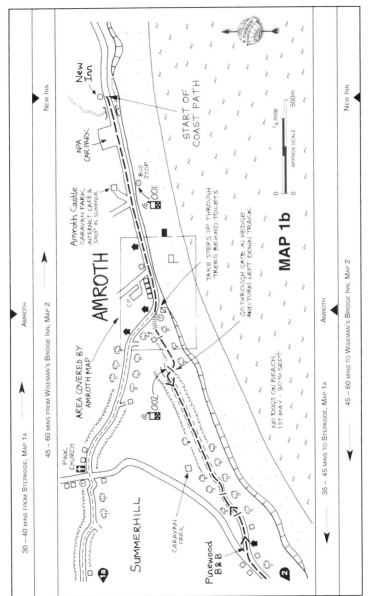

30 – 40 MINS FROM STEPASIDE, MAP 1A ▶

45 – 60 MINS FROM WISEMAN'S BRIDGE INN, MAP 2 ▶

AMROTH ▶

NEW INN ▶

SUMMERHILL

PINK CHURCH

AREA COVERED BY AMROTH MAP

AMROTH

Amroth Castle, Caravan Park, Internet Café & Shop in Summer

BUS STOP

001

NPA CAR PARK

New Inn

START OF COAST PATH

CARAVAN PARK

Pinewood B&B

002

TAKE STEPS UP THROUGH TREES BEHIND TOILETS

GO THROUGH GATE IN HEDGE AND TURN LEFT DOWN TRACK

NO DOGS ON BEACH, 1ST MAY – 30TH SEPT

MAP 1b

◀ 1a

2

35 – 45 MINS TO STEPASIDE, MAP 1A ◀

45 – 60 MINS TO WISEMAN'S BRIDGE INN, MAP 2 ◀

AMROTH ◀

NEW INN ◀

0   1/4 mile   500m
APPROX SCALE

ROUTE GUIDE AND MAPS

ROUTE GUIDE AND MAPS

❏ **Getting to Amroth by car**

If you are coming by car you need to turn off for Stepaside (opposite the turning for Kilgetty). The lane goes down to the village and then goes uphill. About halfway up the hill turn right along a very narrow lane which leads to Summerhill. Go straight over at the crossroads and follow the road downhill to Amroth. The start of the path is at the far eastern end of the village at New Inn but a better place to leave the car is in the free National Park Authority car park. It is just off the seafront road near Amroth Castle and is indicated by a blue 'P' sign.

accommodation. Through a doorway in the wall by the castle there is a small **shop** (April-Oct, daily 9am-5.30pm in the summer months, restricted hours out of season) selling basic supplies and hot and cold snacks; it also offers **internet access** (£1.50 for 30 mins).

Silcox Coaches' **bus** services Nos 350 and 351 connect Amroth with Kilgetty, Saundersfoot and Tenby, and the No 222 runs between here and Carmarthen; see the public transport map and table, pp44-7, for details.

Where to stay, eat and drink

Halfway along the seafront road, simple family-run *Beach Haven Guest House* (☎ 01834-813310; 2T/1F) charges £30 per person for B&B. Two of the rooms have en suite facilities and the other has a bathroom next to it for private use.

There used to be a string of B&Bs on the steep road leading down to the village from Summerhill but these days only *Ashdale* (☎ 01834-813853; Apr-Oct; 1S/ 4D or T, shared facilities), with beds for around £26 per person, and *Mellieha* (☎ 01834-811581, ☐ www.mellieha.co.uk; 3D/1T, all en suite) are operating. Mellieha charges £65-85 per room, single occupancy is £45-50.

If you feel like a break before you've even started, *New Inn* (see Map 1b; ☎ 01834-812368; Mar-Oct bar open all day, food served daily noon-8.45pm) is ideally placed to distract you from the walk. It's a pretty spot with a garden by a stream at the very beginning of the coast path. It's a good place for a pint and they have an extensive menu including curries from £7.50 or, for something less fiery, try one of their

lunchtime baguettes. They close completely between the end of October and March.

Another popular spot is *Temple Bar Inn* (food served daily 11am-10.30pm), in the centre of the village, a bustling place with meals for about £6-10.

Slightly more expensive and perhaps the classiest place in Amroth, the *Amroth Arms* (☎ 01834-812480; bar open daily all day, food served daily 11.30am-2.15pm & Apr-Oct 6-9.30pm) has Welsh pork and local fish dishes. They also issue National Park certificates (see box p11).

The award-winning *Cartwheel Restaurant* (☎ 01834-812100, ☐ cartwheel amroth@aol.com; summer daily 10am to late; winter hours vary) displays the Pembrokeshire Produce Mark guaranteeing the food to be of local origin. Try the scampi at £10.95, the generous mixed grill at £14.95, or honey-roast duck at £15.95. After such a strenuous half mile it's worth treating yourself.

For something cheaper try *Pirate Restaurant and Takeaway* (☎ 01834-812757; daily 9.30am-6pm, to 8.30pm in holidays and high season), which offers toasties, paninis and pizza slices from £3.95.

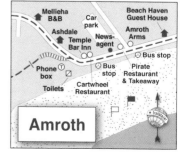

AMROTH TO TENBY

These first **seven miles (11km, 3hrs 10mins-4½hrs)** pass through beautiful and varied scenery, mixing cool cliff-top woodland with small sandy beaches and coves which can be spied through the trees. Don't underestimate this stretch. Although not as rugged as the coastline further north there is enough up and down to make this a tiring introduction especially if you have been slacking in the training!

The path leaves Amroth at its western end where some steps lead up through the trees taking you into a meadow above the cliffs and along a dirt track to **Wiseman's Bridge**. En route you pass *Pinewood* (Map 1b; ☎ 01834-811082, 🖳 www.pinewoodholidaypark.co.uk; Cliff Rd; 2D/1T all en suite) with rooms starting at £25 per person with a £5 single supplement. They also own the neighbouring caravan park but there are no camping facilities.

WISEMAN'S BRIDGE   MAP 2
This is a great spot for a morning break, or lunch if you started from Kilgetty.

The hamlet, which hugs a sandy bay, comprises a scattering of houses, a **phone box**, **public toilets** and, most importantly, *Wiseman's Bridge Inn* (☎ 01834-813236, 🖳 www.wisemansbridgeinn.co.uk; 2T/3D/2D or F/1F sleeping four, all en suite)

which charges £75-85 per room or £50-55 for single occupancy. It's a good idea to book in advance. They also have two **campsites**: the main site has electricity (Mar-Jan; £12-28 for a pitch) but the other one (£12-15; August only), a field, doesn't. The inn does good **food** (daily noon-2.30pm & 6-9pm) but is often very busy in

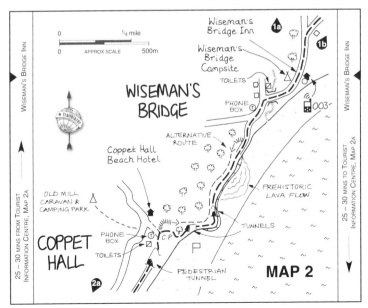

ROUTE GUIDE AND MAPS

the summer; below the restaurant is an arcade with a pool table.

Silcox's **bus** Nos 350 and 351 call here en route to/from Amroth, Kilgetty and Tenby. For full details about public transport see the map and table, pp44-7.

From here the path follows the route of an **old colliery railway** passing through two old tunnels. The railway dates from 1834 when coal from the Stepaside colliery was transported by horse-drawn trams, and later steam engines, to Saundersfoot where it was shipped to the continent. As you walk this stretch look out for the interesting fan-shaped rock formation on the beach. This was produced by wave erosion acting on a fold (anticline in geological terms) in the coal measure strata.

An alternative path passes through shady woodland above the beach to **Coppet Hall** where there is a phone box and public toilet, as well as a B&B (see p81) and campsite, though access is best from Saundersfoot. A third **tunnel** on the other side of the beach car park leads you into the lively seaside town of **Saundersfoot**.

SAUNDERSFOOT   MAP 2a

This is a typical small seaside town pleasantly free of any tackiness. In fact, despite the hustle and bustle, on a summer day Saundersfoot has a rather lazy, even carefree feel to it. Somewhat overshadowed by the more famous seaside town of Tenby, many see Saundersfoot as a quieter alternative to the commotion of its southern neighbour. **Gallery at St Brides** is part of the luxurious St Brides Spa Hotel. Works of art connected to the country – either by Welsh artists, residents or simply having Wales as their subject in some form – are exhibited on the walls of the public areas of the hotel. Anyone is welcome to walk in and look at the paintings.

Services

The **tourist information centre** (☎ 01834-813672, 🖳 saundersfoot.tic@pembrokeshire.gov.uk; Easter/Apr to Oct daily 10am-4pm, Nov to Easter/Apr Thur-Mon 10am-1pm) is in a small building by the car park. There is also a **newsagent**, a small Spar **supermarket** and a **post office**, all of which are scattered around the car park by the harbour. If your feet are suffering

from blisters already there are remedies at the **chemist** on The Strand where you can also find a **bank** with a cashpoint (ATM).

Silcox's **bus** Nos 333, 350, 351 & 361 connect Saundersfoot with Kilgetty, Amroth, Tenby, Pembroke Dock, Carmarthen and Pendine; bus No 381 also stops at the bus station. For full details see the public transport map and table, pp44-7.

Where to stay

Unfortunately, there is a distinct lack of cheap accommodation although *Old Mill Caravan and Camping Park* (Map 2; ☎ 01834-812657; mid Mar to end Oct) charges campers £7/pp; they don't take bookings. It is ten minutes from the coast path near Coppet Hall.

There is another campsite a mile south of Saundersfoot at *Trevayne Farm* (see Map 3; ☎ 01834-813402, 🖳 www.camping-pembrokeshire.co.uk; Apr-Oct); pitches are £4.50-8 per solo camper and £7-12 for two adults sharing a tent; dogs are free. There are toilet/shower and laundry facilities. It is advisable to book, particularly in the main season.

(Opposite) Top: Amroth (see p76), the start of the trail. (Photo © Henry Stedman).
Bottom: Colourful houses perch above Tenby's tranquil harbour (see p82).

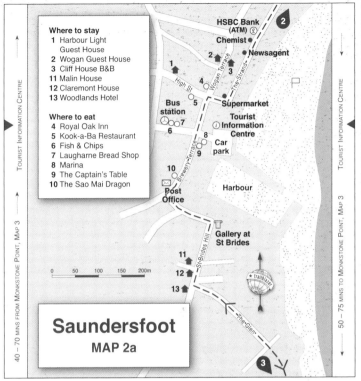

Where to stay
1 Harbour Light
  Guest House
2 Wogan Guest House
3 Cliff House B&B
11 Malin House
12 Claremont House
13 Woodlands Hotel

Where to eat
4 Royal Oak Inn
5 Kook-a-Ba Restaurant
6 Fish & Chips
7 Laugharne Bread Shop
8 Marina
9 The Captain's Table
10 The Sao Mai Dragon

HSBC Bank
(ATM) £
Chemist
Newsagent
Bus station
Supermarket
Tourist Information Centre
Car park
Post Office
Harbour
Gallery at St Brides
trailhoster

High St
Wogan Terrace
The Strand
Brewery Terrace
St Brides Hill
The Glen

0   50   100   150   200m

Saundersfoot
MAP 2a

40 – 70 MINS FROM MONKSTONE POINT, MAP 3

TOURIST INFORMATION CENTRE

TOURIST INFORMATION CENTRE

50 – 75 MINS TO MONKSTONE POINT, MAP 3

In contrast there is plenty of B&B-style accommodation. Before you reach the town, on the other side of the pedestrian tunnel is *Coppet Hall Beach Hotel* (Map 2; ☎ 01834-814467, 🖳 www.coppethallbeach hotel.co.uk; 1S/4T or D/3D/3F, all en suite) with rooms from £35 per person.

In the town you could try *Cliff House* (☎ 01834-813931, 🖳 www.smoothhound .co.uk/hotels/cliffhse; Wogan Terrace; 4D/1T); the rooms are en suite and cost £40 for single occupancy and from £30 per person for two sharing. Close by you'll find *Wogan Guest House* (☎ 01834-812473, 🖳

www.s-h-systems.co.uk/hotels/woganhou .html; Wogan Terrace; 2D/1F sleeping four, all en suite), which, at 300 years old, is reputed to be the oldest building in the village; B&B is £40 per person/£50 single occupancy. Room only is £35 per person.

Harbour Light (☎ 01834-813496, 🖳 www.harbourlightguesthouse.co.uk; 2 High St; 4D/1T/4T or F, seven rooms en suite, two with private facilities) is a large place with beds from £30 per person with a £10 single occupancy supplement.

On the way out of town, on St Brides Hill, are two smart modern options: *Malin*

(Opposite) Top: St Govan's Chapel, hidden down the side of the cliffs in an incredible location. **Bottom**: Impressive cliff erosion – the Green Bridge of Wales (see p100).

House (☎ 01834-812344, 🖳 www.saun dersfoot.co.uk/malinhouse; 19D or T, all en suite) has rooms from £30 to £40 per person as well as an indoor swimming pool and Jacuzzi; *Claremont House* (☎ 01834-813231, 🖳 www.saundersfoothotel.co.uk; 1S/1S or D/3D or T/7D/1T/1F/four suites sleeping up to six, all en suite), just up the hill, charges £70-75 for two sharing, from £55 for a single, the family room costs £115 whilst a suite will set you back £130. Discounts are available for stays of more than one night.

Opposite The Glen, where you turn off to enter the forest, is *Woodlands Hotel* (☎ 01834-813338, 🖳 www.hotelwoodlands.co .uk; 5D/3F, all en suite), a smart but cosy place with light bedrooms that charges £25.50-36 per person for two sharing and £40-50 for single occupancy. They have a licensed bar for guests only and evening meals are served if booked in advance.

Where to eat and drink

There is a plethora of eating dens here. A fantastic pub to look out for with friendly staff is the *Royal Oak Inn* (☎ 01834-812546; food served summer daily noon-2.30pm & 6-9.30pm, to 8.30pm in winter) where there is something for everyone; their traditional fare costs around £9.95 and items from their à la carte menu cost £12.95-20.95; a pint of prawns is £6.95. For a more regular pint they have a selection of real ales. The cosy bar is a good place to unwind after a hard day.

The Captain's Table (☎ 01834-812435; food served daily noon-9.30pm) is renowned for its barbecues with live music, held every Tuesday and Thursday from 6pm in July and August.

Also on Brewery Terrace there is *The Sao Mai Dragon*, a good Vietnamese restaurant (daily 5pm to midnight) which is useful if you arrive late and with an empty belly. It has curries from £4.80 and seafood dishes from £5.20.

For decent **fish and chips** at reasonable rates try *Marina* close to the car park in the centre of the village. There are a couple of other **fish and chip shops** including one by the bread shop (see below).

Kook-a-ba (☎ 01834-813814; daily 6-9.30pm) is a good Australian bar and restaurant with 'Long Neck' ostrich and 'Skippy' kangaroo steaks; something to put a spring in your step for £12.95 and £9.95 respectively. Standard beef steaks start at £11.95.

Packed lunches can be bought at *Laugharne Bread Shop* (☎ 01834-844077; summer daily 9am-4.30pm; Sep-Apr Mon-Sat 9am-4.30pm) where you can get filled baguettes starting at £2 for a simple bacon one.

In **Rhode Wood**, south of Saundersfoot, keep an eye out for red squirrels. At **Monkstone Point** you have the option of a ten-minute detour to the wooded headland. The path to the right after the steps leads to Trevayne Farm Camping (see p80).

The final stretch takes you through more woodland and fields, and also passes the track to Meadow Farm Campsite (see p85), eventually entering **Tenby** above the immaculate sands of North Beach.

TENBY (DINBYCH Y PYSGOD)
MAP 3a, p87

Dinbych y Pysgod (the Little Fort of the Fishes), as it is known in Welsh, has grown from being just a fishing port to a delightful holiday town.

In many respects it is typical of the great British seaside resort, yet it retains a certain charm and sophistication, having resisted stumbling down the road to cheap tackiness as some other seaside towns have done. Immaculate expanses of sand almost surround the town attracting throngs of holidaymakers in the summer. Colourful houses perch above the harbour and South

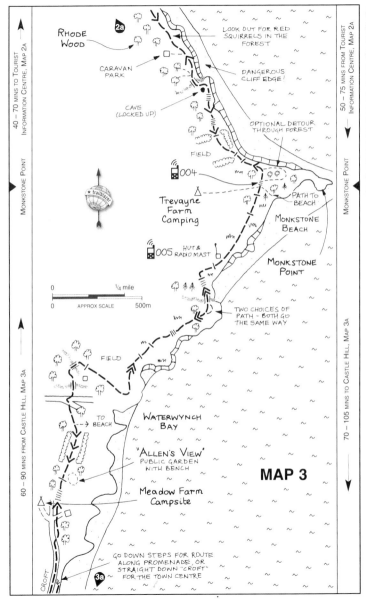

RHODE WOOD

2a

CARAVAN PARK

CAVE (LOCKED UP)

LOOK OUT FOR RED SQUIRRELS IN THE FOREST

DANGEROUS CLIFF EDGE!

OPTIONAL DETOUR THROUGH FOREST

FIELD

004

Trevayne Farm Camping

PATH TO BEACH

MONKSTONE BEACH

005 HUT & RADIO MAST

MONKSTONE POINT

0   ¼ mile
0   APPROX SCALE   500m

TWO CHOICES OF PATH - BOTH GO THE SAME WAY

FIELD

WATERWYNCH BAY

TO → BEACH

"ALLEN'S VIEW" PUBLIC GARDEN WITH BENCH

Meadow Farm Campsite

MAP 3

CROFT

GO DOWN STEPS FOR ROUTE ALONG PROMENADE, OR STRAIGHT DOWN "CROFT" FOR THE TOWN CENTRE

3a

40 – 70 MINS TO TOURIST INFORMATION CENTRE, MAP 2a

MONKSTONE POINT

60 – 90 MINS FROM CASTLE HILL, MAP 3A

50 – 75 MINS FROM TOURIST INFORMATION CENTRE, MAP 2A

MONKSTONE POINT

70 – 105 MINS TO CASTLE HILL, MAP 3A

Beach while the wonderfully well-preserved **medieval town walls** hide a maze of crooked streets.

One of the original three gateways and seven of the original twelve towers which make up the town wall still remain. It was probably built in response to attacks on the town in 1187 and 1260. In the 12th century the Normans built a **castle** on the promontory and though there is little left of it today, built into part of it is **Tenby Museum** (☎ 01834-842809, 🖳 www.tenby museum.org.uk; daily 10am-5pm, weekdays only Nov-Mar; £4, £3 concessions; Castle Hill) where they have two art galleries and exhibitions covering everything from local maritime and social history to displays on archaeology, geology and natural history. They also trace the history of the town from the 10th century, as well as a 'pirate's cell'. You can even find out if you have any ancestors from the local area by checking out their local family-history researcher. An audio tour (£2, refundable deposit £10) is now available and they have a coffee shop (10am-4pm).

Look out for the National Trust's **Tudor Merchant's House** (☎ 01834-842279; April-Oct Sun-Fri and Saturdays of bank holiday weekends, 11am-5pm; admission £2.70; free for members), an old townhouse tucked into tiny Quay St near the harbour. It dates back to the 15th century and still has the original roof beams and a herb garden.

Tenby itself has plenty to keep you busy for a day, even if that means just wandering the streets or exploring the wonderful beaches. It is also the place to catch the boat over to **Caldey Island** and its monastery (see box below).

Services

The **tourist information centre** (☎ 01834-842404, 🖳 tenby.tic@pembrokeshire.gov .uk; Easter to late Oct Mon-Fri 9.30am-5pm, Sat & Sun 10am-4pm, Nov-Easter Mon-Sat 10am-4pm) is down by the entrance to Sainsbury's **supermarket** on Upper Park Rd. There is a £2 non-refundable charge for accommodation booking. There is another conveniently located supermarket at the top of Trafalgar Rd.

There's a **post office** (☎ 01834-843213; Mon-Fri 8.30am-5.30pm; Sat 8.30am-12.30pm) at the northern end of

---

❑ **Caldey Island**

The small island of Caldey (🖳 www.caldey-island.co.uk) is clearly visible just south of Tenby. Monks have been on the island for around 1500 years and about 20 monks from the Reformed Cistercian Community live on the island, attending seven services a day in the private monastery. The first service kicks off at 3.15am!

Boat trips (☎ 01834-844453) to the island from Tenby (Easter-late Oct, Mon-Fri 10am-3pm, the last boat returns about 5pm, every 20 minutes; also Sat May-Sep) do not operate in bad weather. Tickets cost £10/5 (adults/children) return and are sold at the kiosk by Tenby harbour.

There is a surprising amount to see on the island. Everyone is free to explore most of the island outside the monastery grounds including **St Illtud's church** and **Old Priory**. There is a video room where a 15-minute video about the monks' lifestyle shows continuously; there's also a tea room, small museum, post office (with its own official Caldey stamp) and a good bathing beach at Priory Bay. Look out for seals around the lighthouse on the southern tip of the island. Services for the public are held in the island's parish church, **St David's**, at 2.45pm most weekdays.

Chocolate and shortbread (made on the island) as well as other souvenirs are sold in the **gift shop**. Perhaps more surprising is the range of perfumes and toiletries, made by the resident monks, available in the **perfumery shop**. All the products are based on local flowers, herbs and even prickly gorse.

town on Warren St. Another vital port of call for most people is a **bank** of which there are plenty in the centre, including a branch of HSBC on Tudor Sq, a Barclays behind the church, and an Abbey a little further north on the High St; all have **cash-points**. Apart from the ATM in Manorbier, Tenby is the last place you can get money until you reach Pembroke (53 miles/85km away. It is also worth taking into account that many of the pubs and guesthouses along the path to Pembroke do not take debit or credit cards; another good reason to fill your pockets with cash before you leave town.

Another possibly essential stop for many a trekker is the No 25 Café (see p88) which has **internet facilities** (£1/2 for 20/40 mins), as well as wi-fi access, the first since Amroth and the last until Pembroke. Nor are there any shops to speak of until you reach Angle so take a good supply of food unless you plan to eat out every night.

For any medical problems you can always pay a visit to the **health centre** which is in the north of the town on Narberth Rd. There's a **launderette** for your smelly socks just south of St George's St. For entertainment there's no shortage of **pubs** in the town centre, and a **cinema** on White Lion St as you enter the town.

Transport

The **bus station** is on Upper Park Rd while the **train station** is at the bottom of Warren St. Trains run to Pembroke Dock and all the way back to Swansea and London for those who have already had enough.

Bus services (most operated by Silcox) connect Tenby with Amroth (Nos 350/351), Pembroke Dock (Nos 333/358/361), Kilgetty (No 352), Penally (No 380), Haverfordwest (Silcox's No 381 & First's No 349) and other places further afield. See the public transport map and table, pp44-7, for full details.

Where to stay

On the path just to the north of town (see Map 3) is *Meadow Farm Campsite* (☎ 01834-844829, 🖳 www.meadowfarmtenby .co.uk; Mar-Oct) charging £7 per adult per night (children £4). The site has shower and toilet facilities.

Like most seaside towns there are countless B&Bs and guesthouses but they do, of course, get very busy at holiday time. As you enter the town from the north, close to North Beach is *Sea Breezes* (☎ 01834-842753, 🖳 www.seabreezesonline.co.uk; 18 The Norton; 1D/2D or T, all en suite), once a large hotel, now a small guesthouse, with beds from £29 per person; one room can sleep three people. There is a cluster of guesthouses around Warren St and Harding St just above the centre of town. *Lyndale House* (☎ 01834-842836, 🖳 www.lyndale house.co.uk; 1S/3D, all en suite), on Warren St, has rooms for £25-32 per person and *Weybourne Guest House* (☎ 01834-843641, 🖳 www.weybourneguesthouse.co .uk; 14 Warren St, 1T/2D/1F, all en suite) charges from £26 to £35/pp. Packed lunches (about £3) are available if requested in advance. The owners have walked the coast path so are happy to give advice if wanted.

Slightly more expensive is *Sunny Bank Guest House* (☎ 01834-844034, 🖳 www.sunny-bank.co.uk; Harding St; 4D) with en suite rooms from £34 per person (£45 single occupancy), or it's £38 in a room with a four-poster; the nearby *Ivy Bank Guest House* (☎ 01834-842311, 🖳 www.ivybanktenby.co.uk; Harding St; 2T or D/1D or F/2D, all en suite) charges £30-35 per person, single occupancy from £40. Finally in this area, *Kingsbridge House* (☎ 01834-844148, 🖳 www.kingsbridgehouse .co.uk; 3D/1T/3F, all en suite) is a spacious Victorian house with rooms from £26 to £35 per person (£35-65 single occupancy).

Close to the town centre is *Normandie Inn* (☎ 01834-842227, 🖳 www.normandie tenby.co.uk; Upper Frog St; 4D/2F) where all the rooms are en suite and cost £40/pp or £45 for single occupancy – do bear in mind all rooms are above the Normandie's lively late night bar though (see p86). *Bay House* (☎ 01834-849015, 🖳 www.bayhousetenby .co.uk; Picton Tce; 2D/1T or D, all en suite) is an understated, splendidly decorated place charging from £75 to £80 per room including a generous, locally sourced Welsh breakfast. Just off The Esplanade is

Glenholme Guesthouse (☎ 01834-843909, 🖳 www.glenholmetenby .co.uk; Picton Terrace; 1S/7D, all en suite) with rooms for £27.50-32 per person; the single room costs £35; and *Lindholme House* (☎ 01834-843368, 🖳 www.lindholmehouse.co.uk; 27 Victoria St; 6D, all en suite), which charges £25 to £30 per person; single occupancy supplement £5.

Where to eat and drink

There are some great little restaurants in Tenby, most of them on High St and Tudor Sq or at the top end of Upper Frog St. *Plantagenet Restaurant and Quay Room* (☎ 01834-842350; Quay Room open school holidays daily 10am-2.30pm & 5pm to late, Plantagenet open from noon but otherwise the same hours; Easter to mid July and Sep-Oct from 6pm; winter times vary), said to be the oldest house in Tenby, is definitely worth finding if only to have a look at the enormous medieval Flemish chimney, the hearth of which is big enough to seat a couple dining in. It is on the corner of Tudor Sq with the short and narrow Quay Hill.

The menu guarantees local ingredients with home-made sausages a speciality. In addition to some cracking meat dishes including a divine rack of lamb (£21.95) and a sumptuous venison pie (£20.95) they also serve some great vegetarian food. The lunch menu offers cheaper, good-value

snacks including bangers and mash (£8.95). Some of Tenby's finest food is found at *The Blue Ball Restaurant* (☎ 01834-843038; Sun noon-2pm, daily 6.30-9pm, till 9.30pm Fri-Sat). This atmospheric, rustic bistro, on Upper Frog St, serves excellent fish – the menu changes depending on what is available but expect to pay around £15. Alternatively try their homemade faggots with creamed potatoes and pea purée (£9) or their signature dish: pork wellington served with calvados sauce. Puddings are sinfully rich and there's a good selection of real ales and an extensive wine list.

Also on Upper Frog St, *Normandie Inn* (see Where to stay, summer daily noon-9pm; winter hours vary) serves decent steaks and other meats off the grill, and frequently has good meal deals. The colourful modern bar becomes a pulsating late-night venue open till 1am (Wed, Fri & Sat), and occasionally features live music.

Positioned overlooking North Beach is *Vista* (☎ 01834-849636; daily 9am-10.30pm during summer, 9am-5pm winter), which boasts superb harbour views from their outdoor terrace although you get a slight sense you're paying for the location as a decent coffee and pastry here will set you back £3.50. They also offer a small selection of paninis as well as tasty Greek-influenced main dishes, such as beef and butterbean stew, and are licensed. Next to

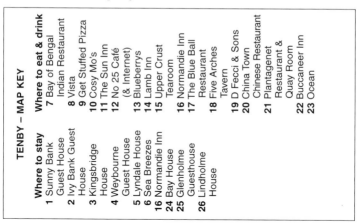

TENBY – MAP KEY

Where to stay
1 Sunny Bank Guest House
2 Ivy Bank Guest House
3 Kingsbridge House
4 Weybourne Guest House
5 Lyndale House
6 Sea Breezes
16 Normandie Inn
24 Bay House
25 Glenholme Guesthouse
26 Lindholme House

Where to eat & drink
7 Bay of Bengal Indian Restaurant
8 Vista
9 Get Stuffed Pizza
10 Cosy Mo's
11 The Sun Inn
12 No 25 Café (& Internet)
13 Blueberrys
14 Lamb Inn
15 Upper Crust Tearoom
16 Normandie Inn
17 The Blue Ball Restaurant
18 Five Arches Tavern
19 D Fecci & Sons
20 China Town Chinese Restaurant
21 Plantagenet Restaurant & Quay Room
22 Buccaneer Inn
23 Ocean

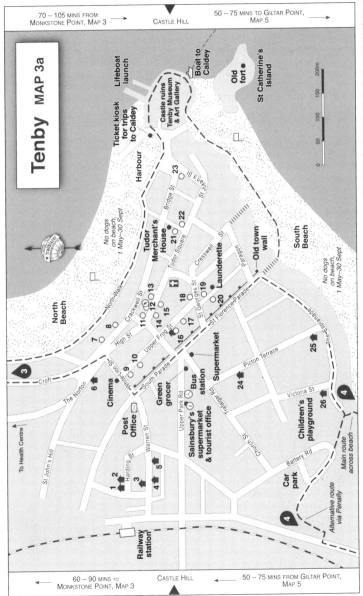

Tenby MAP 3a

70 – 105 MINS FROM MONKSTONE POINT, MAP 3 →

CASTLE HILL

50 – 75 MINS TO GILTAR POINT, MAP 5 →

Lifeboat launch

Ticket kiosk for trips to Caldey

Boat to Caldey

Old fort

St Catherine's Island

Castle ruins Tenby Museum & Art Gallery

Harbour

No dogs on beach, 1 May–30 Sept

North Beach

North Walk

23

Bridge St

St John's

22

Tudor Merchant's House

21

Tudor Square

Cresswell St

St John's

Launderette

Old town wall

South Beach

No dogs on beach, 1 May–30 Sept

Crackwell St

12 13

11

14 15

18

St Georges St

19

20

St John's

Paragon

High St

7 8

9 10

16 17

Upper Frog St

St Florence Parade

Esplanade

25

Croft

3

The Norton

Warren St

Cinema

Greengrocer

Supermarket

South Parade

Bus station

Picton Terrace

24

Post Office

Upper Park Rd

Sainsbury's supermarket & tourist office

Trafalgar Rd

Victoria St

26

To Health Centre

St John's Hill

Harding St

1 2

3

4 5

Church St

Children's playground

Battery Rd

Car park

4

Main route across beach

Alternative route via Penally

4

Railway station

60 – 90 MINS TO MONKSTONE POINT, MAP 3 ←

CASTLE HILL

50 – 75 MINS FROM GILTAR POINT, MAP 5 ←

0   50   100   150   200m

the harbour is *Ocean* (☎ 01834-844536; school holidays daily all day; Easter to Sep daily 9-10.30am, 11am-2.30pm & 6pm to late; winter Tue-Sun 11am-2.30pm & 6pm to late) with simple Italian food including pastas and pizzas, for those who want to load up with carbs before the next leg.

Equally cheap but tasty food can be found on the High St at the *Lamb Inn* (Sun-Thur 11am-5pm, Fri & Sat 11am-8pm; 14 High St) which has a variety of pub food such as jacket potatoes for £3.50 and baguettes from £3.25. Close by is *The Sun Inn* (daily 11am-late, food served daily noon-3pm), a bright and cheerful joint with reasonably cheap food including fisherman's pie for £7, while next door is *No 25 Café* (☎ 01834-842544; daily 9am-5pm, later at weekends in summer) with a range of snacks and sandwiches to eat while you're using their internet (see Services). On the same stretch are *Blueberrys* (☎ 01834-845785; daily 9am-5pm, school holidays also 6-11pm) which will rustle up pasta dishes from £7 and curries from £7.65, and *Upper Crust Tearoom* (☎ 01834-842502; summer daily 10am-5pm, winter Mon-Sat 10am-5pm, closed January), which serves cream teas from £2.50, both clotted and fresh cream.

For more traditional pub grub try the rustic *Five Arches Tavern* (☎ 01834-842513; daily noon-2pm & 6-9pm), on Upper Frog St, where you will find local

fish dishes from £7.25. The *Buccaneer Inn* (☎ 01834-842273; food daily noon-9pm), on St Julian St, is a rowdy place frequently full of Welsh rugby fans, which has a decent beer garden and serves standard pub fare.

Those with oriental tastes should head to Crackwell St, just off High St, for *Bay of Bengal Indian Restaurant* (☎ 01834-843331; daily 5.30-11.30pm). They have a typically extensive Indian menu but are unlicensed so you can bring your own alcohol. The chicken curry is £6.75 and the wonderful views over North Beach are totally free. Alternatively *China Town Chinese Restaurant* (☎ 01834-843557; Lower Frog St; Mon-Sat noon-2pm & 5.30pm-midnight, Sun 12.30-2pm & 6-11.30pm) has the usual array of rice and sweet and sour dishes starting at around £7.

Slightly less sophisticated food can be found at *Get Stuffed Pizza* (☎ 01834-845945; 10 Upper Frog St; daily 5.30-11pm, summer daily noon-11pm) which charges upwards of £6.25, and next door at *Cosy Mo's* (☎ 01834-842929; summer daily 10am-5.30pm, winter Mon-Fri 10.30am-3pm, Sat 10am-4.30pm) which offers all-day breakfasts (£3.95-5.95), jacket potatoes and hot sandwiches from £3.25. Fresh fish and chips can be had from *D Fecci and Sons* (☎ 01834-842484; daily 11.30am-9pm, later on Fri and Sat) on Lower Frog St.

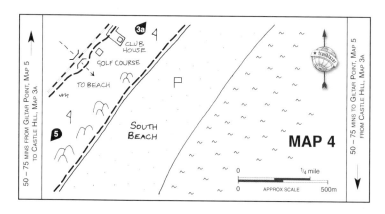

TENBY TO MANORBIER BAY

MAPS 4-8

These **10½ miles (17km, 3-4½ hrs)** are reasonably straightforward. The scenery is tamer than before but no less interesting. The path leaves Tenby at the end of The Esplanade and drops down onto the vast sands of South Beach. The direct route takes you across the beach to Giltar Point in the south. In the unlikely event of an exceptionally high tide or if you are planning on staying in the village of Penally you will need to take the alternative and slightly longer path which follows the track between the railway line and the golf course.

Giltar Point is the first of a number of **MoD firing ranges** and it is occasionally closed to the public (indicated, as with all the firing ranges, by a red flag flying); there is a number you can call to check the times of firing on the range (☎ 01834-845950). If it is open you can climb the steps up through the high dunes onto the cliff top. When it is closed you must take the detour from the beach through the dunes to **Penally**.

PENALLY (PENALUN) MAP 5

Penally has a pretty church set beside the village green. The **post office** in the centre of the village incorporates a small **shop** (Mon-Fri 8am-5.30pm, Sat 8am-noon).

Silcox's No 380 Tenby town **bus** service calls here. First's bus No 349 stops on the road running parallel to the A4139, just to the south-west of the junction to Cross Inn. The **railway station** lies on the main road; there are trains every two hours or so for Pembroke and Pembroke Dock via Manorbier in one direction, and for Swansea via Tenby, Saundersfoot, Kilgetty and Narberth in the other. For details of public transport services see pp44-7.

Where to stay and eat

Should your feet be aching after the first day there are some good places to stay. Campers should head for *Penally Court Farm Campsite* (☎ 01834-845109; Apr-Oct) at the western end of the village. Pitches cost around £15 per tent.

There are also a number of good B&Bs. In the centre of the village up the lane behind the church is *Myrtle House* (☎ 01834-842508, 🖳 myrtlehouse@btinter net.com; 1S/5D/1T/1F, all en suite) where beds are £28-35 per person. *Brambles Lodge* (Map 5, p90; ☎ 01834-842393, 🖳 www.brambleslodge.co.uk; 1S/4D/1T/2F, en suite) can be found in the western corner of Penally, just off the main road. Rates are £30 per person; the single costs £30-33.

Wychwood House (Map 5, p90; ☎ 01834-844387, 🖳 www.wychwoodhouse bb.co.uk; 1D/2F, en suite) at the other end of the village is a very classy place. Rates are from £40 rising to £45 per person in a four-poster bed; single occupancy £55-60. Evening meals (£27.50) are available if booked in advance; there's no licence so bring your own wine.

The budget-busting *Penally Abbey* (☎ 01834-843033, 🖳 www.penally-abbey .com; 11D or T, 6D, all en suite), built on the site of an ancient monastery, has grand rooms for upwards of £148 per room, with a single occupancy discount of £10, and a smart traditional restaurant (daily 7-

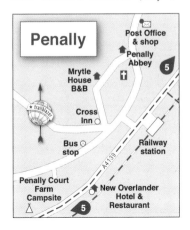

Penally

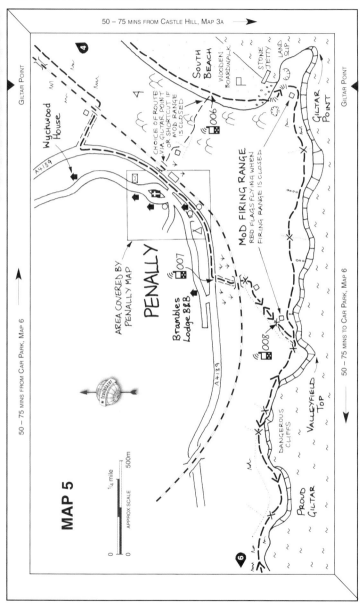

MAP 5

50 – 75 MINS FROM CASTLE HILL, MAP 3A

GILTAR POINT

GILTAR POINT

SOUTH BEACH

LAND SLIP

STONE JETTY

WOODEN BOARDWALK

⌂006

CHOICE OF ROUTE VIA GILTAR POINT OR SHORTCUT IF MOD RANGE IS CLOSED

Wychwood House

A4139

GILTAR POINT

MoD FIRING RANGE
RED FLAGS FLYING WHEN FIRING RANGE IS CLOSED

AREA COVERED BY PENALLY MAP

PENALLY

⌂007

Brambles Lodge B&B

A4139

⌂008

VALLEYFIELD TOP

50 – 75 MINS FROM CAR PARK, MAP 6

DANGEROUS CLIFFS

PROUD GILTAR

50 – 75 MINS TO CAR PARK, MAP 6

★ trailblazer

¼ mile

500m

APPROX SCALE

0

0

8.45pm) that's also open to non-residents.

Cross Inn (☎ 01834-844665; food daily noon-2.30pm & 6-8.30pm) offers a mouthwatering selection of pub meals; they also do breakfasts from 9.30am by arrangement (call in or phone the day before).

On the main A4139 road is *New Overlander Hotel and Restaurant* (☎ 01834-842868 ⌨ www.newoverlander.co .uk; 5D, all en suite), which charges £70-80 per room; the de luxe room is £85-95; there

is no discount for single occupancy. Rates include breakfast. The restaurant (summer daily 9.30am-9pm; winter daily 5.30-9pm but also as much as possible during the day) is a smart little place with a garden and glass conservatory in which to enjoy a drink. Try their minty lamb steak for £10.25, or their steak and ale pie for £9.25. For £5.75 their sautéed mushrooms topped with melted Camembert are fantastic. Breakfast for non residents costs from £3.95.

From Penally you must follow the main road a short distance before joining a track that goes under the railway line and back up onto the coast path proper. The path continues over low grassy cliff tops, passing the pretty sandy bay of **Lydstep Haven**. At **Lydstep** there's an optional 20-minute detour to the open headland of Lydstep Point with views along the coast in both directions.

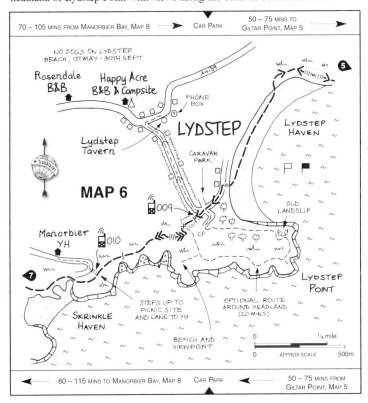

70 – 105 MINS FROM MANORBIER BAY, MAP 8 → CAR PARK

50 – 75 MINS TO GILTAR POINT, MAP 5 →

NO DOGS ON LYDSTEP BEACH, 1ST MAY – 30TH SEPT

Rosendale B&B

Happy Acre B&B & Campsite

A4139

PHONE BOX

LYDSTEP

LYDSTEP HAVEN

Lydstep Tavern

CARAVAN PARK

OLD LANDSLIP

★ trailblazer

MAP 6

009

Manorbier YH

010

LYDSTEP POINT

SKRINKLE HAVEN

STEPS UP TO PICNIC SITE AND LANE TO YH

OPTIONAL ROUTE AROUND HEADLAND (20 MINS)

BENCH AND VIEWPOINT

0   ¼ mile

0   APPROX SCALE   500m

◄ 80 – 115 MINS TO MANORBIER BAY, MAP 8 CAR PARK ◄

50 – 75 MINS FROM GILTAR POINT, MAP 5

ROUTE GUIDE AND MAPS

ROUTE GUIDE AND MAPS

LYDSTEP   MAP 6, p91

Lydstep Haven is dominated by an unat-
tractive caravan park though the small village of Lydstep itself is reached by following the coast path up from the beach. There
is a **phone box**. First's No 349 **bus** stops by
the Tavern. Silcox's No 358 Tenby service
also calls in Lydstep. For details see the
public transport map and table, pp44-7.

Happy Acre B&B and Campsite (☎
01834-870150, 💻 www.happy-acre-bandb-
lydstep-tenby.wales.info; 2T/1F sleeping
four, all en suite) is convenient and charges
£25-35 per person for two sharing; single
occupancy £30-40. They also allow **camping** (May-Sep) and charge £12 per tent with
two adults (£10 for one person with a tent).
They may offer luggage transfer so contact
them for details. Just up the road is
Rosendale Guesthouse (☎ 01834-870040,
💻 www.rosendalepembrokeshire.co.uk; 3T
/3D, all en suite), which is a decent B&B
charging £32.50-35/pp (£40-45 for single
occupancy). They can offer luggage transfer.

Lydstep Tavern (☎ 01834-871521;
food summer daily noon-9pm, winter daily

noon-2.30pm & 6-9pm; bar open daily
summer noon-midnight, winter noon-3pm
& 6-11pm) is on the bend of the main road
with fine local beers and ciders to accompany snacks and meals (most of which are
home made), which can be enjoyed in its
pleasant garden. Their Sunday lunch (£8.95
including dessert) is served noon-3.30pm in
the summer and to 2.30pm in the winter
months. They can cater for people with particular dietary requirements.

Budget travellers should head for
Manorbier Youth Hostel (☎ 0845-371 9031,
💻 manorbier@yha.org.uk; open all year), a
little further along the coast path, some 200
metres from the beach at Skrinkle Haven. It
has 69 beds but is often full in the summer
months. The rather unfortunate but striking
sardine-tin appearance of the hostel is thanks
to its original use as a 1950s NATO storage
building. Thankfully the interior is actually
quite habitable now. Prices start at £11.95 for
members during the low season but rise to
£17.95 at peak times. The hostel is licensed
and serves meals.

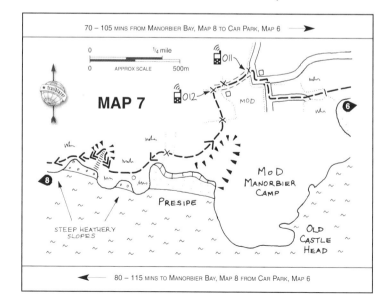

70 – 105 MINS FROM MANORBIER BAY, MAP 8 TO CAR PARK, MAP 6 ➤

MAP 7

80 – 115 MINS TO MANORBIER BAY, MAP 8 FROM CAR PARK, MAP 6

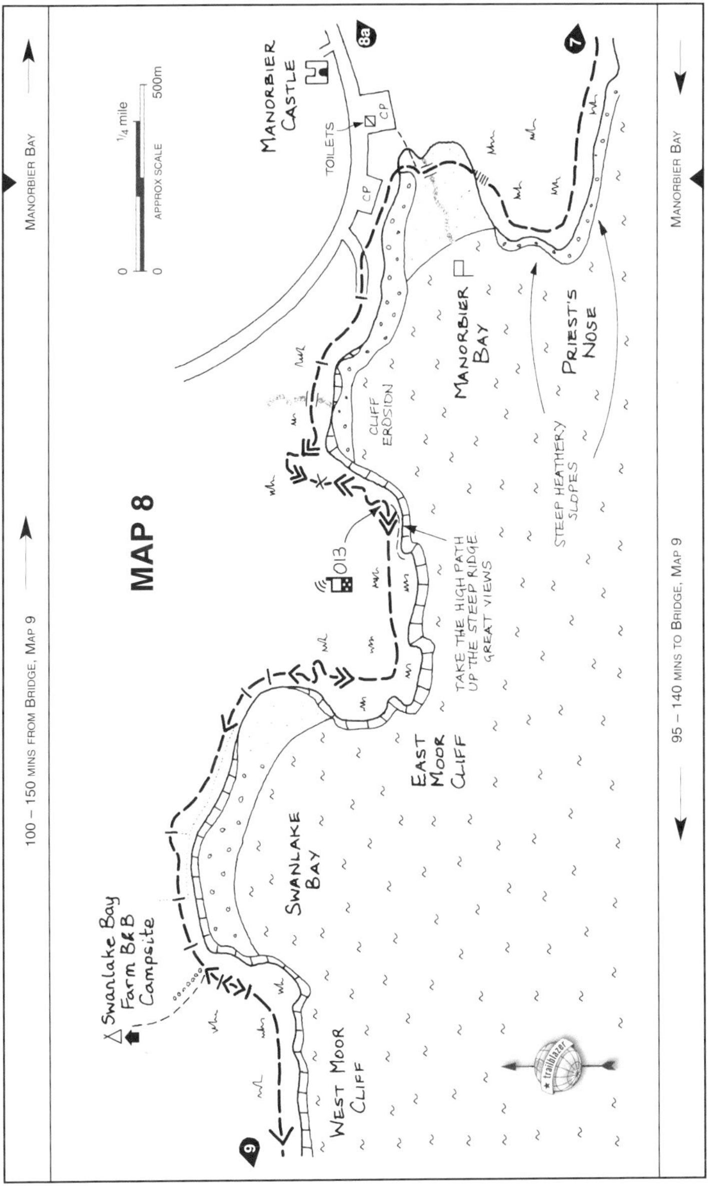

MAP 8

MANORBIER BAY

MANORBIER BAY

100 – 150 MINS FROM BRIDGE, MAP 9

MANORBIER CASTLE

8a

TOILETS

CP

CP

CLIFF EROSION

MANORBIER BAY

PRIEST'S NOSE

STEEP HEATHERY SLOPES

7

013

TAKE THE HIGH PATH UP THE STEEP RIDGE GREAT VIEWS

EAST MOOR CLIFF

SWANLAKE BAY

Swanlake Bay Farm B&B Campsite

WEST MOOR CLIFF

9

0   APPROX SCALE   ¼ mile

0   500m

95 – 140 MINS TO BRIDGE, MAP 9

ROUTE GUIDE AND MAPS

ROUTE GUIDE AND MAPS

The cliffs up to **Skrinkle Haven** are impressive but then the path heads inland to avoid another MoD enclosure. The stretch to **Manorbier Bay** follows some beautiful coast, the path contouring steep heathery slopes that drop straight into the sea.

MANORBIER (MAENORBYR) MAP 8a

Pronounced 'manor-bee-er' this village boasts a windswept sandy beach and an impressive, well-preserved **castle** (see box below) as well as an attractive 12th-century church. It also has a B&B, a **shop** with long opening hours and an **ATM** at the top of the village, as well as a good pub, which is a saving grace on a rainy day. There are **public toilets** in the car park.

Silcox's No 333 and No 358 **bus** services call here, as does First's No 349. **Trains** stop at the railway station every couple of hours but it is a bit inland (about two miles) so not that convenient. For full details see the public transport map and table, pp44-7.

Where to stay and eat

Castlemead Hotel (☎ 01834-871358; 💻 www.castlemeadhotel.com; 3T/3D/2F, all en suite) is the first building on the right as you enter the village by the lane from the beach. This is a luxurious option, with B&B starting from £43/pp. Their restaurant is open to non-residents in the evenings (Mon-Sat 6-8.30pm, booking recommend-

ed in summer and on bank holiday weekends) and for lunch (noon-2pm) on Sundays.

For hungry tummies, on the right-hand side past Castlemead Hotel, *Castle*

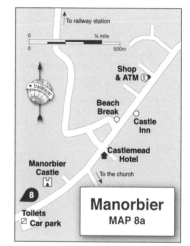

Manorbier
MAP 8a

To railway station

Shop & ATM £

Beach Break

Castle Inn

Castlemead Hotel

Manorbier Castle

To the church

8

Toilets
Car park

❑ **Manorbier Castle**

History is visible everywhere you go in Pembrokeshire, from standing stones and Iron-Age hill-forts to the numerous castles dotted around the countryside.

The birthplace of Gerald of Wales, a 12th-century scholar who described Manorbier as 'the pleasantest spot in Wales', this fine castle stands in a wonderful location close to the beach, just off the coast path. Life-size wax figures and appropriately contemporary music piped throughout much of the building help visitors get a feel for what the castle and its pleasant walled gardens must have been like in Gerald's day. If the castle seems vaguely recognisable, that could be because it has been used as a set in various films including *I Capture the Castle* and the 1989 version of *The Lion, the Witch and the Wardrobe*.

Visitors to Manorbier Castle (☎ 01834-871394; 💻 www.manorbiercastle.co.uk) can explore the castle, including the turrets and dungeons, from Easter to the end of September, daily 10am-6pm and over the October half-term. The castle is also open every weekend in October. However, it may be closed on Saturdays for private functions so check in advance. Admission £3.50.

Inn (☎ 01834-871268; food summer daily noon-3pm & 6-9.30pm, Sep-Oct noon-2pm & 6-9pm, Oct-Easter 6-9pm) has an extensive menu including homemade cawl (see box p16) for £4.95 and steak and kidney pie for £9.50. It also has a pool table in the winter months.

On the other side of the road is *Beach Break* (☎ 01834-871709; summer daily 9am-7pm, winter daily 10am-5pm) with soups (£3.50), the dish of day (£6) and baked potatoes from £3.75. Cream and Welsh teas are available later till 5pm for £3.75.

A mile and a half (2km) further along the coast path, *Swanlake Bay Farm* (see Map 8, p93; ☎ 01834-871204, 🖳 www .swanlake-bay.co.uk; 3D/2T/1F, most with private facilities) offers B&B from £30 per person. Three-course evening meals are available for £15 per person if booked in advance. They allow **camping** (costs vary according to the size of the tent but work out at about £3 per person) but there are no facilities other than a water tap.

MANORBIER BAY TO FRESHWATER EAST   MAPS 8-9

This short section of **four miles (6km, 1¹/₂-2hrs)** takes in two wild windswept headlands which sandwich **Swanlake Bay**, a sandy beach backed by steep slopes and farmland. Short but strenuous accurately describes this section. No sooner do you drop down the side of one steep cliff than you find yourself climbing up another. It can make for slow progress if you have a heavy pack. The broad sands of **Freshwater East** make a welcome sight.

It is worth bearing in mind that budget accommodation is pretty thin on the ground from here until Pembroke and the same can be said for any other services you may be looking for. Forward planning is essential. Book all your accommodation well in advance especially in the high season.

FRESHWATER EAST   MAP 9

Freshwater East is a peculiar place. A number of houses lie scattered among the wooded slopes above the bay while the steep road up from Trewent Park is lined by yet more homes. In fact there is little here other than houses.

If you need basic supplies you can pick these up from **The Longhouse** (daily, hours variable depending on the season), a bar and café in Trewent Park, which sells snacks, soft drinks and hosts the occasional evening BBQ. There are **public toilets** and a **phone box** in the village.

If you are staying here it is worth using the footpath that cuts in to the village just before the coast path drops down to the beach. Otherwise you have to walk down and then back up the steep road to reach the village.

Silcox's No 387 and 388 Coastal Cruiser **bus** services call here on the way round the coast via Pembroke Dock, Angle,

Hundleton and Stackpole. For further information see pp44-6.

The Georgian country mansion *Portclew House* (☎ 01646-672800; 🖳 www .portclewhouse.co.uk; 1S/3T/2D/1F) is a grand place boasting en suite only rooms with internet facilities. They also serve great breakfasts. Rates are £28-34 per person. Opposite is *Upper Portclew Farm* (☎ 01646-672112; May-Sep) which allows **camping** in one of its fields overlooking the bay, with tent pitches costing £10 (£5 for a solo camper). There are reasonable facilities and decent hot showers.

Closer to the path, half a mile west of Freshwater East, is *East Trewent Farm* (☎ 01646-672127, 🖳 www.easttrewentfarm .co.uk; 2D/1T, en suite) with rates from £30 per head, £40 for single occupancy.

Well worth the detour from the path, the food at *Freshwater Inn* (☎ 01646-672828; food daily noon-2pm & 6-9pm)

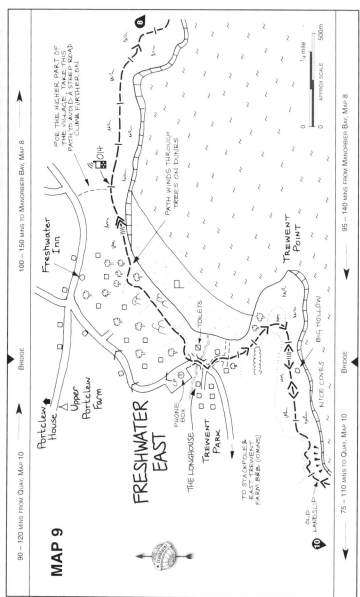

MAP 9

90 – 120 MINS FROM QUAY, MAP 10 — BRIDGE — 100 – 150 MINS TO MANORBIER BAY, MAP 8

75 – 110 MINS TO QUAY, MAP 10 — BRIDGE — 95 – 140 MINS FROM MANORBIER BAY, MAP 8

FOR THE HIGHER PART OF THE VILLAGE, TAKE THIS PATH TO AVOID A STEEP ROAD CLIMB FURTHER ON

PATH WINDS THROUGH TREES ON DUNES

Freshwater Inn

Portclew House

Upper Portclew Farm

FRESHWATER EAST

THE LONGHOUSE

TREWENT PARK

PHONE BOX

CP

TOILETS

TREWENT POINT

BIG HOLLOW

NICE CONES

TO STACKPOLE & EAST TREWENT FARM B&B (10MINS)

OLD LANDSLIP

0   500m
0   ¼ mile
APPROX SCALE

trailblazer

comes with a wide choice and big helpings including some fine baguettes. The tranquil beer garden with views out to sea is a great space to while away an evening with a pint of Double Dragon (£2.40).

FRESHWATER EAST TO BROAD HAVEN (FOR BOSHERSTON)
MAPS 9-12

The scenery really is spectacular for the next **6½ miles (10km, 2-3hrs)** to Broad Haven (not to be confused with the village of Broad Haven further north). It begins with more tortuous 'up-and-downs' as the cliffs twist and turn their way west of Freshwater East.

Between Trewent Point and **Greenala Point** some fantastic contorted green cliffs, coves and blowholes line the coastline. Once past Greenala Point the path follows the high top of a long steep cliff before dropping down to Stackpole Quay.

The scenery changes dramatically as you pass **Stackpole Quay**. Leaving the old red sandstone behind, the path moves into carboniferous limestone country where the cliffs drop precipitously into the sea. Flat grassy tops here make the walking easier on the feet.

Barafundle Bay is probably one of the most beautiful beaches along the entire walk with lush woodland dropping down to its southern edge. It's a great

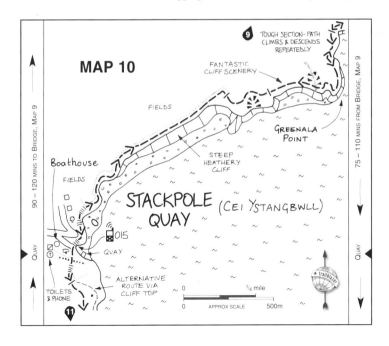

spot for a picnic lunch on a nice day. If it's raining or you don't feel like hump-
ing a hamper round you're better off stopping at the ***Boathouse*** (Map 10; ☎
01646-672672; Easter-Oct daily 9.30am-5.30pm; hot food noon-4pm; teas and
cakes 4-5.30pm) at Stackpole Quay to take advantage of their hot bacon rolls
(£2.95) and haddock chowder (£4.95). If it's sunny try the dressed crab salad
(£9.95) instead. All their food is home made and, where possible, locally
sourced. The Coastal Cruiser **bus** services (see pp44-6) stop at the car park if
you have had enough of walking.

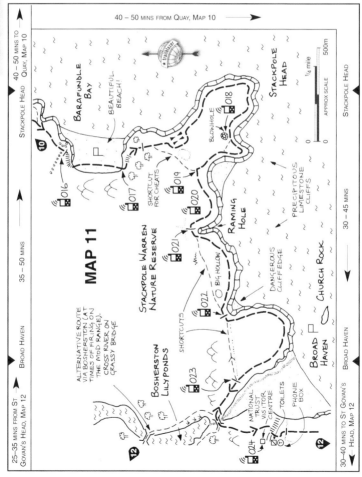

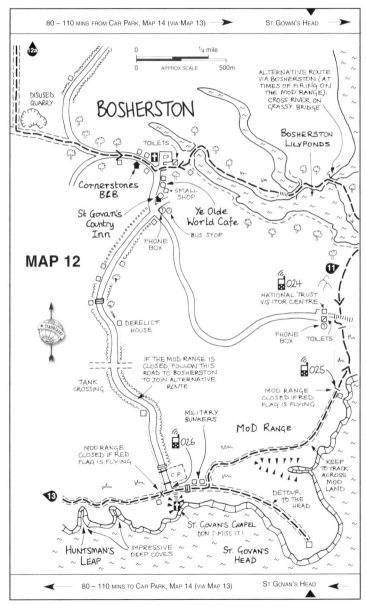

ROUTE GUIDE AND MAPS

12a

DISUSED
QUARRY

0   ¼ mile
0   500m
APPROX SCALE

BOSHERTON

ALTERNATIVE ROUTE
VIA BOSHERSTON (AT
TIMES OF FIRING ON
THE MOD RANGE),
CROSS RIVER ON
GRASSY BRIDGE

BOSHERSTON
LILYPONDS

TOILETS
CP

Cornerstones
B&B

SMALL
SHOP

St Govan's
Country
Inn

Ye Olde
World Cafe

BUS STOP

PHONE
BOX

MAP 12

11

024
NATIONAL TRUST
VISITOR CENTRE

DERELICT
HOUSE

PHONE
BOX   TOILETS

IF THE MOD RANGE IS
CLOSED, FOLLOW THIS
ROAD TO BOSHERSTON
TO JOIN ALTERNATIVE
ROUTE

TANK
CROSSING

025

MOD RANGE
CLOSED IF RED
FLAG IS FLYING

MILITARY
BUNKERS

MoD RANGE

MOD RANGE
CLOSED IF RED
FLAG IS FLYING

026

CP

KEEP
TO TRACK
ACROSS
MOD
LAND

13

DETOUR
TO THE
HEAD

HUNTSMAN'S
LEAP

IMPRESSIVE
DEEP COVES

ST. GOVAN'S CHAPEL
DON'T MISS IT!

ST. GOVAN'S
HEAD

The path continues on through **Stackpole Warren Nature Reserve**, before leading you to the wonderful beach at **Broad Haven**. The Coastal Cruiser **bus** services (see pp44-6) stop at Broad Haven. There is a National Trust Visitor Centre as well as **toilets** and a **phone box**.

There is limited accommodation and food at Bosherston (see opposite; 15 to 20 minutes from Broad Haven if walking on the western side of the ponds), which is on the alternative road detour route (see below).

BROAD HAVEN TO MERRION   MAPS 12-14

There is a choice of route here. The route proper continues across the cliff tops through the Castlemartin **MoD firing range**, said to be one of NATO's most important training areas in Europe. Covering 5880 acres it also hides some of the finest limestone cliff scenery in Britain. Unfortunately it is closed to the public when firing is taking place. It is well worth checking the opening times (☎ 01646-662367) since the detour is a monotonous trudge along a boring road.

There are two points where the path may be closed (indicated by a red flag). The first is just above Broad Haven beach and the other is at St Govan's. At both points there are roads which take you to Bosherston and on to the alternative road route described below.

Via Stack Rocks   Maps 12, 13, 14

If the range is open it is **8¹/₂ miles (13.5km, 3-3¹/₂hrs)** to Merrion, following the jeep track along the flat limestone cliff tops. The cliffs, when you can see them, are spectacular but signs along the track warn you to stick to the path through the firing range. There are many rewards to walking this route as opposed to the road detour, the first of which is at St Govan's.

St Govan's Chapel (Map 12), sitting just before the sentry box into the MoD range, should not be missed. It's in an extraordinary location hidden down some steep stone steps in a cleft. A tiny stone chapel, cold, dark and empty inside, it is squeezed between sheer rocky cliffs which seem to prevent it from falling into the heaving sea below.

On entering the Castlemartin firing range follow the jeep track across open grassland and scrubland with vertical limestone cliffs to your left all the way to the dead-end road at **Stack Rocks** (Map 14) or Elegug Stacks, two impressive sea stacks sitting a short way offshore. A little further on, past the car park, is the natural arch known as the **Green Bridge of Wales**, a spectacular sight when the waves are crashing around it and the gulls are wheeling above the cliff tops. It's only a three-minute detour from the coast path.

From here you must follow the lane which takes you inland across the firing range to the main B4319 road. Turn right and walk for quarter of a mile to **Merrion** (see opposite).

Detour route via Bosherston   Maps 12, 12a, 14

If the Castlemartin firing range is closed you must follow the road north via Bosherston. The village of Bosherston and the lily ponds of the same name are the only real highlights if you are going this way. Otherwise these **five miles (8km, 1hr 40mins-2 hrs)** comprise a rather tedious trudge along roads hemmed in by high hedges. If you have the time, it really is worth waiting for the trail through the firing range to reopen.

From Broad Haven, where the main path crosses the stone bridge at the southern tip of the lily ponds (see p98), you must follow the path inland up the east bank of the beautiful lake, crossing the three bridges over the arms of the lake and up the steep rocky track to **Bosherston**.

BOSHERSTON   MAP 12, p99

If you are taking the road detour either from Broad Haven or St Govan's you will pass through this quaint little village with its photogenic **church**. Even if you are taking the cliff-top route through the military firing range it is worth making the short detour to the village. This is partly because it is the only place with any accommodation along this stretch and also because it gives you the opportunity to explore the intricate creeks and woodland of **Bosherston lily ponds**. These peaceful lakes, reed beds and heavily wooded slopes contrast greatly with the crashing waves on the beach. It's a great place to spot wildlife. Otters can sometimes be seen at dusk if you are quiet and there is plenty of birdlife from coots and moorhens to herons and buzzards.

The No 387/388 Coastal Cruiser **bus** services go via Bosherston on the looping journey between Pembroke Dock and St Govan's Head. See public transport map and table pp44-6 for further details.

The village itself is compact with a tiny **shop**, **phone box** and **toilets**.

At the end of the main street is *St Govan's Country Inn* (☎ 01646-661311, 🖳 www.stgovanscountryinn.webeden.co.uk;

food served daily Apr to end Oct noon-9.30pm; Nov-Mar Mon-Fri noon-2.30pm & 5.30-9pm, Sat & Sun noon-9.30pm; 2T/1D/1F, all en suite). They do B&B from £80 for two sharing a room in the smart en suite rooms upstairs; single occupancy costs £45. In terms of food St Govan's is a hugely and deservedly popular place with a vast and delicious menu, including lamb shank in rosemary and a red wine jus (£9.95) and at least three authentic curries (up to eight on their monthly curry nights). They also have a wide range of well-kept cask ales, though stock fewer in the winter months.

Opposite the church there is B&B at *Cornerstones* (☎ 01646-661660; 1S/1T/1D or F, all with private facilities) from £35/pp for two sharing and £40 for the single room.

Apart from St Govan's the other place serving food is *Ye Olde World Café* (☎ 01646-661216; daily 9am-6pm); it has a wide variety of snacks which you can eat in their big front garden. The owner, who was 88 at the time of writing and still working at the café, received an MBE in the June 2009 Honours List for her services to hospitality and tourism. The café was started by her parents and has been open nearly 90 years.

Here the road heads west past a disused quarry before heading north through farmland (Map 12a, p102 and then west along the very straight and boring B4319 road to the turn off for **Merrion** where you rejoin the main coast path.

MERRION   MAP 14, p105

Merrion sits along a hilly ridge. Milford Haven estuary is in the distance to the north while to the south is the MoD's vast

Castlemartin firing range. The village has a laidback friendly feel but there is little for the weary walker.   *(cont'd on p104)*

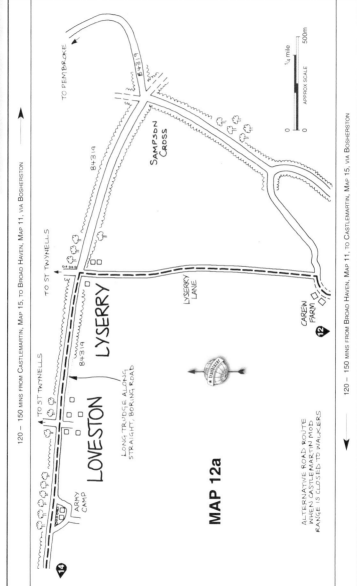

ROUTE GUIDE AND MAPS

120 – 150 MINS FROM CASTLEMARTIN, MAP 15, TO BROAD HAVEN, MAP 11, VIA BOSHERSTON

120 – 150 MINS FROM BROAD HAVEN, MAP 11, TO CASTLEMARTIN, MAP 15, VIA BOSHERSTON

TO PEMBROKE

B4319

SAMPSON CROSS

TO ST TWYNELLS

B4319

LYSERRY LANE

LYSERRY

CAREW FARM

12

TO ST TWYNELLS

LOVESTON

LONG TRUDGE ALONG STRAIGHT, BORING ROAD

B4319

ARMY CAMP

14

MAP 12a

ALTERNATIVE ROAD ROUTE WHEN CASTLEMARTIN MOD RANGE IS CLOSED TO WALKERS

¼ mile
APPROX SCALE
0   500m
0

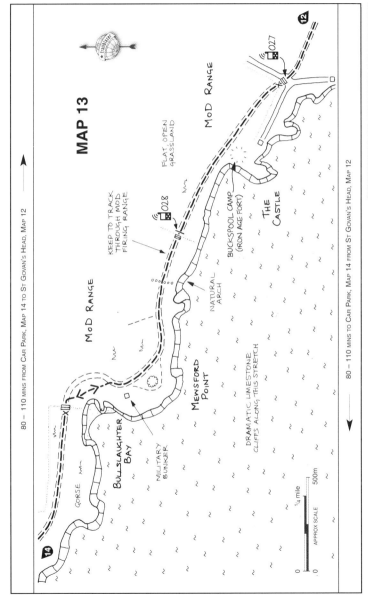

MAP 13

80 – 110 MINS FROM CAR PARK, MAP 14 TO ST GOVAN'S HEAD, MAP 12

MoD RANGE

MoD RANGE

MoD RANGE

FLAT OPEN GRASSLAND

027

028

KEEP TO TRACK THROUGH MoD FIRING RANGE

NATURAL ARCH

BUCKSPOOL CAMP (IRON AGE FORT)

THE CASTLE

MEWSFORD POINT

DRAMATIC LIMESTONE CLIFFS ALONG THIS STRETCH

MILITARY BUNKER

BULLSLAUGHTER BAY

GORSE

80 – 110 MINS TO CAR PARK, MAP 14 FROM ST GOVAN'S HEAD, MAP 12

¼ mile

500m

APPROX SCALE

0

12

14

(cont'd from p101) Merrion has a **phone box** and two B&Bs. *The Old Smithy* (☎ 01646-661310; 1D/1T or F), is a smart and welcoming place charging £30/pp; there is one bathroom for both rooms as well as a shower room downstairs. Their big back garden is also open to **campers** at £8 per person; campers can secure breakfast for a small fee by asking nicely in advance. The owner will also cook guests an evening meal for about £8.50 if you book in advance. *Hayston House* (☎ 01646-661462, 🖥 www.haystonfarmhouse.co.uk; 1D private bathroom) on the same road offers B&B accommodation in the main house for £70, or self-catering in their smart coach house apartment (1D en suite) for £50. Enquire about rates for single occupancy.

MERRION TO ANGLE   MAPS 14-20

Some beautiful scenery can be found along these **12 miles (19km, 4hrs 50mins-6¹/₂hrs)** but you must work for it. After the relatively easy walking of the previous section the going once again gets tougher with plenty of ups and downs along the southern side of the Angle peninsula. Remember to bring plenty of **food and water** as there is nowhere to find any along this stretch until you get to West Angle, only an hour or so from the end.

Things begin easily enough as you leave Merrion. There are two options: either head west for the quicker route along the main B4319 road to **Castlemartin**, or north to follow the country lanes through the village of **Warren**, where there is a nice church, St Mary's. Country lanes are always preferable to main roads but the truth is you really won't miss much if you choose to take the quicker, main road route.

Along the road between Warren and Castlemartin the MoD have kindly set aside a 'spectator area' from where you can safely watch the army shooting at things. On a quieter note the Golden Plover Art Gallery (Mon-Fri 10am-6pm) exhibits and sells watercolours of Pembrokeshire and elsewhere. The workshop is also open to visitors.

You quickly reach **Castlemartin** (Castellmartin, Map 15) where there is a tiny **post office** as well as a **phone box**. The only **bus** service coming this way is the Coastal Cruiser (No 387 and No 388); see pp44-6 for details.

From Castlemartin follow the lane across farmland and through enormous grassy dunes to the magnificent beach at **Freshwater West** (the Coastal Cruiser buses, see above, also call here), renowned as being one of Pembrokeshire's finest sweeps of sand. The relentless crashing of the surf makes this a popular haunt for surfers but it is not a safe place for swimming. The beach and dunes behind it have also had starring roles on the screen; in *Harry Potter and the Deathly Hallows* a full-sized house, Shell Cottage, was created at the northern end of the beach, whilst in Ridley Scott's Robin Hood film *Nottingham*, starring Russell Crowe, the dunes hosted a giant battle sequence featuring 600 extras.

At the bridge just past the car park (where there are some toilets) there are two options. You can turn left after the bridge and follow the wonderful beach north or continue along the road which winds its way through high sand dunes. At times the road almost seems to get swallowed up by the shifting sands.

(cont'd on p110)

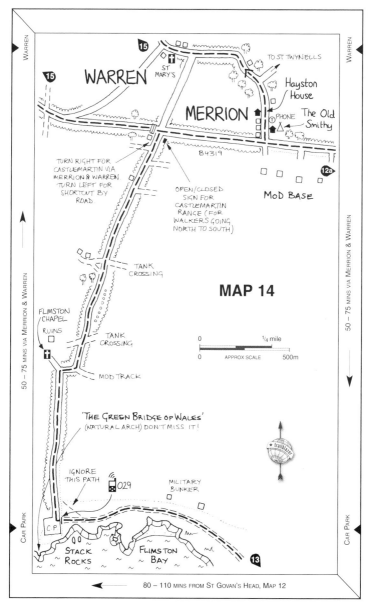

WARREN

15

ST MARY'S

TO ST TWYNELLS

Hayston House

MERRION

PHONE

The Old Smithy

B4319

TURN RIGHT FOR CASTLEMARTIN VIA MERRION & WARREN.
TURN LEFT FOR SHORTCUT BY ROAD

OPEN/CLOSED SIGN FOR CASTLEMARTIN RANGE (FOR WALKERS GOING NORTH TO SOUTH)

MOD BASE

12a

TANK CROSSING

MAP 14

FLIMSTON CHAPEL RUINS

TANK CROSSING

MOD TRACK

0   ¼ mile

0   APPROX SCALE   500m

'THE GREEN BRIDGE OF WALES' (NATURAL ARCH) DON'T MISS IT!

trailblazer

IGNORE THIS PATH

029

MILITARY BUNKER

C.P.

STACK ROCKS

FLIMSTON BAY

13

WARREN

WARREN

50 – 75 MINS VIA MERRION & WARREN

50 – 75 MINS VIA MERRION & WARREN

50 – 75 MINS VIA MERRION & WARREN

CAR PARK

CAR PARK

80 – 110 MINS FROM ST GOVAN'S HEAD, Map 12

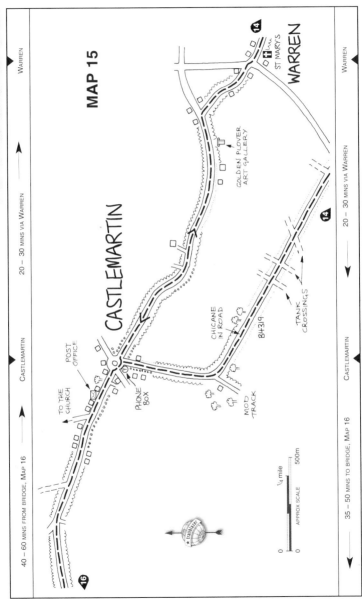

MAP 15

CASTLEMARTIN

WARREN

◀ WARREN

20 – 30 MINS VIA WARREN ▲

◀ CASTLEMARTIN

40 – 60 MINS FROM BRIDGE, MAP 16 ▲

TO THE CHURCH

POST OFFICE

PHONE BOX

MOD TRACK

CHICANE IN ROAD

B4319

TANK CROSSINGS

ST MARYS

WARREN ▶

20 – 30 MINS VIA WARREN ▶

CASTLEMARTIN ◀

35 – 50 MINS TO BRIDGE, MAP 16 ▼

GOLDEN PLOVER ART GALLERY

14

14

16

¼ mile

500m

APPROX SCALE

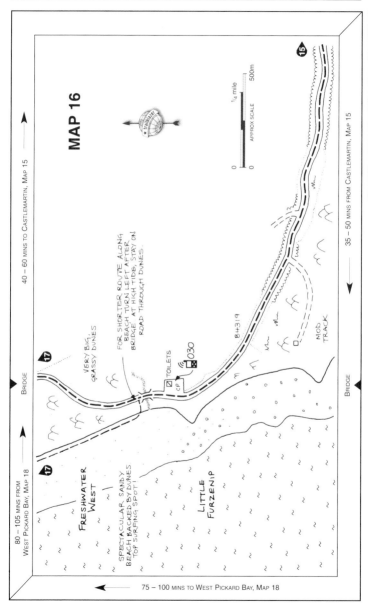

MAP 16

40 – 60 MINS TO CASTLEMARTIN, MAP 15

35 – 50 MINS FROM CASTLEMARTIN, MAP 15

ROUTE GUIDE AND MAPS

APPROX SCALE

0   ¼ mile

0   500m

VERY BIG, GRASSY DUNES

FOR SHORTER ROUTE ALONG BEACH TURN LEFT AFTER BRIDGE AT HIGH TIDE, STAY ON ROAD THROUGH DUNES.

B4319

MOD TRACK

TOILETS

CP

BRIDGE

BRIDGE

FRESHWATER WEST

80 – 105 MINS FROM WEST PICKARD BAY, MAP 18

SPECTACULAR SANDY BEACH BACKED BY DUNES TOP SURFING SPOT!

LITTLE FURZENIP

75 – 100 MINS TO WEST PICKARD BAY, MAP 18

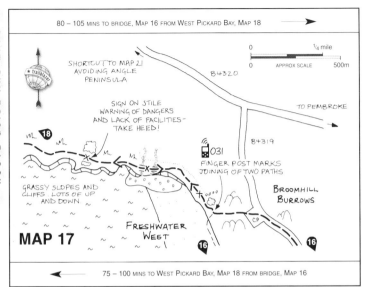

80 – 105 MINS TO BRIDGE, MAP 16 FROM WEST PICKARD BAY, MAP 18 ➤

SHORTCUT TO MAP 21
AVOIDING ANGLE
PENINSULA

B4320

TO PEMBROKE

SIGN ON STILE
WARNING OF DANGERS
AND LACK OF FACILITIES –
TAKE HEED!

031
FINGER POST MARKS
JOINING OF TWO PATHS

B4319

18

GRASSY SLOPES AND
CLIFFS . LOTS OF UP
AND DOWN

BROOMHILL
BURROWS

MAP 17

FRESHWATER
WEST

CP

16

16

◄ 75 – 100 MINS TO WEST PICKARD BAY, MAP 18 FROM BRIDGE, MAP 16

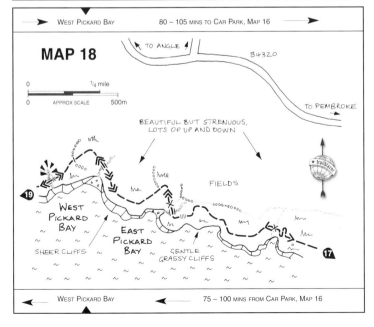

➤ WEST PICKARD BAY   80 – 105 MINS TO CAR PARK, MAP 16 ➤

MAP 18

TO ANGLE

B4320

TO PEMBROKE

BEAUTIFUL BUT STRENUOUS,
LOTS OF UP AND DOWN

FIELDS

19

WEST
PICKARD
BAY

EAST
PICKARD
BAY

SHEER CLIFFS

GENTLE
GRASSY CLIFFS

17

◄ WEST PICKARD BAY   ◄ 75 – 100 MINS FROM CAR PARK, MAP 16

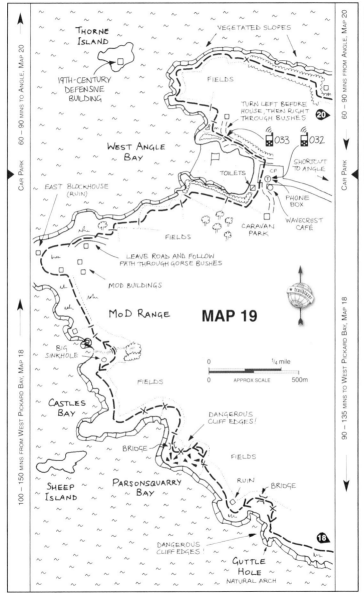

THORNE ISLAND

19TH-CENTURY DEFENSIVE BUILDING

VEGETATED SLOPES

FIELDS

TURN LEFT BEFORE HOUSE, THEN RIGHT THROUGH BUSHES

20

033   032

SHORTCUT TO ANGLE

WEST ANGLE BAY

TOILETS

EAST BLOCKHOUSE (RUIN)

FIELDS

CARAVAN PARK

PHONE BOX

WAVECREST CAFÉ

LEAVE ROAD AND FOLLOW PATH THROUGH GORSE BUSHES

MOD BUILDINGS

MoD RANGE

MAP 19

BIG SINKHOLE

FIELDS

0   1/4 mile

0   APPROX SCALE   500m

CASTLES BAY

DANGEROUS CLIFF EDGES!

BRIDGE

FIELDS

RUIN   BRIDGE

SHEEP ISLAND

PARSONSQUARRY BAY

18

DANGEROUS CLIFF EDGES!

GUTTLE HOLE

NATURAL ARCH

60 – 90 MINS TO ANGLE, MAP 20

CAR PARK

100 – 150 MINS FROM WEST PICKARD BAY, MAP 18

60 – 90 MINS FROM ANGLE, MAP 20

CAR PARK

90 – 135 MINS TO WEST PICKARD BAY, MAP 18

(cont'd from p104) Whichever way you choose the paths meet at the northern end of the beach and climb up above grassy, heathery slopes with wonderful views back across the sands. Although not as high or precipitous as other parts of the coastline this section is beautiful all the same. It is a wild and remote stretch of coast and is probably the least frequented.

If you are behind schedule you can avoid the entire Angle peninsula by continuing along the main road north from Freshwater West, taking the first left and next right to bring you onto Angle Bay. However, it would be a real shame to do so and miss out on some superb scenery.

For those still circumnavigating the Angle peninsula the cliffs become more and more spectacular as you head west, passing the natural arch of **Guttle Hole** and the grassy **Sheep Island**. Look out for the ruins of **East Blockhouse** constructed as a defence building during the reign of Henry VIII.

At **West Angle Bay** *Wavecrest Café* (Map 19, p109; seasonal) serves large, cheap baguettes (from £2.20); there are **toilets** and a **phone box** and the Coastal Cruiser **buses** (see pp44-6) stop here but there's little else.

Once again there is the option of a shortcut since Angle village is agonisingly close, almost within touching distance along the road leading east. Die-hards who want to 'do' the whole path must continue on around the northern half of the peninsula. The consolation is that the walking is less strenuous, passing above gentle slopes and on through some beautiful woodland on the steep water's edge. To the west, looking very much like Alcatraz, is **Thorne Island** with its 19th-century military defensive building which was once the venue for the World Hopscotch Championships. Rumours are constantly circulating about plans to turn the forbidding fortress into a luxury five-star hotel accessible by cable car from the mainland but these have so far failed to come to fruition and it seems unlikely you'll encounter any rich and famous folk hiding away here any time soon. Tired legs will be pleased to reach the village of **Angle**.

ANGLE   MAP 20

Angle is nothing to get too excited about but it is pleasant enough with boats bobbing in the pretty little estuary and some old castle ruins by the stream. Fishing is the main industry and seaweed is also harvested here as it is used as a principal ingredient of the Welsh speciality, laverbread (see box p16).

There is a well-supplied **shop** (☎ 01646-641037, 🖥 www.anglevillageshop .co.uk; Mon-Sat 8am-6pm, Sun 8am-1pm; extended hours in the summer months) on the main street opposite the school, which sells camping gear, a wide range of produce and grocery items, snacks and drinks (the shop is licensed to sell alcohol). It is also possible to order food in advance through

their website; debit cards are accepted and they will do cashback. There are also some public **toilets** in the village but little else.

The Coastal Cruiser **buses** (387/388) stop here as does, at weekends in the main season, the **Haven Link Waterbus** (Angle to Dale £7.50/4 return/single, £4/2 for children under 16; 1hr); the ferry departs 2/day. See public transport map and table, pp44-7, for details.

Campers will find *Castle Farm Campsite* (☎ 01646-641220; Easter-Oct) the perfect spot to pitch at just £3.50 per person. It's situated in the field to the right just before you cross the bridge into the village. Toilets and showers are available.

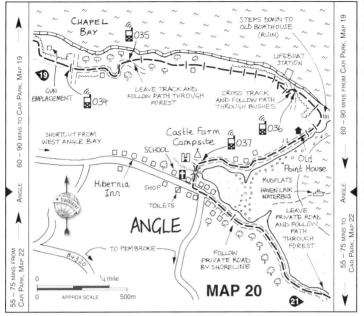

MAP 20

CHAPEL BAY

035

034

GUN EMPLACEMENT

LEAVE TRACK AND FOLLOW PATH THROUGH FOREST

STEPS DOWN TO OLD BOATHOUSE (RUIN)

LIFEBOAT STATION

CROSS TRACK AND FOLLOW PATH THROUGH BUSHES

036

SHORTCUT FROM WEST ANGLE BAY

Castle Farm Campsite

037

SCHOOL

Hibernia Inn

SHOP

TOILETS

ANGLE

Old Point House

MUDFLATS

HAVEN LINK WATERBUS

LEAVE PRIVATE ROAD AND FOLLOW PATH THROUGH FOREST

B4320

TO PEMBROKE

FOLLOW PRIVATE ROAD BY SHORELINE

0   ¼ mile
0   APPROX SCALE   500m

21

60 – 90 MINS FROM CAR PARK, MAP 19

ANGLE

55 – 75 MINS TO CAR PARK, MAP 22

19

60 – 90 MINS TO CAR PARK, MAP 19

ANGLE

55 – 75 MINS FROM CAR PARK, MAP 22

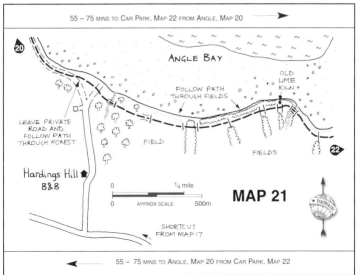

55 – 75 MINS TO CAR PARK, MAP 22 FROM ANGLE, MAP 20

20

ANGLE BAY

OLD LIME KILN

FOLLOW PATH THROUGH FIELDS

LEAVE PRIVATE ROAD AND FOLLOW PATH THROUGH FOREST

FIELD

FIELDS

22

Hardings Hill B&B

SHORTCUT FROM MAP 17

0   ¼ mile
0   APPROX SCALE   500m

MAP 21

55 – 75 MINS TO ANGLE, MAP 20 FROM CAR PARK, MAP 22

Regarding **B&B accommodation**, there are only two options, one of which you'll pass just before you enter the village. The *Old Point House* (☎ 01646-641205; 2S/2D) is an ancient (16th century according to some estimates) place with friendly owners. Rustic and eccentric, this place charges £35-45 per person for reasonable rooms with shared facilities, though one double is en suite.

The alternative is the very pleasant and welcoming *Harding's Hill* (Map 21; ☎ 01646-641232; 2F), a little way out of town though only a short walk up from the coast path. Each of the rooms has a double and a single bed; they charge £30 per person (there is no single supplement).

As for **food**, the *Old Point House* (food served daily noon-2.30pm & 6.30-9pm) has great grub and probably the best chips in Pembrokeshire. The gulls are pretty fond of them too so be on your guard if you are eating in the garden. The chowder is a delicious starter (£4.50) as is, maintaining the fishy theme, the hake with laverbread and cockle sauce.

In the centre of the village, *Hibernia Inn* (☎ 01646-641517; daily noon-2pm & 7-9pm, closed on Mondays in winter) has less character but it still offers decent pub grub from its extensive menu for around £8.

ANGLE TO HUNDLETON   MAPS 20-25

The sad truth is that after such wonderful coastal scenery things really do go downhill from here until Sandy Haven, just under 30 miles (48km) away. If you feel you can skip this part of the Pembrokeshire Coast Path (or even the section between here and Herbrandston or Dale) and still hold your head up high when you get home, consider the public transport options: either take the Coastal Cruiser bus to Pembroke/Pembroke Dock, then First's 349 to Haverfordwest and finally the Puffin Shuttle (Acorn Travel/Richards Bros) to Herbrandston (for Sandy Haven), or the Haven Link Waterbus – to Milford Haven, or as far as Dale – to avoid the oil refineries and urban sprawl that blights the Milford Haven estuary (no doubt Milford Haven was once a beautiful harbour, described by Nelson as one of the world's finest but sadly it has been very spoilt). However, services are fairly infrequent for both: see the public transport map and table, pp44-7 for details.

These **nine miles** (**14km, 3-4¹/₂ hrs**) begin pleasantly following the shoreline of **Angle Bay** through some nice woodland and fields. However, on the way to **Fort Popton** on the other side of the bay the first of two oil refineries looms above you belching out acrid fumes.

To be fair, passing through some beautiful old oak and beech woodland wherever it can the path does its best to avoid any possible eye contact with this blot on the landscape but at times the stench of crude oil is hard to miss. The path crosses farmland and then joins a small lane before passing the churches at **Pwllcrochan**.

Having left the oil refinery you now have the old power station site to walk around. Again the path does well to hide in the woodland but even so the scenery is nothing compared to what has gone before or is to come further ahead.

Leaving the power station site, the path continues across farmland passing the two creeks (locally known as 'pills') at Goldborough mudflats.

(cont'd on p116)

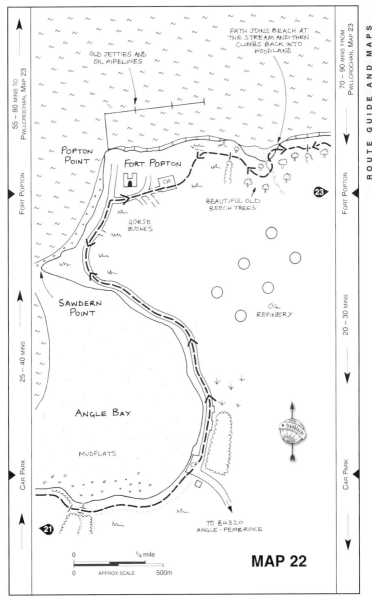

OLD JETTIES AND
OIL PIPELINES

PATH JOINS BEACH AT
THE STREAM AND THEN
CLIMBS BACK INTO
WOODLAND

Popton
Point

FORT POPTON

CP

BEAUTIFUL OLD
BEECH TREES

23

GORSE
BUSHES

SAWDERN
POINT

OIL
REFINERY

ANGLE BAY

MUDFLATS

CP

21

TO B4320
ANGLE - PEMBROKE

trailblazer

0   ¼ mile
0   APPROX SCALE   500m

MAP 22

55 – 80 MINS TO
PWLLCROCHAN, MAP 23

FORT POPTON

25 – 40 MINS

CAR PARK

70 – 90 MINS FROM
PWLLCROCHAN, MAP 23

FORT POPTON

20 – 30 MINS

CAR PARK

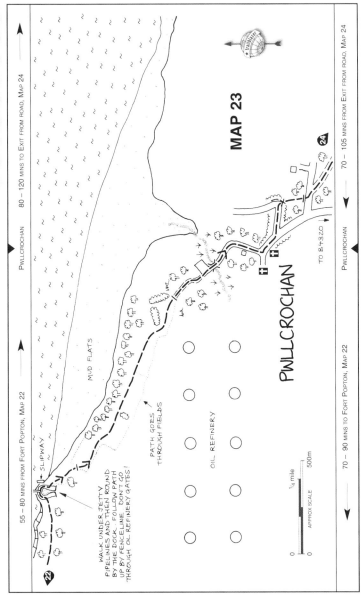

MAP 23

80 – 120 MINS TO EXIT FROM ROAD, MAP 24

70 – 105 MINS FROM EXIT FROM ROAD, MAP 24

PWLLCROCHAN

PWLLCROCHAN

TO B4320

24

55 – 80 MINS FROM FORT POPTON, MAP 22

70 – 90 MINS TO FORT POPTON, MAP 22

SLIPWAY

MUD FLATS

PATH GOES
THROUGH FIELDS

OIL REFINERY

PWLLCROCHAN

WALK UNDER JETTY
PIPELINES AND THEN ROUND
BY THE DOCK. FOLLOW PATH
UP BY FENCELINE. DON'T GO
THROUGH OIL REFINERY GATES!

22

¼ mile

500m

APPROX SCALE

0

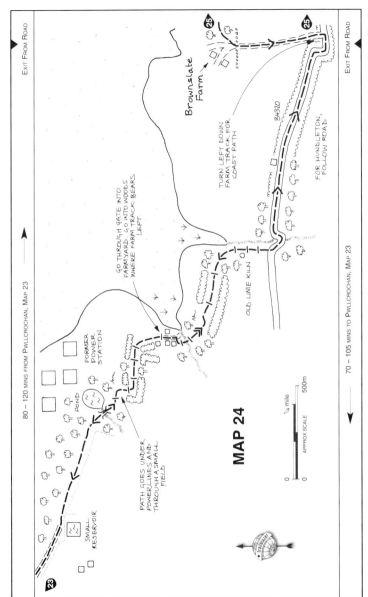

EXIT FROM ROAD

EXIT FROM ROAD

Brownslate Farm

GO THROUGH GATE INTO FARMYARD. GO INTO WOODS WHERE FARM TRACK BEARS LEFT

TURN LEFT DOWN FARM TRACK FOR COAST PATH

B4320

FOR HUNDLETON, FOLLOW ROAD

OLD LIME KILN

FORMER POWER STATION

POND

PATH GOES UNDER POWERLINES AND THROUGH A SMALL FIELD

SMALL RESERVOIR

MAP 24

80 – 120 MINS FROM PWLLCROCHAN, MAP 23

70 – 105 MINS TO PWLLCROCHAN, MAP 23

¼ mile

500m

APPROX SCALE

0

0

(cont'd from p112) The path then joins the Goldborough Rd, a country lane that climbs steeply up to the village of **Hundleton**.

The coast path actually heads down the farm track to Brownslate Farm a few hundred metres short of the village.

HUNDLETON   MAP 25

Hundleton (about a two-mile walk) has little to offer and it is probably better to carry on to Pembroke which isn't far away.

The post office has closed but the **phone box** and **bus stop** (for the Coastal Cruiser 387/388 services; see pp44-6) can be found in the centre next to the green.

The only place to stay and eat in the centre of the village is *Highgate Inn Hotel* (☎ 01646-685904, 🖥 lewissandie@aol.com; 2D/4T, all en suite; food served Apr-Oct daily noon-2pm & 6-9pm, Nov-Mar Thur-Sun noon-2pm & 6-9pm). The rooms are £65; up to £55 for single occupancy. They serve good solid pub grub such as pies and sausages and mash; their Sunday lunch is £9.95.

Heading east along the B4320 road to Pembroke is the charming, ivy-clad *Bowett Farmhouse* (☎ 01646-683473, 🖥 www .bowettfarmhouse.co.uk; 1S/1D/1T or D), set on a 250-acre dairy farm, with B&B accommodation from £35/pp. It is easiest to reach it from Quoits Mill which is further along the coast path from Hundleton.

One mile to the west of Hundleton, there's *Speculation Inn* (☎ 01646-661306; food served daily noon-3pm & 6-8pm; closed on Monday in winter). The menu is limited but unusual with homemade rabbit pie (£12.95), pigeon pie (£13.95) and chicken pie (£9.95); the portions are generous and you can pick up a decent pint of Reverend James Ale.

HUNDLETON TO HAZELBEACH   MAPS 25-29

From Hundleton it's **10¹/₂ miles (17km, 3¹/₂-4¹/₂ hrs)** to Hazelbeach on the other side of the Milford Haven estuary. This may not be the most stimulating stretch of the coast path but there are some pleasant bits.

From Brownslate Farm the path continues across fields to **Quoits Mill** before passing through the housing estate of **Monkton** where there is a small shop selling simple snacks and drinks. Silcox's No 356 & 357 **bus** services call here; see pp45-6 for details. The road then drops down into Pembroke with the impressive and well-preserved **Pembroke Castle** the first thing you see.

PEMBROKE (PENFRO) MAP 26, p119

Pembroke, birthplace of Henry VII (1457-1509), is steeped in history and comes as a pleasant surprise. Stretched out along one long street on top of a ridge by the river, there are plenty of pubs and places to stay.

The 900-year-old Norman **castle** (see box p118) is the focal point of the town, standing guard over the river and well worth a visit. Down on Commons Rd you can see the remains of **Gun Tower** and **Gazebo Tower**; medieval defensive towers which formed part of the old town wall.

Next to them is a 200-year-old **lime kiln**, one of many scattered along the Pembrokeshire coast. (The lime was scattered on the fields to 'sweeten' the acidic soil round here, with some going into the local buildings as mortar.)

Services
Pembroke Tourist Information Centre (☎ 01437-776499, 🖥 pembroke.tic@pem brokeshire.gov.uk; Easter-Oct Mon-Fri 10am-4pm, Sat 10am-1pm, Nov-Easter

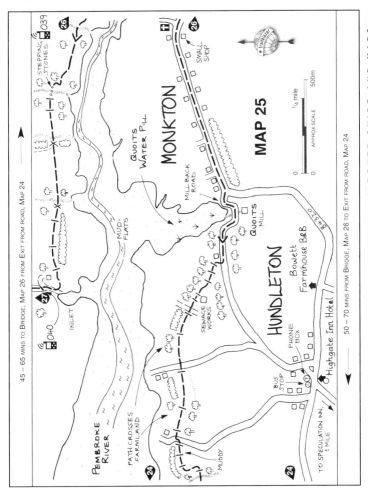

MAP 25

Tue-Sat 10am-1pm) is on Commons Rd. The TIC shares premises with the **library** which offers free **internet access**.

There are a number of **banks** as well as a **post office**, plenty of **shops** including **Mendus Pharmacy** and a Somerfield **supermarket**. These, and indeed almost everything else of interest to the trekker, can be found on Main St.

Transport

Silcox's **bus** Nos 356, 358, 387 & 388 depart from in front of Somerfield supermarket and outside the castle on Main St. First's No 349 service also calls here.

The **train station** is at the far end of the town past the roundabout on Station Rd. There are regular services to Pembroke Dock or back to Tenby, Kilgetty and

❑ Pembroke Castle

The mighty Pembroke Castle (☎ 01646-681510; 🖳 www.pembroke-castle.co.uk; daily 9.30am-6pm Apr-Sep, 10am-5pm Mar & Oct, 10am-4pm Nov-Feb, last entry 45 mins before closing; admission £3.50), birthplace of Henry VII, is a picture-book, turreted castle overlooking the town and the river estuary. It is one of many Norman castles in Pembrokeshire built in the 11th century to keep the Welsh at bay and can proudly claim to be the only one that never fell to the Welsh.

It has been the scene of many a bloody battle; most famously in 1648 during the Civil War. The local mayor, John Poyer, caused consternation in parliament when he switched his allegiances, deciding to support the king. A rather annoyed Oliver Cromwell marched over, blew up the town walls and took Poyer prisoner.

During the summer there are a number of organised events within the castle walls, including falconry and archery displays, battle re-enactments and Shakespeare plays.

Swansea for connections elsewhere. See the public transport map and table, pp44-7, for further details.

Where to stay

There are plenty of places to spend the night. Campers will have to head up the steep B4319 road for about half a mile to find *Windmill Hill Farm Campsite* (☎ 01646-682392, 🖳 www.windmillhillcaravanpark .co.uk; open all year); rates start from £4 per person.

The very comfortable and friendly *High Noon Guest House* (☎ 01646-683736, 🖳 www.highnoon.co.uk; Lower Lamphey Rd; 3S/1T/3D/2F) has been operating since 1958. Beds £24.50-35 per person. Most rooms are en suite but some share facilities.

There are several places on Main St including the amazingly good-value *Beech House* (☎ 01646-683740, 🖳 www.beech housepembroke.com; 78 Main St; 1S/1T/ 1D/1F, shared shower room or bathroom), a fine B&B boasting comfy rooms, a pool room and a great breakfast ... and all for the hostel-type price of £18.50 per person – or £10 for kids! Next door is the more expensive but still reasonable-value *Woodbine B&B* (☎ 01646-686338, 🖳 andrea@pem brokebedandbreakfast.co.uk; 2D en suite/ 1D, T or F with private bathroom), where the rate is £30 per person, or £35 for single occupancy.

At the eastern end of Main St is the *Old Cross Saws Inn* (☎ 01646-682475; 6T)

with rooms from £20/pp without breakfast (breakfast can be served if requested in advance). Some rooms are en suite and some share a bathroom. Nearby *Penfro B&B* (☎ 01646-682753, 🖳 www.penfro .co.uk; 1T/2D, all with private facilities) is a Grade 2 listed Georgian mansion dating back to 1760, with big high-ceiling rooms and a large back garden. The rooms are highly individual: rates are per room and depend on which room you stay in but start at £65; the largest room is £85.

A little further on is the smart but expensive *Coach House Hotel* (☎ 01646-684602, 🖳 www.coachhousehotel.uk.com) with 19 en suite rooms including two singles. Prices start from £37.50/pp; a single costs £50.

The *Old King's Arms Hotel* (☎ 01646-683611, 🖳 www.oldkingsarmshotel.co.uk; Main St; 14S/4D/1T, all en suite) is Pembroke's oldest hotel, dating back to the 15th century. It's a quite luxurious place with satellite TV in every room. Expect to pay £45-60 for a single, or £40 per person for two sharing.

Close by are two more upmarket hotels: *Middlegate Hotel* (☎ 01646-622442, 🖳 www.themiddlegate.co.uk; 41-43 Main St; 1S/3D, all en suite) charges £29-34 per person, and *Lion Hotel* (☎ 01646-684501; 5S/3T/5F, all en suite), where B&B costs from £35 for a single, £30 per person for two sharing. Four of their family rooms sleep three people and one sleeps four.

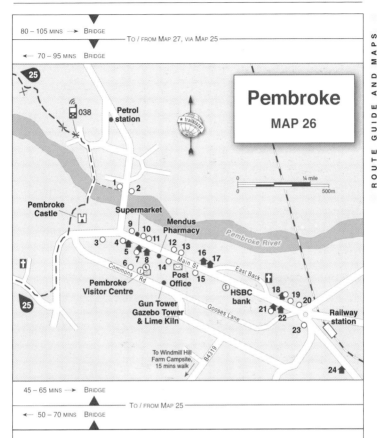

80 – 105 MINS → BRIDGE

TO / FROM MAP 27, VIA MAP 25

← 70 – 95 MINS BRIDGE

25

038

Petrol station

Pembroke
MAP 26

trailblazer

¼ mile
500m

Pembroke Castle

Supermarket

9 10 Mendus Pharmacy

11

12 13

16

17

Pembroke River

1 2

3 4

5

6 7 8

14

Main St

Post Office

15

East Back

HSBC bank

Commons Rd

Pembroke Visitor Centre

Gun Tower Gazebo Tower & Lime Kiln

Gooses Lane

18 19

21 20

22

23

Railway station

25

To Windmill Hill Farm Campsite, 15 mins walk

B4319

24

45 – 65 MINS → BRIDGE

TO / FROM MAP 25

← 50 – 70 MINS BRIDGE

PEMBROKE – MAP KEY

Where to stay
5 Lion Hotel
7 Old King's Arms Hotel
8 Middlegate Hotel
16 Beech House
17 Woodbine B&B
18 Coach House Hotel
21 Old Cross Saws Inn
22 Penfro B&B
24 High Noon Guest House

Where to eat & drink
1 Cornstore Café
2 Waterman's Arms
3 Haven Coffee Shop
4 Eleven
6 Pembroke Carvery & Chinese Takeaway
7 Old King's Arms Hotel
9 Rowlies
10 Mr Wong Chinese
11 Jay's Sandwich Shop

12 Monsoon Tandoori Takeaway
13 Pembroke Kebab House
14 Middlegate
15 Brown's Snack Bar
18 Griffins Bistro
19 Top of the Town
20 Royal Oak
21 Old Cross Saws Inn
23 Hope Inn

ROUTE GUIDE AND MAPS

Where to eat and drink

There is a wide variety of choice for food in Pembroke: *Eleven* (Mon-Thu 9am-6pm, Fri-Sat 9am-9pm, Sun 9am-5pm) is a cheerful place serving a variety of meals including a tasty sweet chilli chicken stir fry. They also have a late bar at weekends. Almost opposite, *Rowlies* (☎ 01646-686172; Mon-Sat 9am-8pm) claims to serve the best all-day breakfast (£3.75) in town; their extensive menu also includes fish and chips.

Not surprisingly, many of the pubs and hotels do food. The *Old King's Arms Hotel* (see Where to stay; food daily noon-2.30pm, Mon-Sat 7-10pm, Sun 7-8.30pm) has a good restaurant in a rustic, dimly lit room with a variety of dishes including duckling at £14.75 and steaks at £20.75. At the other end of Main St is the Coach House Hotel (see Where to stay) with an expensive à la carte menu in their award-winning *Griffins Bistro* (daily 7.30-9am, noon-2pm & 7-9.30pm).

Also along Main St you'll find *Brown's Snack Bar* (☎ 01646-682419; Mon-Sat 9am-5pm, Sun in August 9am-5pm), a Pembroke institution that's been serving locals since 1928; the décor is more 1970s but the food is fine and the service friendly. Most remarkable of all, however, are the staff: Constance 'Connie' Brown opened the shop with her husband and, at the time of writing, was still working in the kitchen! She was awarded the MBE in 2006, celebrated her 100th birthday in August 2007 and 80 years in business in 2008. *Jay's Sandwich Shop* (☎ 01646-683838; Mon-Fri 6am-3pm, Sat 8am-3pm) is a good spot to get a packed lunch for the day and has several vegetarian options.

Meanwhile there are a number of cafés and coffee shops, including the simple *Haven Coffee Shop* (☎ 01646-685469; Easter-Sep Mon-Sat 10am-4pm, Oct-Easter Mon-Sat 10.30am-3.30pm) opposite the castle – a no-frills place but one with a great outdoor seating area behind offering snacks for under £3.

The best café though is probably *Cornstore Café* (☎ 01646-684290; daily 10am-5pm, lunch 11.30am-4pm), set back from the main drag and overlooking the castle, where you can pick up home-made cakes for £1-2, paninis for £3.95 and jacket potatoes for £5-5.50.

Also on Main St, *Middlegate* (see Where to stay; daily 9.15am-3pm, to 6pm in summer) is OK for lunch, with eggs, chips and sausage costing just £3.50; they also have some vegetarian dishes.

At the road's eastern end, *Old Cross Saws Inn* (see Where to stay; Mon-Fri 5-8pm) does standard pub food and also shows the football.

There are also a number of fast-food outlets along Main St including *Mr Wong* (☎ 01646-622425; daily 5-11pm) near Somerfield, *Pembroke Kebab House* and *Monsoon Tandoori Takeaway* (☎ 01646-687766; daily 5-11pm) next door, and *Top of the Town* (☎ 01646-622332; Mon-Sat 10am-10pm), a well-regarded chippy, at the street's eastern end. There's also *Pembroke Carvery and Chinese Takeaway* (☎ 01646-686224; Mon-Sat noon-2pm & 5.30-9.30pm, Sun noon-9pm), a large restaurant on Commons Rd, with typical Chinese fare from around £7 and English food, such as steaks from £14, to eat in or take away. On Sunday they do a roast lunch from noon to 4pm.

Good places for a pint include the *Royal Oak* (☎ 01646-682537; bar open Mon-Fri & Sun 2pm-midnight, Sat noon-1am) and *Hope Inn* (bar open daily 11am-11pm) both of which are at the far eastern end of Main St by the roundabout.

At the other end of town is the *Waterman's Arms* (☎ 01646-682718; opening hours vary but are generally daily noon-11pm, food noon-3pm & 6-9pm) where you can enjoy fish pie (£9), cawl (£7.50), or fresh fish (£8.50 upwards) with a pint of Brains IPA (£2.60) whilst sitting on their outdoor deck overlooking the Pembroke River and castle.

THE DAUGLEDDAU AND THE LANDSKER BORDERLANDS

The one part of the national park that is completely by-passed by the coast path, thanks to the Cleddau Bridge, is the Daugleddau estuary. This is a shame because it is also one of the most beautiful and quietest parts. In stark contrast to the rest of the coastline there are no dramatic cliffs or crashing waves. Instead the intricate creeks and waterways are sheltered by heavily wooded banks, offering peaceful walks far from the rest of the crowds who flock to the coast.

This part of Pembrokeshire is known as the Landsker Borderlands. The invisible Landsker Line separates the Welsh-speaking north of Pembrokeshire from the southern half where the Norman influence is predominant. Along this invisible line are a number of Norman castles and fortresses, one of which can be seen at Carew on the banks of the estuary east of Pembroke. To this day southern Pembrokeshire has a distinctly English feel to it earning itself the unofficial title of 'Little England Beyond Wales'.

Walks

Unfortunately, circumnavigating the entire estuary is a little complicated since the western side is distinctly lacking in rights of way. Most of it would have to be walked on roads, many of which are not even that close to the estuary. It is best to explore the eastern side by following part of the Landsker Borderlands Trail and starting your walk from Cresswell Quay.

● **Transport** Cresswell Quay is on Silcox Coaches' Route No 361 (Pembroke Dock to Tenby). Alternatively you could get a taxi if you have a bit of spare cash; Cresswell Quay is about six miles (10km) from Pembroke. To return to the coast path catch the bus to Pembroke Dock or back to Tenby, Kilgetty or Saundersfoot. The Haven Link Waterbus (see p45) calls at Lawrenny. See pp44-7 for further information.

● **Accommodation** In Lawrenny there are en suite rooms (£34-37 per person, single occupancy supplement £10) at *Knowles Farm* (☎ 01834-891221, 🖥 www.lawrenny.org.uk; 3D).

Important! It is paramount that you **check the tide tables** for the following walks since the path at Garron Pill and the stepping stones at Cresswell Quay are submerged at high tide. Aim to reach Garron Pill as the tide is falling so that you have time to reach the crossing at Cresswell Quay before it comes back in.

A short walk via Garron Pill and Lawrenny (see map p122)

A shorter 6^1/2-mile (10km, 2^3/4-3^1/4 hrs) walk is described here for coast-path walkers who are looking for an easy day. (Note the times below are cumulative.)

From **Cresswell Quay** head north up the left-hand lane. After crossing Cresswell Bridge take the first left up a steep hill through woodland. Follow this lane bordered by hedges. Ignore the left turn and go straight over at the crossroads where there is a **postbox**. The lane drops down through woodland to reach another set of crossroads. Turn left here to reach **Garron Pill** estuary (1-1^1/4 hrs). Turn right if staying at Knowles Farm (see above).

At the car park by the estuary walk directly onto the mudflats and after five minutes look out for the less than obvious path cutting up into the shore-side forest and over a **stile**. Follow the path through woodland, past a **shed** and south along the wooded shoreline of the main Daugleddau estuary; the heather

ROUTE GUIDE AND MAPS

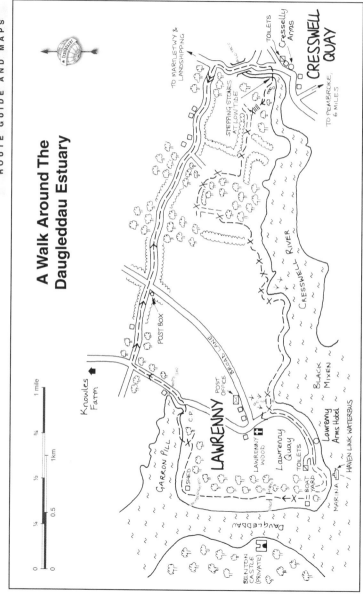

A Walk Around The
Daugleddau Estuary

and oak trees here have been stunted by the prevailing wind. Across the water is the white tower of **Benton Castle** poking through the trees.

The path then crosses another stile and comes out on a track which you follow through the boatyard and onto the road at **Lawrenny Quay** (1¼-1¾hrs). Between 1780 and 1860 Lawrenny Quay was an important shipbuilding site. Follow the lane past Lawrenny Arms Hotel. After ten minutes the path leaves the road on the right-hand side just before reaching the village of **Lawrenny**. It's worth popping up to the village to see the pretty **Norman church**. On the other side of the estuary, by the way, is the privately owned Benton Castle. The Haven Link Waterbus (see p44-7) sails from here and calls at Neyland, Milford Haven, Angle and Dale.

Back on the path, hop over the stone wall and cross the wooden boardwalk through the reed bed. The path follows the edge of the field, passes a marshy inlet and then continues through more fields, crossing a number of stiles before reaching a farm track next to woodland. Go up the **farm track** and turn right following the hedgerow before crossing a stile into the woods. Another stile takes you back into another field.

Follow the edge of the woodland and then bear left following another hedgerow. Cross through a small field to reach another farm track. Leave the track at the sharp left-hand bend and follow the steps down through some beautiful woodland to reach the **stepping stones** across the Cresswell River and back to **Cresswell Quay** (2¾-3¼hrs).

By now you deserve some liquid refreshment in the wonderfully traditional *Cresselly Arms* (☎ 01646-651210; bar open daily noon-3pm & 5-11pm). However, they do not serve food.

A long walk via Landshipping If your feet are not too tired from the coast path you could try the long circular walk from Cresswell Quay, up the lane to Martletwy and on to Landshipping Quay. From here the Landsker Borderlands Trail can be followed back along the shoreline passing the pretty village of Lawrenny on the way. This walk is 13½ miles (22km) and takes about six hours.

From Pembroke the path passes through woodland and farmland before dropping steeply down Treowen Rd and Pembroke St to **Pembroke Dock**.

PEMBROKE DOCK (DOC PENFRO)
MAP 27

Pembroke Dock won't win any beauty contests but study it a little closer and you will find it is a place with a short but interesting history.

The town sprung up quite suddenly in the early 1800s when the Royal Navy came to the tiny hamlet of Paterchurch, built a dockyard and then started constructing ships. In 1814 the first terraced row (**Front St**) was built to house the workers. The coast path runs along the road. A number of defensive fortifications sprang up to protect

the town. One of the two **Martello Towers** can be seen off Front St. These days the oil industry provides most of the employment and the ferry terminal for boats to Ireland keeps a steady flow of visitors going through the town.

Services

There is a **tourist information point** in the ferry terminal.

As you would expect there are also a number of **shops** in town, though the place is not quite the shoppers' paradise you might have been hoping for. There are three **banks** with cashpoints and a **post office** (☎ 01646-621202; Mon-Fri 9am-5.30pm, Sat 9am-12.30pm) near each other on Dimond St; all the shops and best places to eat are here as well. There is free **internet access** at the **library** (Mon, Fri 9.30am-7pm, Tue-Thur 9.30am-5pm, Sat 9.30am-12.30pm, closed Sun).

Pembroke Dock is not short of big **superstores**: Asda is across the road after leaving Front St, Kwiksave and Lidl lie just to the north while Tesco can be found off London Rd.

Near Tesco is Pembrokeshire Outdoors, a convenient place to pick up **camping/ backpacking equipment**. On Water St, near Asda, there is a **health centre**.

Transport
There are three **bus stops**, one outside Tesco, one on Laws St and the other on Albion Sq, which is not square at all but decidedly road-shaped. Most services (Silcox's No 333, 356, 357, 358, 361, 387 & 388, and First's No 349) stop on Laws St; check in advance for the other stops.

For the **train station** walk to the far eastern end of Dimond St. This is the terminus of the line from Swansea; services arrive/depart every couple of hours, less frequently on Sunday. See the public transport map and table, pp44-7, for full details.

Adventurous types might want to take a day trip to Rosslare in Ireland. Passenger-only fares are around £25 each way. Contact **Irish Ferries** (see p142) for details and bookings.

Where to stay
Rates at *Roxana Guest House* (☎ 01646-683116, 🖳 www.roxanaguesthouse.hotels .officelive.com; 2S/1T/3F, all with private facilities) on Victoria Rd just off Treowen Rd, start from £25 per person.

At the bottom of the hill on Pembroke St is *Dolphin Hotel* (☎ 01646-685581; 3D/5T/2F). It's not in the nicest part of town but the rooms are en suite (£25-30 per person) and they boast they serve the best breakfasts in town.

On London Rd there are a number of places offering accommodation: at No 23 *The Welshman's Arms* (☎ 01646-685643, 🖳 www.thewelshmansarms.co.uk; 4S/1D/1T/ 2F, all with private facilities) charges from £25 per person but they do not provide breakfast. The bar is open Mon-Fri from 5pm and from noon on Sat and Sun; food is served Mon-Fri 5.30-8.30pm & Sat/Sun noon-7.30pm.

At the other end of the scale, the most luxurious option is *Cleddau Bridge Hotel* (Map 28, p127; ☎ 01646-685961, 🖳 www .cleddauhotel.co.uk; 40 rooms, all en suite). It is on Essex Rd just before the toll booth on the bridge and has single rooms for £73 or double/twin rooms for £93 for two sharing; discounts are available for stays of longer than two nights.

Where to eat and drink
For a curry head for the *Made In India Restaurant* (☎ 01646-681821; daily 5.30-11.30pm; 9 Pembroke St) and for Chinese/Cantonese food try *Tasty House* (☎ 01646-686132, Tue-Sun 5-10.30pm, to 10pm on Sun, 28 Queen St).

Best Kebab House (☎ 01646-686149; Mon-Sat 5pm-midnight, Sun to 11pm), on Dimond St, is good for late-night hunger; there's a branch of *McDonald's* near Tesco.

On Dimond St there is a good café, *The Coffee Pot* (☎ 01646-622314; Mon-Fri 9am-5pm, Sat 10am-5pm) with great toasties, and a reasonable bakery, *Snowdrop* (☎ 01646-683373, Mon-Sat 8am-4pm), which sells baguettes from £2.30.

Along the same road you will find *Davina's* (☎ 01646-682974; Mon-Sat 10am-3pm, Sun noon-3pm) with some standard but reasonably priced dishes including lasagne or scampi from £6.50.

More unusual fare is found at *La Brasseria* (☎ 01646-687643; daily from 9am; reservations are required in the evening) which, in addition to standard all-day breakfasts (£4.95) and baguettes (£3.95), offers such treats as lamb shank (£12.95), or swordfish with creamed garlic and white wine sauce (£8.95).

On the corner of Front St, right on the official coast path, *Ship Wright* (☎ 01646-

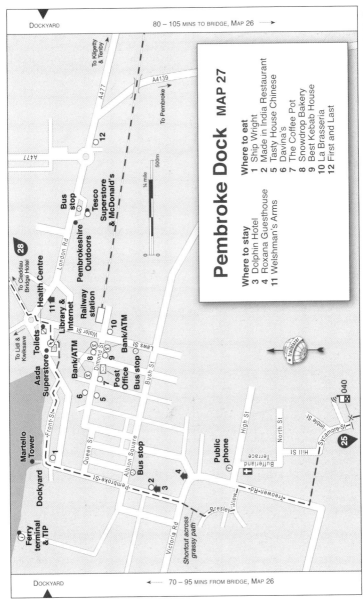

DOCKYARD

80 – 105 MINS TO BRIDGE, MAP 26

Pembroke Dock MAP 27

Where to stay
3 Dolphin Hotel
4 Roxana Guesthouse
11 Welshman's Arms

Where to eat
1 Ship Wright
2 Made in India Restaurant
5 Tasty House Chinese
6 Davina's
7 The Coffee Pot
8 Snowdrop Bakery
9 Best Kebab House
10 La Brasseria
12 First and Last

To Kilgetty & Tenby

A4477

A4139

To Pembroke

12

¼ mile

500m

Bus stop

Tesco Superstore & McDonald's

London Rd

Pembrokeshire Outdoors

To Cleddau Bridge Hotel

28

Health Centre

11

Library & Internet

Railway station

Water St

10

Bank/ATM

Laws St

To Lidl & Kwiksave

Toilets

Asda Superstore

Front St

Bank/ATM

8

9

Dimond St

7

Post Office

Bush St

Bus stop

6

5

Martello Tower

Dockyard

1

Queen St

Albion Square

Bus stop

Pembroke St

2

3

4

Public phone

High St

North St

Butterland Terrace

Hill St

Sycamore St

25

040

Trewoon Rd

Victoria Rd

Presley View

Shortcut across grassy path

Ferry terminal & TIP

DOCKYARD

70 – 95 MINS FROM BRIDGE, MAP 26

682090; bar open all day; food served daily noon-2.30pm & 6-9.30pm) has won awards for their fine atmosphere and good food. Front St used to be home to a number of old taverns that served as drinking dens for the dockyard workers back in the early 1800s. The Ship Wright is the only survivor.

The *First and Last* (☎ 01646-682687) pub is next to the roundabout where the road heads north to the Cleddau Bridge. It is the first and last pub on this side of Milford Haven harbour, hence the name. It's open all day and serves food, such as toasties, daily from noon to 2.30pm but not in the evening; it has some great real ales.

After negotiating the streets of Pembroke Dock you must cross the **Cleddau Toll Bridge**. Don't worry; environmentally friendly walkers go for free! It also takes them much longer to cross than it does the motorists so they can really savour the experience.

Half a mile after crossing Cleddau Bridge you cross a second, smaller bridge. Immediately you reach the end of this bridge, the path doubles back on your left to take you along the top of the wooded slope. The path eventually brings you to the top of the quiet town of Neyland, from where it's a straightforward march along the shoreline road through the village of Llanstadwell to Hazelbeach.

NEYLAND   MAP 28

Having crossed the Cleddau toll bridge and left Pembroke Dock behind you, Neyland is nothing to get excited about, being only marginally less ugly than Pembroke Dock and certainly less interesting.

The modern marina is the only attractive part of the town – and the path avoids that! From the big car park at the end of the marina village you can follow the main street up the hill for five minutes to reach the **post office** and a **small supermarket**.

If you are looking for a bed you are probably better off back in Pembroke Dock as there is little choice here.

First's No 349 **bus** service and Silcox's No 356 stop here. The **Haven Link Waterbus** stops at Neyland Quay; tickets are available on board. See the public transport map and table, pp44-7.

HAZELBEACH   MAP 29, p128

The only bus service passing through here is Silcox's No 356 but the **Haven Link Waterbus** stops at the jetty. See the public transport map and table, pp44-7, for details.

Ferry House Inn (☎ 01646-600270, 🖳 www.smoothhound.co.uk/hotels/ferry inn.html; 1S/1D/2T/2F, all en suite) has **B&B** at £42 (single) and £32.50 per person for two sharing. It is also the best place to get **food** (daily noon-2pm & Mon-Sat 6-9pm), served in a nice conservatory with harbour views, albeit including the refinery and power station. Despite this, Hazelbeach is a lot prettier than Neyland.

HAZELBEACH TO SANDY HAVEN   MAPS 29-34

After nigh on 20 miles (30km) negotiating oil refineries, power stations and conurbations, the bad news is that there is more of the same for the next **8½ miles (14km, 2¾-4hrs)** to Sandy Haven. The good news is that the good stuff begins again from Sandy Haven. The coast path heads up a small lane beside Ferry House Inn, passing through fields and woodland. You may be surprised to

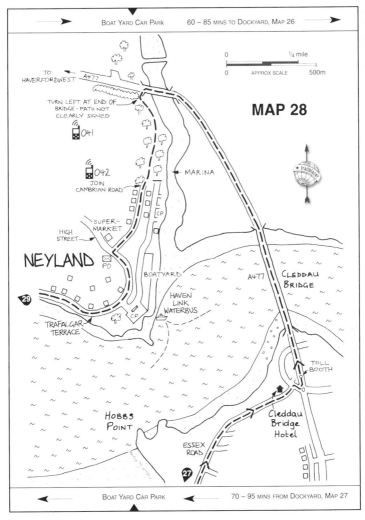

realise that there is a second vast oil refinery to the right. To be fair to the refinery and/or the path designers, they have done their best, too, to shield you from the worst of the industrial eyesores, though occasionally it fails, such as when you come to an ugly red bridge over the LNG pipelines (see box p132), or have to pass through a pedestrian tunnel above yet more pipelines.

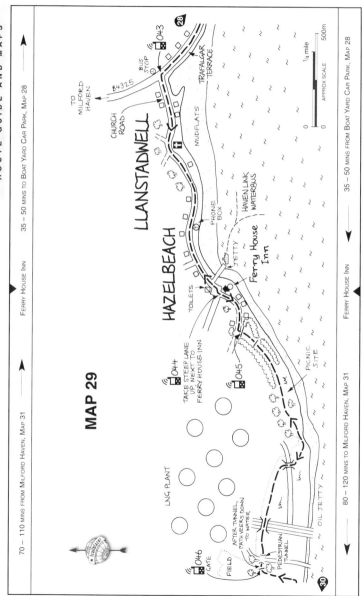

MAP 29

LLANSTADWELL

HAZELBEACH

TO MILFORD HAVEN

B4325

CHURCH ROAD

BUS STOP

TRAFALGAR TERRACE

043

MUDFLATS

PHONE BOX

HAVEN LINK WATERBUS

JETTY

Ferry House Inn

TOILETS

TAKE STEEP LANE UP, NEXT TO FERRY HOUSE INN

044

045

PICNIC SITE

LNG PLANT

AFTER TUNNEL, PATH VEERS DOWN TO WATER

PEDESTRIAN TUNNEL

GATE

FIELD

046

OIL JETTY

28

30

APPROX SCALE

¼ mile

500m

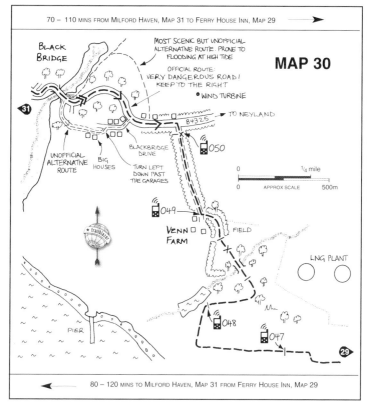

BLACK BRIDGE

MOST SCENIC BUT UNOFFICIAL ALTERNATIVE ROUTE. PRONE TO FLOODING AT HIGH TIDE

MAP 30

OFFICIAL ROUTE: VERY DANGEROUS ROAD! KEEP TO THE RIGHT

● WIND TURBINE

B4325 ➤ TO NEYLAND

31

050

UNOFFICIAL ALTERNATIVE ROUTE

BIG HOUSES

BLACKBRIDGE DRIVE

TURN LEFT DOWN PAST THE GARAGES

0 ────── ¼ mile

0 ────── 500m
APPROX SCALE

049

VENN FARM

FIELD

trailblazer

LNG PLANT

PIER

048

047

29

Eventually, however, you come to the path leading to **Venn Farm** and then follow the farm track to the main B4325 road. From here, the official path takes you along a twisting road with some dangerous blind bends and no pavement. It can be hair-raising but unfortunately as yet the authorities have not been able to organise a better alternative.

There are, though, two other (better but as yet unofficial) routes; one involves taking a left down Blackbridge Drive, followed by another left down past some garages and several rather grand houses to the Black Bridge. The other involves crossing the B4325 after 100m and taking the country footpath on the right. Upon reaching the edge of the estuary (at a T junction), turn left onto a bridleway and head back to the road adjacent to Black Bridge. The bridleway is prone to flooding on some high tides. However you get to the bridge, once you're there it's just a case of climbing up the opposite bank and so on into...

MILFORD HAVEN (ABERDAUGLEDDAU)

MAP 31

The town of Milford Haven, named after the harbour on which it lies, is a relatively modern place. It dates back to 1790 when it was settled by a group of American whalers who provided whale oil for London's street lamps.

The town later became an important fishing port and although fishing is still of importance here, it is now the nearby pipeline constructions and the refineries, supplemented by a little tourism, that bring in the money.

For a greater insight into the town's history visit the small **Milford Haven Museum** (☎ 01646-694496; Easter-Oct, Mon-Sat 11am-5pm; admission £1.50) by the dockyard.

Also in the docks is a working **seal hospital** (see Map 32, p134) built into an oil refinery storage tank. A sign outside usually tells you whether any seals are resident; visitors are welcome.

The enormous harbour, lauded by both Vice-Admiral Horatio Nelson and Daniel Defoe (author of *Robinson Crusoe*), is one of the natural wonders of the British Isles but over the last few decades the authorities have allowed the oil giants to monopolise it, as anyone who has walked from Angle can testify. Two new LNG terminals (see box p132) were opened in 2009, meaning that in total there are four terminals, two gas and two oil, and the jetties and pipelines visibly scar the coastline.

The harbour has been renovated and is now home to a number of facilities, including Charlie's Restaurant (see p133), in the old sail loft, and **Waterfront Gallery** (☎ 01646-695699; Mon-Sat 10am-5pm, free), a not-for-profit showcase of the best in local art.

Services

Milford Haven is the last of the big towns around the estuary. From here there is little chance of getting any provisions until Broad Haven, about 30 miles (48km) away, although there are small shops-cum-post offices at Dale and Marloes (the former open mornings only). The next cash machine is also at Marloes (in the pub) with another at Broad Haven.

Charles St is where you'll find most of the shops and services including the post office. The **tourist information centre** (☎ 01646-690866, ✉ milford.tic@pembroke shire.gov.uk; Apr-Oct Mon-Fri 10am-4pm, Sat 10am-1pm, Nov-Mar Mon, Wed, Fri & Sat 10am-1pm) also used to be here but from the end of October 2009 it moved to Cedar Court, Haven's Head Business Park and is in the same building as the **library** (☎ 01437-771888; Mon-Fri 9.30am-5pm, to 6.30pm on Thurs, Sat 9.30am-1pm) which offers free **internet access**.

You will find the **launderette** (Mon-Sat 8am-5.30pm, last wash 4.30pm) at No 17, a Kwiksave **supermarket** as well as the majority of **banks**, most with **cashpoints**. There's also a **pharmacy**, Harbourside, on Hamilton Terrace, and a big Tesco **superstore** in the retail park by the docks.

Transport

Opposite Tesco is the **train station** with services to Haverfordwest, Swansea, Cardiff and London. Silcox's No 356 **bus** service to Pembroke stops on Charles St, Hamilton Terrace and outside Tesco. The No 300 service goes round town and to Herbrandston, and First's No 302 service goes to Haverfordwest. The **Puffin Shuttle** (315/400) departs from Robert St and the **Haven Link Waterbus** calls at the dock; tickets are available on board. For further information see the public transport map and table, pp44-7.

Where to stay

Where the coast path enters the main part of town there's bed and breakfast for £22-25 per person at *1 Pier Rd* (☎ 01646-694531; 1S/1T/2D, shared facilities) just off The Rath.

Belhaven House Hotel (☎ 01646-695983, ✉ www.westwaleshotel.com; 29 Hamilton Terrace; 3S/2T/4D, all en suite) charges £38.50-45 for a single or £30-40 per person for two sharing. Also on Hamilton Terrace is *Lord Nelson Hotel* (☎ 01646-695341, ✉ www.lordnelsonmilford .com) with 32 en suite rooms at £55 for a

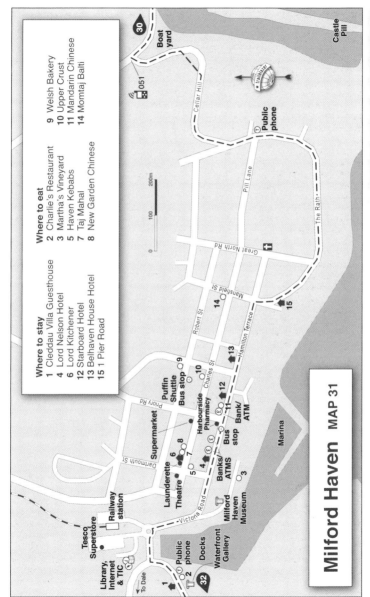

Where to stay
1 Cleddau Villa Guesthouse
4 Lord Nelson Hotel
6 Lord Kitchener
12 Starboard Hotel
13 Belhaven House Hotel
15 1 Pier Road

Where to eat
2 Charlie's Restaurant
3 Martha's Vineyard
5 Haven Kebabs
7 Taj Mahal
8 New Garden Chinese
9 Welsh Bakery
10 Upper Crust
11 Mandarin Chinese
14 Momtaj Balti

Milford Haven MAP 31

single, doubles at £75, and family rooms at £85-95 and *Starboard Hotel* (☎ 01646-692439; 4S/3T/1F), 21 Hamilton Terrace, which has rooms (most of which have en suite facilities) for £25 per person.

On Charles St, *Lord Kitchener* (☎ 01646-692741; 2T/1F sleeping four, all en suite) charges £15-20 per head.

After passing the dockyard on the way into **Hakin** you'll find *Cleddau Villa Guesthouse* (☎ 01646-690313; 4D, shared bathroom) at 21 St Anne's Rd, with good-value accommodation for £22 per person. However, at the time of writing the owner was considering retiring though she hopes the guesthouse will continue to operate, so check in advance.

Where to eat and drink

For Indian food head to *Momtaj Balti* (☎ 01646-690880; daily 5-11pm) at the eastern end of Charles St.

❏ **LNG at Milford Haven**
Never the prettiest part of the coast path, the section around Milford Haven has been subjected to some pretty extensive development caused by the construction of two new Liquid Natural Gas (LNG) terminals, South Hook and Dragon. The terminals were necessary as, following years of plenty, in 2006 Britain became a net importer of gas for the first time as its own sources ran dry. In 2009 the Queen officially inaugurated South Hook Terminal, easily Europe's largest LNG terminal, and the first LNG supertankers from Qatar made their maiden journeys to Milford Haven.

The gas arrives by ship in liquid form as this reduces its volume, making the entire process economically viable. Upon arrival, the cargo is transferred into LNG storage tanks and converted back into gaseous form, after which it is pumped through the country using the existing network. When the Milford Haven LNG plants come fully on stream, 30% of the entire country's gas requirements will be imported in this way. By 2020 it is estimated that imports will account for 80% of the UK's gas needs. The terminals have joined the two operational refineries and an oil terminal that already exist in the area.

Whilst the economic benefits are manifold not everyone is entirely happy with the new development; concerns have been raised about both the environmental impact of such extensive construction, and the safety of the residents who call this area their home. To back up their argument they point to claims by James Fay, a professor at Massachusetts Institute of Technology, that an LNG spill could endanger 20,000 lives. However, the developers argue, how much environmental impact can one have on an area that used to have five oil refineries? Furthermore, with each delivery of gas arriving in a double-hulled ship that will be heavily protected, and with extensive systems already in place guarding the existing refineries and terminals, fears about the security of the operation should also be allayed.

The question for walkers, however, is how much of an impact all this development is going to have on the coast path? At the time of walking, the changes to the path brought about by all the ongoing construction were surprisingly minimal and indeed there were only a few places where the construction was actually visible; the authorities did a good job in shielding walkers from the ugliest sections.

The greatest impact so far has been on the region's accommodation: with so many workers having relocated temporarily to this area of Pembrokeshire to help with the construction, it can sometimes be very difficult to find a bed for the night. Hopefully, by the time you read this, the workers will have returned home and the situation will have returned to normal but, if not, book early if you want to stay in a B&B between Pembroke and Milford Haven.

Alternatively, just down the road from the Torch Theatre (undergoing renovations at the time of writing) is the *Taj Mahal* (☎ 01646-698998; Sun-Thur 5pm-midnight, Fri & Sat to 1am). Opposite, for fast food there's *Haven Kebabs* (☎ 01646-694747), open Mon-Fri 5pm-midnight Sat/Sun 5pm-2.30am.

There's also *Mandarin Chinese* (☎ 01646-693336, 20 Hamilton Terrace, daily 5-10.30pm except Tuesday) for chicken fried rice and the like, and *New Garden Chinese* (☎ 01646-692493; Charles St; daily 5-11pm) where dishes start at £4.20.

During the day the *Welsh Bakery* (☎ 01646-695183; Mon-Fri 8am-4.30pm, Sat 8.30am-4pm), on Robert St, does a roaring trade with its good-value no-nonsense menu; sandwiches cost from £2 and buns start at just 50p. The *Upper Crust* bakery (☎ 01646-697713; Mon-Sat 8am-5pm, to 4pm in the winter) is on Charles St.

Down by the dockyard is the swish *Martha's Vineyard* (☎ 01646-697083, 🖵 www.marthasmilfordmarina.co.uk; food served daily noon-2pm & 6-9.15pm, bar open daily 11am-12.30am, till 1.30am Fri-Sat, till 11.30pm Sun) with a smart upstairs bar and restaurant where all food is guaranteed to be of local origin. The lounge bar terrace has an extensive menu and the restaurant specialises in fish; main courses generally cost between £12.95 and £18.95. The restaurant is popular with locals so book in advance.

Charlie's Restaurant (☎ 01646-690098; daily noon-2pm & 6.30-8.30pm), by the docks, also specialises in fish dishes.

West of the main town centre, on St Anne's Rd in Hakin, there's fish & chips at *Hake Inn* (Map 32, p134; ☎ 01646-690075; Mon-Fri noon-1.30pm & 5.30-9pm, Sat noon-2pm & 5.30-8.30pm).

You'll be pleased to hear that **Milford Haven** and the housing estate of **Hakin** are the last of the big urban areas that you have to walk through. The scenery improves a little once past **Gelliswick Bay** as you follow a concrete path through trees and scrubland and past the enormous liquid natural gas terminal (see box opposite) up the slopes.

Thankfully, the path once again does its best to shield you from the worst of the industrial scenery, though the pretty beach of **Sandy Haven** is still a very welcome sight. Ahead you can see the harbour opening out with Angle peninsula on the left and Dale peninsula on the right.

Herbrandston (see below) lies on the high-tide detour route (see p136) and is only a short distance from the main coast path at Sandy Haven.

HERBRANDSTON   MAP 33, p135

This quiet little village can be reached by following the lane up from Sandy Haven campsite (see Map 34 p137). It has a **post office** (☎ 01646-692203), incorporating a small **shop** (Mon-Fri 8am-6pm, Sat 9am-1pm, Sun 9am-11.30am), in the centre of the village by the church hall, and a good pub, Taberna Inn, where you can sit and wait for the tide to go out, rather than taking the long-winded alternative route.

The very useful **Puffin Shuttle bus**, (315/400) which serves all the coastal villages as far as St David's, stops on the main road opposite the Taberna Inn. Silcox's No 300 Milford Haven town service also calls here. See the public transport map and table, pp44-7, for full details.

Taberna Inn (☎ 01646-693498; bar daily noon-11pm, food served daily noon-2pm & 6-9pm; 1S/1D/1F, shared bathroom) is a very friendly place to stay and eat – with real ale – boasting an interesting menu with many of the ingredients farmed or caught locally. However, in the winter months they don't serve food on Sunday evenings. The rate for B&B is from £25/pp.

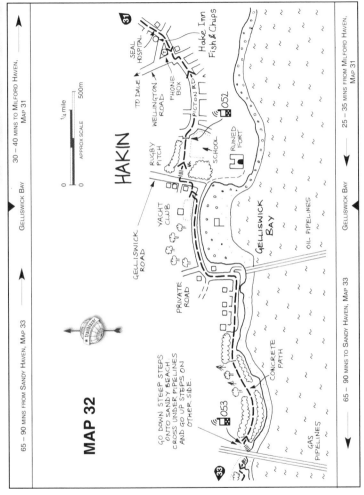

MAP 32

HAKIN

65 – 90 MINS FROM SANDY HAVEN, MAP 33 ——— GELLISWICK BAY ——— 30 – 40 MINS TO MILFORD HAVEN, MAP 31

65 – 90 MINS TO SANDY HAVEN, MAP 33 ——— GELLISWICK BAY ——— 25 – 35 MINS FROM MILFORD HAVEN, MAP 31

GO DOWN STEEP STEPS ONTO SANDY BEACH. CROSS UNDER PIPELINES AND GO UP STEPS ON OTHER SIDE.

GAS PIPELINES

CONCRETE PATH

GELLISWICK BAY

OIL PIPELINES

PRIVATE ROAD

GELLISWICK ROAD

YACHT CLUB

RUGBY PITCH

SCHOOL

RUINED FORT

PICTON RD

WELLINGTON ROAD

PHONE BOX

TO DALE

SEAL HOSPITAL

Hake Inn Fish & Chips

½ mile
500m
APPROX SCALE

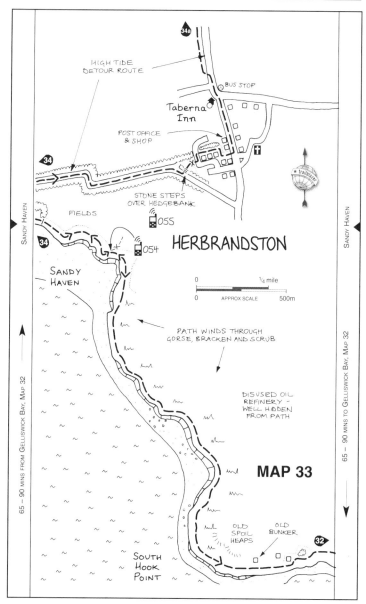

34a

HIGH TIDE
DETOUR ROUTE

BUS STOP

Taberna Inn

POST OFFICE
& SHOP

34

STONE STEPS
OVER HEDGEBANK

trailblazer

SANDY HAVEN

SANDY HAVEN

FIELDS

055

34

054

HERBRANDSTON

SANDY
HAVEN

0   ¼ mile

0   500m
APPROX SCALE

PATH WINDS THROUGH
GORSE, BRACKEN AND SCRUB

DISUSED OIL
REFINERY –
WELL HIDDEN
FROM PATH

MAP 33

65 – 90 MINS FROM GELLISWICK BAY, MAP 32

65 – 90 MINS TO GELLISWICK BAY, MAP 32

OLD
SPOIL
HEAPS

OLD
BUNKER

32

SOUTH
HOOK
POINT

ROUTE GUIDE AND MAPS

SANDY HAVEN   MAP 34

East bank Sandy Haven is a beautiful spot with a sandy beach and a long creek, or 'pill', stretching inland. Right on the coast path is **Sandy Haven Caravan and Camping Park** (☎ 01646-698844, 🖳 www .sandyhavencampingpark.co.uk; Easter to early Sep) with pitches from £6 per person.

West bank Just up the lane from Sandy Haven, **Skerryback Farm** (☎ 01646-636598, 🖳 www.pfh.co.uk/skerryback; 2D or T) offers B&B from £30 (with a £5 single occupancy supplement).

About a mile from the trail, **Bicton Farm** (☎ 01646-636215; 1S/2D/1T) charges from £30 per person in the doubles (both en suite) or £25-27 in the other rooms which share a bathroom. They don't serve evening meals but are happy to give residents a lift to and from the Brook Inn (see p138), St Ishmaels.

SANDY HAVEN TO DALE   MAPS 34-37

These **5$\frac{1}{2}$ miles miles (9km, 2-3hrs)** are quite easy going and, although not spectacular, the scenery is a vast improvement on the industrial landscape around Pembroke Dock and Milford Haven.

The cliffs at the beginning of this section are quite low compared to the rest of the coastline so there is nothing too strenuous. If you have timed it right you will be able to cross the stepping stones across **Sandy Haven Pill** at low tide (see box below). If, however, you find yourself faced with a barrier of water at high tide you will have to take the long road detour described below.

HIGH TIDE DETOUR AT SANDY HAVEN (VIA RICKESTON BRIDGE)
MAPS 34, 33, 34a & 34

This detour will add an extra **four miles (6km, 1$\frac{1}{2}$ hrs)** to your day. From the campsite at Sandy Haven follow the lane up the hill. Just after the second right-hand bend there is a stone stile and steps on the left which takes you into a small field where a few horses often graze. Cross the field, over another stile and cross the road, following the path behind a line of houses. This brings you out into the centre of **Herbrandston** (see p133).

Turn left and go past Taberna Inn and walk on a path parallel to the road north down the hill over Clay Bridge to **Rickeston Bridge**. Ignore the turn-offs

---

❏ **Warning – high-tide obstacles**

It is worth giving advance warning here of two significant obstacles on the next section. The inlet at Sandy Haven and the estuary at The Gann near Dale, four miles (6km) further west, can both be crossed at low tide but at high tide the crossing points are completely submerged necessitating lengthy detours along roads. The trick is to cross the stepping stones at Sandy Haven as the tide is going out. In this way you have time to reach the next crossing near Dale before the tide has had time to come back in. For example, if low tide is at 2pm you should be able to cross at 1pm. The tide won't have cut off the next crossing near Dale until about 6pm giving you plenty of time to reach it. Tide times are posted all over the place, in shops, on noticeboards and in the national park's annual newspaper *Coast to Coast*.

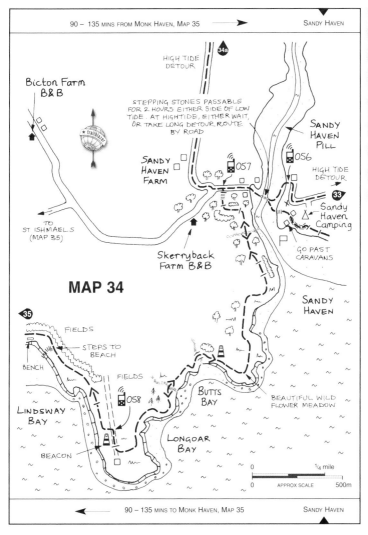

90 – 135 MINS FROM MONK HAVEN, MAP 35 ➞ SANDY HAVEN

34a

HIGH TIDE
DETOUR

STEPPING STONES PASSABLE
FOR 2 HOURS EITHER SIDE OF LOW
TIDE. AT HIGHTIDE, EITHER WAIT,
OR TAKE LONG DETOUR ROUTE
BY ROAD

Bicton Farm
B&B

★ trailblazer

SANDY
HAVEN
FARM

057

SANDY
HAVEN
PILL

056

HIGH TIDE
DETOUR

33

TO
ST ISHMAEL'S
(MAP 35)

Sandy
Haven
Camping

GO PAST
CARAVANS

Skerryback
Farm B&B

MAP 34

SANDY
HAVEN

35

FIELDS

STEPS TO
BEACH

BENCH

FIELDS

058

BUTTS
BAY

BEAUTIFUL WILD
FLOWER MEADOW

LINDSWAY
BAY

LONGOAR
BAY

BEACON

0   ¼ mile

0   500m
APPROX SCALE

◀ 90 – 135 MINS TO MONK HAVEN, MAP 35 SANDY HAVEN

to the right and follow the road round to the left to the **cottages** at Sandyhill.
Climb the steep hill and take the next left. Just after passing Sandy Haven
Farm turn left towards Sandy Haven. The coast path proper leaves the road on
your right up some steps through woodland.

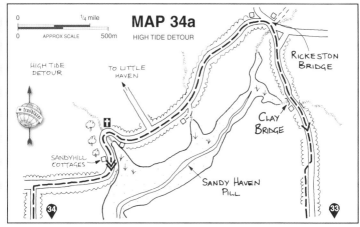

Once across the stepping stones the path takes you into some waterside woodland. It continues along the edge of a number of fields above low cliffs passing the ugly beacon above **Butts Bay**.

The scenery becomes more spectacular around **Lindsway Bay**, a lovely sandy beach protected by steep cliffs on all sides. The quickest way to **St Ishmael's** is to follow the public footpath from Lindsway Bay (look out for a bench by the coast path marking the trail to the village). The route from Monk Haven is slightly longer unless you are coming from Musselwick.

ST ISHMAEL'S (LLANISMEL) MAP 35

St Ishmael's is a pretty village with a friendly pub: ***Brook Inn*** (☎ 01646-636277; food served daily noon-11pm; Oct-Mar 4-11pm) has quite an extensive menu and a good choice of real ales including their own Brook Inn Ale.

The **Puffin Shuttle bus** (Acorn's No 315) stops by Brook Inn; see public transport map and table, pp44-7, for details.

The **post office** is up the hill at the northern end of the village.

At **Watch House Point** there are old military bunkers and lookout buildings which can provide very welcome shelter in wet weather. The coast path carries on, past the remains of a curious Victorian watchtower, to **Monk Haven**, a pretty little wooded valley with an impressive castle-like wall guarding the bay. It also provides another access point to St Ishmael's.

The path now follows gentle slopes overgrown with gorse, hawthorn and bracken to the farm buildings at **Musselwick**. From the small raised pond in the farmyard the path cuts down through shady trees to the stony beach. When there are exceptionally high tides the beach route is impassable and you will have to follow the short detour up the farm track from the raised pond following the fence line round to The Gann.

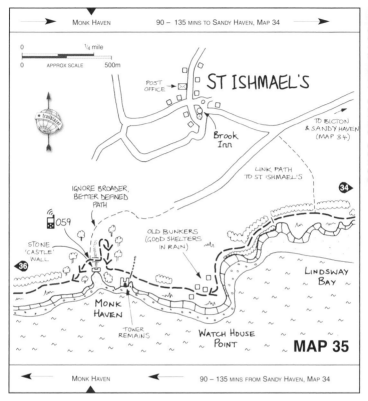

ROUTE GUIDE AND MAPS

MONK HAVEN — 90 – 135 MINS TO SANDY HAVEN, MAP 34 →

0 ¼ mile
0 APPROX SCALE 500m

POST OFFICE

ST ISHMAEL'S

TO BICTON & SANDY HAVEN (MAP 34)

Brook Inn

LINK PATH TO ST ISHMAEL'S

34

IGNORE BROADER, BETTER DEFINED PATH

059

OLD BUNKERS (GOOD SHELTERS IN RAIN)

STONE 'CASTLE' WALL

36

LINDSWAY BAY

MONK HAVEN

TOWER REMAINS

WATCH HOUSE POINT

MAP 35

← MONK HAVEN — 90 – 135 MINS FROM SANDY HAVEN, MAP 34

If you've come by any route save the high tide one, the next obstacle is the plank crossing of the creek at **The Gann**. As with Sandy Haven you will need to have checked the tide times as the crossing is only possible at low tide (see box p136). At high tide you must take the detour route by the road (described below). Once over the other side the path takes you across the shingle beach to the road and down to the village of **Dale**.

HIGH-TIDE DETOUR (VIA MULLOCK BRIDGE)   MAP 36, p140

This second detour, around The Gann estuary near Dale, will add a further **2½ miles (4km, 1hr)** to your day. Turning off the trail at Musselwick, follow the signposted track east, turning north at the first opportunity to continue on to Slatehill Farm.

Negotiating the path through the farm buildings, you carry on heading north and, with Whiteholme's Farm on your left, cross the farmland to the road at **Mullock Farm**.   *(cont'd on p142)*

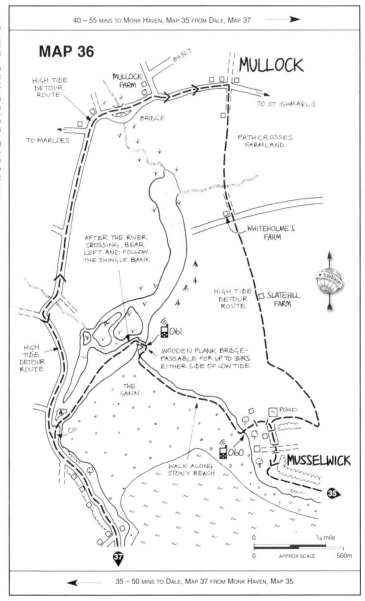

ROUTE GUIDE AND MAPS

MAP 36

HIGH TIDE
DETOUR
ROUTE

MULLOCK
FARM

B4327

MULLOCK

BRIDGE

TO ST ISHMAEL'S

TO MARLOES

PATH CROSSES
FARMLAND

AFTER THE RIVER
CROSSING, BEAR
LEFT AND FOLLOW
THE SHINGLE BANK

WHITEHOLME'S
FARM

HIGH TIDE
DETOUR
ROUTE

SLATEHILL
FARM

trailblazer

061

HIGH
TIDE
DETOUR
ROUTE

WOODEN PLANK BRIDGE -
PASSABLE FOR UP TO 3HRS
EITHER SIDE OF LOW TIDE.

THE
GANN

POND

CP

060

MUSSELWICK

WALK ALONG
STONY BEACH

35

0   ¼ mile

0   500m
APPROX SCALE

37

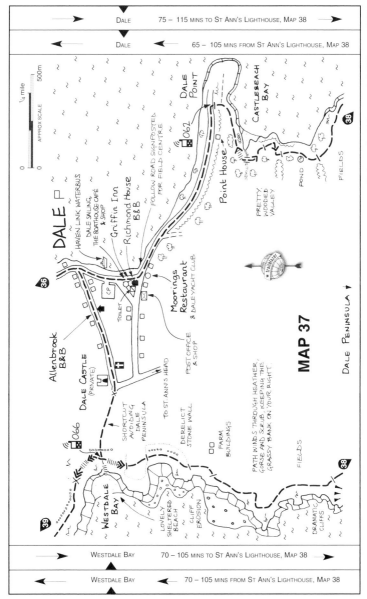

DALE — 75 – 115 MINS TO ST ANN'S LIGHTHOUSE, MAP 38 →

DALE ← 65 – 105 MINS FROM ST ANN'S LIGHTHOUSE, MAP 38

DALE POINT

CASTLEBEACH BAY

38

062

POINT HOUSE

PRETTY, WOODED VALLEY

POND

FIELDS

500m

¼ mile

APPROX SCALE

0

0

HAVEN LINK WATERBUS

DALE SAILING, THE BOATHOUSE CAFÉ & SHOP

DALE 🏠

GRIFFIN INN

RICHMOND HOUSE B&B

FOLLOW ROAD SIGNPOSTED FOR FIELD CENTRE

36

CP

TOILET

MOORINGS RESTAURANT & DALE YACHT CLUB

POST OFFICE & SHOP

ALLENBROOK B&B

DALE CASTLE (PRIVATE)

066

SHORTCUT AVOIDING DALE PENINSULA

To ST ANN'S HEAD

DERELICT STONE WALL

FARM BUILDINGS

PATH WINDS THROUGH HEATHER, GORSE AND SCRUB, KEEPING THE GRASSY BANK ON YOUR RIGHT

MAP 37

DALE PENINSULA ▶

FIELDS

38

39

WESTDALE BAY

LOVELY SHELTERED BEACH

CLIFF EROSION

DRAMATIC CLIFFS

WESTDALE BAY — 70 – 105 MINS TO ST ANN'S LIGHTHOUSE, MAP 38 →

WESTDALE BAY ← 70 – 105 MINS FROM ST ANN'S LIGHTHOUSE, MAP 38 *(cont'd from p139)* From here walk down the lane joining the B4327 road just before **Mullock Bridge**. After the bridge simply follow the road all the way to Dale, rejoining the coast path proper at the car park by the estuary.

DALE   MAP 37, p141

Dale is a small village but it's alive with tourists in the summer months. Sitting on the neck of the Dale peninsula, it overlooks a sheltered bay popular with water-sports enthusiasts.

If you want to have a go you can try everything from surfing and sailing to canoeing, kayaking and coasteering (see box p167) at **West Wales Watersports** (☎ 01646-636642; 💻 www.surfdale.co.uk; see box p154). They offer tuition for beginners as well as equipment hire.

Dale Sailing (☎ 01646-603110, 💻 www.dale-sailing.co.uk) operates a number of sea safaris, subject to the weather, some of which can be booked in advance but some are first come first served. Contact them for details.

There is a small **shop** (Mon-Fri 9.15am-4pm, Sun 9am-1pm) at the **post office** which can be found just around the corner from Griffin Inn. Another **shop** (Wed-Sat 9am-1pm), which has internet access, can be found at Dale Boathouse.

At weekends in the main season **Haven Link Waterbus** (Dale to Angle 1hr; £7.50/4 return/single; £4/2 children under 16) leaves for Angle twice a day. The **Puffin Shuttle bus** (No 315/400) also stops here. See the public transport map and table, pp44-7, for details.

Where to stay and eat

There are few places to stay so booking in advance is recommended.

Richmond House B&B (☎ 01646-636662, 💻 www.richmond-house.com;

1D/2T/1F) charges £65/pp for two sharing an en suite room and £45 for single occupancy; the family room sleeps four and costs £110.

Along the road towards Dale Castle is ***Allenbrook*** (☎ 01646-636254, 💻 www.allenbrook-dale.co.uk; 1S/1T/1D/1D or T), a fairly grand country house, which charges from £35-40 per person in its smart rooms, some of which are en suite and some have a private bathroom. They do not take children aged under 15.

Griffin Inn (☎ 01646-636227) is the only pub. They do food throughout the year (daily 12.30-2pm, Mon-Sat 6-8.30pm), apart from Monday lunchtime from October to March, and the bar is open Mon-Fri noon-3pm & 5-11pm, Sat/Sun noon-11pm with extended opening hours during the summer months. You can't miss it, sitting at the southern end of the village overlooking the water. The menu is limited but there are some tasty dishes, including locally caught prawns served by the pint. Bookings are requested for groups of eight or more.

Close by is ***Moorings Restaurant*** (☎ 01646-636362; Wed-Sat 6pm to late, open for Sun lunch from 12.30pm) situated in Dale Yacht Club, once again specialising in locally caught seafood.

Snacks are available at ***The Boathouse Café*** which is open daily in the summer only.

DALE TO MUSSELWICK SANDS (FOR MARLOES) MAPS 37-41

This beautiful section is **12 miles (19km, 5-6hrs)** so it is tempting to shorten it by missing out the Dale peninsula. If you follow the official path around the peninsula it is 5¹/₂ miles (9km, 2¹/₄ hrs) to Westdale Bay. If you take the short-cut it is less than a mile (1km, 15 mins). Purists will want to do the whole thing and will be well rewarded since there is some beautiful scenery. The peninsula protects Milford Haven harbour from the worst the Atlantic can throw at it. The eastern side is a mixture of gentle cliffs, small wooded valleys and pretty bays while the wind battered western side is characterised by high, rugged cliffs.

From Dale Yacht Club at the southern end of the village the route follows the lane to Point House and then on across farmland before dropping down to a pretty little bay surrounded by woodland.

Just past Watwick Point and its ugly beacon is the lovely **Watwick Bay**, then more farmland and low cliffs. At **Mill Bay** there is a stone on the field's edge commemorating the landing of Henry Tudor and his 55 ships and 4000 men from France, on 7 August 1485, after 14 years in exile. From Mill Bay Henry marched east where he got the better of Richard III in the Battle of Bosworth on 22 August 1485. He then became Henry VII, founder of the Tudor dynasty.

St Ann's lighthouse, which is now a set of holiday homes, marks the northern lip of the Milford Haven harbour. North from here the cliffs are precipitous and in places are crumbling into the sea so take great care. The path passes through scrubland and heathland along the level cliff top, eventually dropping steeply to pretty **Westdale Bay**. People do swim here but it is not the safest place for a dip since there are strong undercurrents as the big warning sign indicates.

The path skirts an old disused aerodrome, rapidly becoming overrun with gorse and bracken, before arriving high above the great sweep of **Marloes Sands**, one of the finest beaches in Pembrokeshire. The islands of Gateholm, Grassholm and Skomer can all be seen on the western horizon.

Hostellers should look out for a path above **Raggle Rocks** which leads to the youth hostel (see p148; five minutes from the coast path). The coast path continues on an easy course above some spectacular cliffs with twisted, folded rock dropping into the heaving sea below. This part of the coast is a marine nature reserve and with the proximity of some important breeding islands is a great place to spot seabirds.

At **Martin's Haven** there are public toilets, a National Trust visitor centre with information about the wildlife of the area as well as a Wildlife Trust Information Centre, known as Lockley Lodge (Apr-mid Sep, Tue-Sun 9am-12.15pm & 12.45pm-4pm or until the last boat returns). Just to the north of the centre, within the wall, is a stone engraved with a ring-cross design dating from somewhere between the 7th and 9th centuries; you'll see further examples of these at the lapidarium of the cathedral at St David's (see p166). The Puffin Shuttle (Nos 315/400) **bus** services stop here.

From Martin's Haven you can take a boat trip to Skomer (see box p144), where you have an even greater chance of spotting wildlife, particularly puffins.

The path then follows the fairly level cliff top to **Musselwick Sands**, another wonderful sandy beach with sheer cliffs all around. En route you pass West Hook Farm Campsite (see p148) but access is only possible along the road (see Map 40, p147).

At the southern end of the bay next to a picnic bench there is a path leading down to the beach and another one heading inland to the village of Marloes.

❏ Skomer, Skokholm and Grassholm islands

Lying to the west of the Marloes peninsula are three barren islands brought to life by the thousands of sea birds which breed on the sheer cliffs. All of them can be visited quite easily with guided walks available on Skomer and Skokholm.

Skomer, a national nature reserve and a marine nature reserve, with its coastline peppered with caves and blowholes, is the largest of the three and is closest to the mainland. It also has the widest variety of bird species of all the islands with razorbills, guillemots, kittiwakes, storm petrels, fulmars, shags and cormorants festooning the cliffs. The puffins and manx shearwaters breed in burrows on the cliff tops with pictures from one of the burrows relayed to a monitor in the island centre. There are 100,000 manx shearwaters making up at least a third of the world's population. There are also peregrine falcons and short-eared owls which can often be seen during the daytime.

If you prefer the odd mammal or two there are grey seals on the rocky shoreline while porpoises and dolphins can often be spotted from the boat to the island. There are also plenty of rabbits and some other small mammals, most notably the Skomer vole (see box p67), a sub-species of bank vole, unique to the island. For the botanist the island is carpeted in bluebells, heather, thrift and sea campion, creating a riot of colour in the spring. For further details about the flora and fauna see pp62-72.

Skomer is managed by the Wildlife Trust of South and West Wales (WTSWW; see p61 and box p60). At the time of writing it is the only island where you can stay overnight; for details call WTSWW (☎ 01239-621600).

Skokholm, to the south, is smaller but no less noisy with the relentless chatter of seabirds. About 30,000 pairs of manx shearwater breed on Skokholm. You can land on the island but can't wander around as you please. You must join one of the guided walks (see below) organised by the WTSWW who manage the island.

Grassholm, an RSPB reserve, is a rocky outcrop 11 miles (7km) from the mainland. It's Wales's only gannetry, home to 30,000 pairs of gannets in the summer breeding season when it can be hard to see the rock for the gannets. Although you can't land on the island you can take a boat trip around it.

Getting to the islands Dale Sailing (see p142) offer a number of cruises including trips to **Skomer** from Martin's Haven on the *Dale Princess*. It costs £10 per person for the boat trip and an additional £7 to land (Easter to Oct, daily 10am, 11am, noon; no landings on Mondays). Bookings aren't necessary. Guided day trips (9am-5pm) to **Skokholm** operate from Martin's Haven (£30 for boat and landing) on certain dates in summer; bookings must be made through WTSWW (see above). Dale Sailing also offer a 3-hour cruise around **Grassholm** (Mondays 1pm & 5pm; £30) from Martin's Haven. See 🖵 www.pembrokeshire-islands.co.uk for further details.

(Opposite) Top: Looking out to sea beyond Gateholm Island on the path between Dale and Musselwick Sands. Skokholm is in the distance. **Bottom**: Crossing Sandy Haven Pill at low tide (see p136).

(Overleaf) Top: St Ann's Lighthouse. **Bottom**: Striped cliffs beyond St Ann's Head.

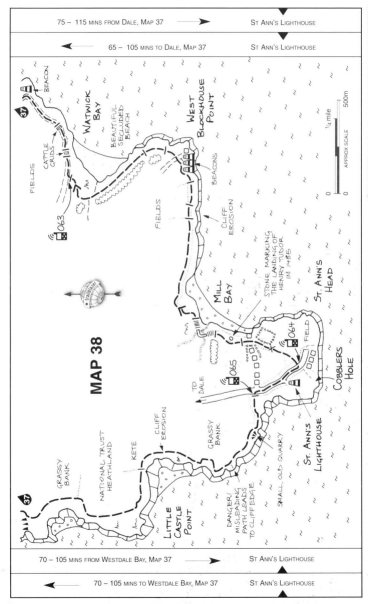

ROUTE GUIDE AND MAPS

75 – 115 mins from Dale, Map 37 ——→   St Ann's Lighthouse

←—— 65 – 105 mins to Dale, Map 37   St Ann's Lighthouse

BEACON

WATWICK BAY

CATTLE GRIDS

FIELDS

BEAUTIFUL SECLUDED BEACH

WEST BLOCKHOUSE POINT

BEACONS

CLIFF EROSION

FIELDS

063

MAP 38

½ mile
500m
APPROX SCALE

MILL BAY

STONE MARKING THE LANDING OF HENRY TUDOR IN 1485

St Ann's Head

064

FIELD

COBBLERS HOLE

TO DALE

065

St Ann's Lighthouse

GRASSY BANK

NATIONAL TRUST HEATHLAND

CLIFF EROSION

KETE

GRASSY BANK

DANGER! MISLEADING PATH LEADS TO CLIFF EDGE

SMALL OLD QUARRY

LITTLE CASTLE POINT

GRASSY BANK

70 – 105 mins from Westdale Bay, Map 37 ——→   St Ann's Lighthouse

←—— 70 – 105 mins to Westdale Bay, Map 37   St Ann's Lighthouse

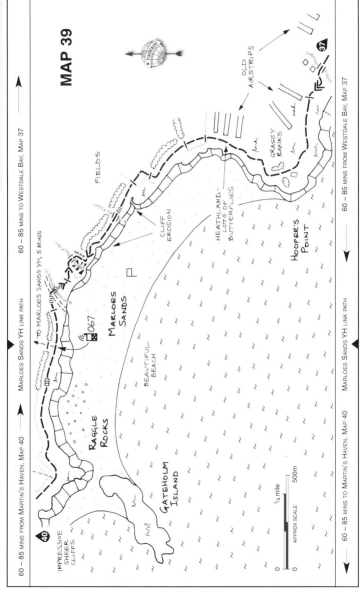

MAP 39

60 – 85 MINS TO WESTDALE BAY, MAP 37

MARLOES SANDS YH LINK PATH

60 – 85 MINS FROM MARTIN'S HAVEN, MAP 40

60 – 85 MINS FROM WESTDALE BAY, MAP 37

MARLOES SANDS YH LINK PATH

60 – 85 MINS TO MARTIN'S HAVEN, MAP 40

*Trailblazer

OLD AIRSTRIPS

GRASSY BANKS

HOOPER'S POINT

HEATHLAND – LOTS OF BUTTERFLIES

FIELDS

CLIFF EROSION

MARLOES SANDS YH, 5 MINS

TO MARLOES SANDS

067

MARLOES SANDS

BEAUTIFUL BEACH

RAGGLE ROCKS

GATEHOLM ISLAND

IMPRESSIVE SHEER CLIFFS

¼ mile

500m

APPROX SCALE

0

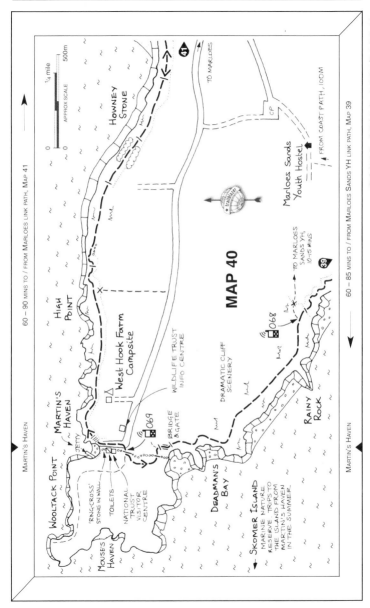

MARTIN'S HAVEN

60 – 90 MINS TO / FROM MARLOES LINK PATH, MAP 41

TO MARLOES

HOWNEY STONE

CP

Marloes Sands Youth Hostel

FROM COAST PATH, 100M

MAP 40

TO MARLOES SANDS YH, 10-15 MINS

39

HIGH POINT

West Hook Farm Campsite

WILDLIFE TRUST INFO CENTRE

068

DRAMATIC CLIFF SCENERY

RAINY ROCK

BRIDGE & GATE

069

WOOLTACK POINT

MARTIN'S HAVEN

JETTY

'RING-CROSS' STONE IN WALL

TOILETS

NATIONAL TRUST VISITOR CENTRE

MOUSE'S HAVEN

DEADMAN'S BAY

SKOMER ISLAND

MARINE NATURE RESERVE. TRIPS TO THE ISLAND FROM MARTIN'S HAVEN IN THE SUMMER.

MARTIN'S HAVEN

60 – 85 MINS TO / FROM MARLOES SANDS YH LINK PATH, MAP 39

APPROX SCALE

500m

¼ mile

trailblazer

MARLOES   MAP 41

Marloes, around half a mile inland from the path, is not an especially attractive village although the strange **clocktower** is quite interesting, looking as though it needs to be on top of something like a town hall rather than sitting solemnly in a small field by the side of the road. The main **church** is also very pretty and worth a look.

There is a **post office** and **shop** (Mon-Sat 8am-1pm & 2.30-6pm, Sun 9am-4pm) as well as a **phone box** opposite the pub. The **Puffin Shuttle bus** (315/400) stops outside Lobster Pot Inn; see public transport map and table, pp44-7, for details.

Marloes Sands Youth Hostel (see Map 40; ☎ 0845-371 9333) has 26 beds at £13.50 for members and is a self-catering-only property. It is not actually in the village and rather than coming from Musselwick Sands it is much easier to reach it from Marloes Sands (see Map 39; a five-minute walk) where a signpost points the way from the coast path.

Also outside the village itself, a mile and a half (2km) before Musselwick Sands near Martin's Haven (see Map 40), there is **camping** from £5/pp at *West Hook Farm* (☎ 01646-636424; Easter-end Oct); the site has shower/toilet facilities and there is also a shed where campers can sit and cook meals, though equipment isn't provided.

In the village on Glebe Lane there's the highly commended, pink-painted *Foxdale* (☎ 01646-636243, 🖳 www.foxdaleguesthouse.co.uk; 3D en suite/1T private

bathroom) which offers B&B accommodation at £33.50 per person for two sharing a room. There is a £15 single supplement; they also offer **camping** (Apr-Sep) for £5 per person. The site has toilet, shower and laundry facilities.

Opposite the post office is the homely *Albion House B&B* (☎ 01646-636365; 1S/1D/1T/1F) with rooms, some en suite, from £30 per person. At *Clock House* (☎ 01646-636527, 🖳 www.clockhousemarloes.co.uk; 1S/3D/2T, all en suite) B&B costs £40 per person for two sharing a room or £40 for the single or £55 for single occupancy of a double/twin room. They also have a good selection of snacks in the *café/restaurant* (daily 11am-4pm, lunch noon-3pm), and are open 6.30-8pm for evening meals Tue-Sat in high summer. You should book to guarantee a table in the evening.

The social centre of the village is undoubtedly *Lobster Pot Inn* (☎ 01646-636233; food served daily noon-3pm & 6-8.30pm; 2D/1F sleeping three), which has revamped itself as a fashionable bar complete with dark brown leather sofas, big screens and a gastro pub menu including standard pub fare with vegetarian options as well as specials; main dishes cost around £10.95. They also have decent Welsh beer on tap (the bar is open daily noon-11pm). The pub also does B&B with en suite rooms for £60-70; there is no discount for single occupancy.

MUSSELWICK SANDS TO BROAD HAVEN   MAPS 41-45

It is **8¹/₂ miles (14km, 3¹/₂-4¹/₂ hrs)** from the link path for Marloes village to Broad Haven following the easy path above the cliffs. The next port of call is **St Brides Haven (Sainffraid)**, a sheltered little bay where you will find toilets, a phone box, a church and a cluster of houses but little else. The extravagant-looking castle across the fields is actually the stately home of the St Brides estate.

The next stretch continues along easy-to-follow cliff tops. Once past **Mill Haven** things get a little tougher. The cliffs grow higher and the path roller-coasters its way up and down, passing **Brandy Bay**, a tiny little cove sheltered by frighteningly sheer cliffs. Take care here as the path is very close to the edge.

(cont'd on p152)

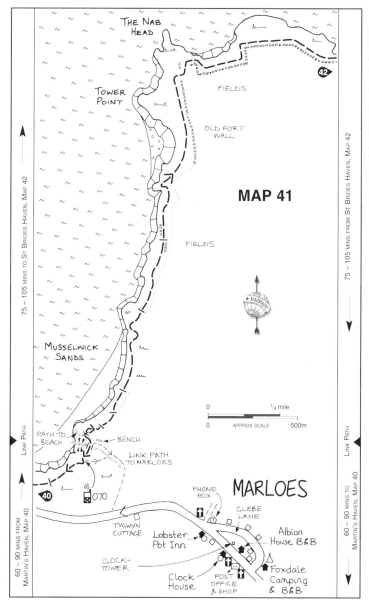

THE NAB
HEAD

TOWER
POINT

FIELDS

OLD FORT
WALL

MAP 41

75 – 105 MINS FROM ST BRIDES HAVEN, MAP 42

75 – 105 MINS TO ST BRIDES HAVEN, MAP 42

FIELDS

MUSSELWICK
SANDS

0   1/4 mile
0   500m
APPROX SCALE

LINK PATH

PATH TO
BEACH

BENCH

LINK PATH
TO MARLOES

070

MARLOES

PHONE
BOX

GLEBE
LANE

TYGWYN
COTTAGE

Lobster
Pot Inn

Albion
House B&B

CLOCK-
TOWER

Clock
House

POST
OFFICE
& SHOP

Foxdale
Camping
& B&B

LINK PATH

60 – 90 MINS TO
MARTIN'S HAVEN, MAP 40

60 – 90 MINS FROM
MARTIN'S HAVEN, MAP 40

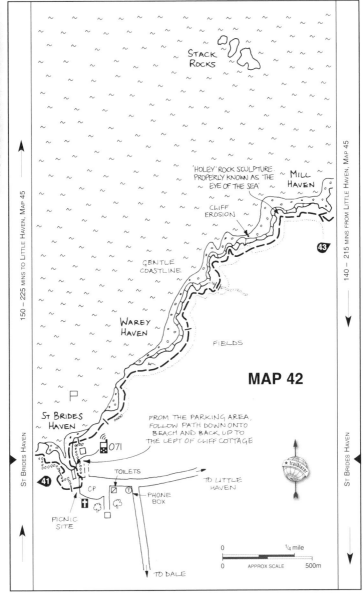

ROUTE GUIDE AND MAPS

150 – 225 MINS TO LITTLE HAVEN, MAP 45

140 – 215 MINS FROM LITTLE HAVEN, MAP 45

STACK ROCKS

'HOLEY' ROCK SCULPTURE PROPERLY KNOWN AS 'THE EYE OF THE SEA'

MILL HAVEN

CLIFF EROSION

43

GENTLE COASTLINE

WAREY HAVEN

FIELDS

MAP 42

P

St BRIDES HAVEN

071

FROM THE PARKING AREA, FOLLOW PATH DOWN ONTO BEACH AND BACK UP TO THE LEFT OF CLIFF COTTAGE

St BRIDES HAVEN

St BRIDES HAVEN

41

TOILETS

TO LITTLE HAVEN

CP

PHONE BOX

PICNIC SITE

★ trailblazer

0   ¼ mile

0   APPROX SCALE   500m

TO DALE

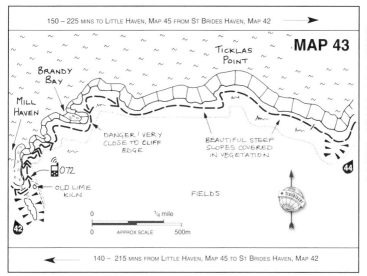

150 – 225 MINS TO LITTLE HAVEN, MAP 45 FROM ST BRIDES HAVEN, MAP 42 →

MAP 43

TICKLAS POINT

BRANDY BAY

MILL HAVEN

DANGER! VERY CLOSE TO CLIFF EDGE

BEAUTIFUL STEEP SLOPES COVERED IN VEGETATION

072

OLD LIME KILN

FIELDS

44

42

0 — ¼ mile
0 — 500m
APPROX SCALE

← 140 – 215 MINS FROM LITTLE HAVEN, MAP 45 TO ST BRIDES HAVEN, MAP 42

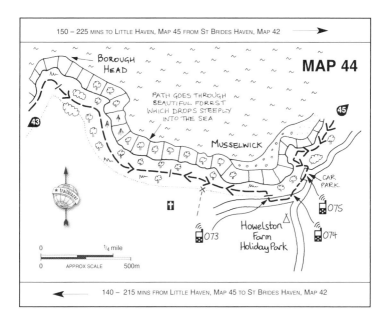

150 – 225 MINS TO LITTLE HAVEN, MAP 45 FROM ST BRIDES HAVEN, MAP 42 →

MAP 44

BOROUGH HEAD

PATH GOES THROUGH BEAUTIFUL FOREST WHICH DROPS STEEPLY INTO THE SEA

MUSSELWICK

43

45

CAR PARK

075

073

074

Howelston Farm Holiday Park

0 — ¼ mile
0 — 500m
APPROX SCALE

← 140 – 215 MINS FROM LITTLE HAVEN, MAP 45 TO ST BRIDES HAVEN, MAP 42

(cont'd from p148) Eventually the path settles down above high, vegetated cliffs at **Ticklas Point**. You can now see the immense sweep of St Brides Bay with Ramsey Island in the far distance.

Once past the mighty **Borough Head** with its 75-metre (246ft) slopes dropping steeply into the sea, the path enters some beautiful forest of oak, beech and pine which cling to the steep cliff side. Howelston Farm Campsite (see below) is off the first road to the right after joining the road. The pretty village of **Little Haven** is a bit further on down the hill. From here it's a steep climb up the road out over the hill into **Broad Haven**, its bigger sister village.

LITTLE HAVEN (ABER BACH) MAP 45

Squeezed between two steep hillsides around a tiny cove, Little Haven is a lovely place. It may be smaller than Broad Haven over the hill but is far more appealing and has a good number of pubs to distract the exhausted walker.

Services

For food supplies or a post office you will need to carry on to Broad Haven which is only ten minutes away over the hill.

The **Puffin Shuttle bus** (No 400) stops by Castle Hotel; see pp45-6 for details.

Where to stay

For camping try *Howelston Farm Holiday Park* (see Map 44; ☎ 01437-781818; Mar-Nov); however, they prefer families and groups so a pitch costs £16-19 per tent sleeping up to four people.

Down in the centre of the village, near the post office, *St Brides Inn* (☎ 01437-781266, 🖳 www.stbridesinn.co.uk; 2D, both en suite) charges £30-35/pp for B&B.

Further up Settlands Hill is *Haven Fort Hotel* (☎ 01437-781401; Apr-Oct; 2S/1D/3F, all with private facilities) which charges £36 per person for two sharing and £42 for a single room. The rooms have a view of the bay but they do not have a television, though there is a TV room. Further along this road and actually closer to Broad Haven is *Atlantic View* (☎ 01437-781589, 🖳 www.atlantic-view.co.uk; 2T/3D); all the rooms have private facilities and they charge from £70 per room. It also has a small **campsite**; pitches cost from £6 per tent plus £2 per head.

Where to eat and drink

St Brides Inn (see Where to stay) has good food on offer (daily noon-2pm & 6-9pm) including sea bass with chorizo mash (£14.75), though the menu changes regularly; they do barbecues in the summer. The bar itself is generally open Sun-Fri 11am-3pm & 6-11pm and all day on Saturday.

The *Swan Inn* (☎ 01437-781880; food served Mon-Sat noon-2pm & 6-9pm) sits overlooking the small bay and is the first pub you see as you come in from the coast path; the characterful restaurant serves sandwiches from £5.60 and faggots at £9. In the evening fresh fish dishes start at £16.95. The bar is open daily 11am-3pm & 5-11pm.

The Castle Hotel (☎ 01437-781445, 🖳 www.littlehavencastle.co.uk; daily 10.30am-midnight, food served daily all day in school summer holidays; rest of year daily noon-2pm & 6-9pm) has an extensive menu, including Little Haven dressed crab (£11.95) and braised lamb (£12.95), and a nice beer garden where you can watch the waves crashing on the small beach. Despite the name they no longer offer accommodation.

Away from the beach is the *Nest Bistro* (☎ 01437-781728, 🖳 thenestbistro@hotmail.com; Mar-Oct Tue-Sat 7-8.30pm), a quality fish restaurant offering great monkfish, sea bass and turbot dishes from £15.50. Booking is advised.

Captain Morgan's (*Ceri's*; daily 9am-5pm) sells everything from sandwiches to hot meals and an all-day breakfast and sources food from local suppliers.

BROAD HAVEN (ABER LLYDAN)
                              MAP 45

The wonderful beach is the highlight here. The village itself would not win any beauty contests but it has a nice air about it all the same. Popular with holidaymakers who come for the endless expanse of sand, you may well be tempted to take a dip to soothe those aching feet.

The small **supermarket** (daily 8am-9pm) on the seafront is probably the only place you will need since it incorporates the **post office** (Mon, Tue, Thur & Fri 9am-1pm & 2-5.30pm, Wed & Sat 9am-12.30pm) and has a Link **cash machine** too.

The supermarket also has an array of **first-aid** bits and bobs which may be useful for anyone suffering from blisters. The next cash machine, chemist and shop are not until St David's, 17 miles (27km) away, though there is a small shop at Solva.

There is an expensive (£5/hr) **internet** terminal at Broad Haven Youth Hostel (see p154). Slightly better value is the wi-fi service provided by the Anchor Guesthouse (see p154), at 50p for 10 minutes.

The **Puffin Shuttle bus** (No 400) and Silcox's No 311 stop here; see public transport map and table, pp44-7, for details.

ROUTE GUIDE AND MAPS

Where to stay

Broad Haven Youth Hostel (☎ 0845-371 9008, 📧 broadhaven@yha.org.uk) has space for 77 people. The rate for members is £19.95 per person. The hostel is licensed and serves meals.

Nearby, backing onto the car park, is **Albany Guesthouse** (☎ 01437-781051; 27 Milmoor Way; 1D/2D or T, all en suite; Easter to end Sep) charging from £30 per head, £32 for single occupancy. Luggage transfer is available for a fee.

Anchor Guesthouse (☎ 01437-781476, 📧 www.anchorguesthouse.co.uk; 1S/3T/2D/1D or F, all en suite) is a large place on the seafront. Rates are £35-40 per person; single occupancy supplement £10. The family room sleeps four. Packed lunches are available if requested in advance; evening meals are served daily in the main season but at weekends only at other times. Advance bookings are recommended.

Where to eat and drink

Galleon Inn (☎ 01437-781152; food served daily noon-2.30pm & 6-8.30pm, all day in the school summer holidays) is the most popular spot with a menu on which everything costs £4.99. It also has a good selection of real ales; the bar is open daily noon-10.30pm.

The Royal (☎ 01437-781249; food served Thur-Sat from 6pm, also Sat & Sun lunch from 12.30pm) serves a variety of staple meals including lasagnes, curries and roasts; the bar is open daily noon-11pm. The pub is opposite the Slash Pond, an old culm pit originally opened in 1859.

For cheaper, quicker fare look behind Galleon Inn for **Seaview Takeaway** which serves fish and chips.

BROAD HAVEN TO NEWGALE   MAPS 45-49

This short stretch of **seven miles (11km, 2¹/₂-3¹/₄ hrs)** follows easy ground over low cliffs, passing a number of intimate little coves before arriving at the wonderful Newgale Sands, two miles (3km) of uninterrupted sand battered by Atlantic rollers.

From Broad Haven the cliffs get steadily higher as you head north with the easy-to-follow path running through scrubland. At the rocky outcrops known as **Haroldston Chins** there's a great bench (dedicated to Paul Blick, one of the men who helped to found the coast path and its first warden); if the weather's fine, there's no better place to stop for a while.

❏ **Surfing**

Some of the best surfing in Britain can be found at places like Broad Haven and Newgale as the uninterrupted swell from the Atlantic comes rolling in. Even if you have never caught a wave before there are a number of patient instructors who will try to get you standing up on that board in the space of a day.

Newsurf (☎ 01437-721398, 📧 www.newsurf.co.uk) specialises in surfing tuition but also offers surfboard and wetsuit hire. They also have **hot showers** for their customers.

West Wales Watersports (see p142), in Dale, offers half-day courses in surfing, windsurfing, canoeing and sailing with equipment hire too. Alternatively try **TYF** (📧 www.tyf.com) in St David's (see p167). They also have equipment for hire and offer tuition in windsurfing, canoeing, sailing and coasteering (see box p167).

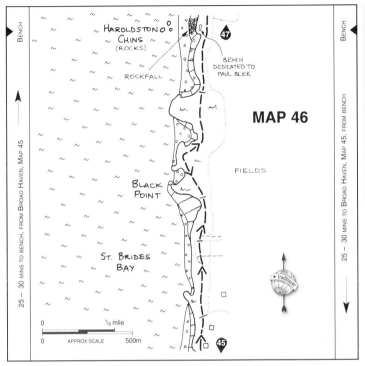

The route then turns inland to join the road around ***Druidstone Villa*** (☎ 01437-781221; 💻 www.druidstone.co.uk; 2S/8D/1F; some rooms are en suite; some share facilities), an excellent place to stay, where a bed costs from £35 to £70 per person; booking in advance is essential in school summer holidays and at weekends. They also have a bar and restaurant open to non-residents (booking essential for the latter; food served daily 12.30-2.30pm & 7.30-9.30pm).

Just past the villa look out for **The Roundhouse**. Tours of this 'eco-friendly' little building are by arrangement only; contact Druidstone Villa if you're interested.

There is a lovely beach at **Druidstone Haven** which tends to stay reasonably quiet since most people head for the beaches either side at Broad Haven and Newgale. If you feel the need for a break from walking the **Puffin Shuttle bus** (No 400) stops here. From Druidstone Haven the path climbs over the top of an enormous grassy sand dune and then continues along the cliff top. Much of this section is falling into the sea with large land slips and erosion cutting into the coast path. Watch out for diversions and sudden drops.

ROUTE GUIDE AND MAPS

NOLTON HAVEN   MAP 47

Nolton Haven is an enchanting little cove and hamlet and a good spot to have lunch, especially if it's raining.

There is a rather good pub here, the *Mariner's Inn* (☎ 01437-710469; 1S/3D or T/3F), which does B&B for £38 per person, £48 for the single room or single occupancy, and £28 for bed only. The bar is open Apr-Oct daily noon-3pm & 6-11pm Nov-Mar evening only, and they also do good food (summer daily 12.30-2.15pm & 6.30-8.30pm) from Indian to seafood. Fish and chips are £8.95 and the jacket potatoes are excellent.

The **Puffin Shuttle bus** (No 400) stops here by the car park; see pp44-6 for details.

From Nolton Haven the path climbs steeply above high grassy slopes with views of **Newgale Sands** ahead. At the southern end of this immense beach you will find a **disused mine** still with the old red-brick chimney and spoil heaps. Coal was exported from Nolton Haven by sea for 25 years before the mine closed at the turn of the 20th century.

At the mine you have a choice. You can clamber down the very precarious path to the beach, or head up the steep slope to continue along the heathery cliff top. Both routes have their merits. The beach is spectacular with nearly two miles (3km) of straight walking. The cliff route gives you the chance to admire the beach from up high and you still have the chance to walk along the top half of the beach once you climb down from the high ground. If planning to camp at South Wood Cottage (see below) the cliff route may be better.

If you choose to walk along the beach bear in mind that loose, dry sand is tiring to walk on. Furthermore, about a third of the way along, the cliff juts right out which could prove tricky to negotiate if the tide's in. As it is almost two miles (3km) of walking it's a good idea to walk close to the sea where the sand is damper and firmer. **Newgale** village lies at the far northern end of the beach.

NEWGALE (NÎWGWL) MAP 49, p159

This is one of the most popular spots for surfers which is not surprising considering it has two miles of immaculate beach continually pounded by Atlantic surf. The village itself is just a collection of houses stretched along the northern end of the beach and up the hill.

Services

There is a **phone box** next to the Duke of Edinburgh pub on the seafront. If you want to try your hand at surfing contact **Newsurf** (see box p154).

The **Puffin Shuttle bus** (No 400) stops here as does Richards Brothers/ Summerdale No 411; see public transport map and table, pp44-7, for details.

Where to stay and eat

(Note that Newgale YMCA, two miles north of Newgale and off the coast path, now operates only as an outdoor centre).

Behind the Duke of Edinburgh is *Newgale Camping Site* (☎ 01437-710253, 🖳 www.newgalecampingsite.co.uk; Mar-Oct) which charges £5 per person; they don't take bookings. There is a shower (50p) and toilet block.

About half a mile back from the seafront road on Woodhill Rise is *South Wood Cottage* (off Map 48, p158; ☎ 01437-710620; 1D private bathroom) which charges £30 per person. The single occupancy rate is £40 but the full rate (£60) is charged for single occupancy in July and August. They also do luggage transfer.

(cont'd on p160)

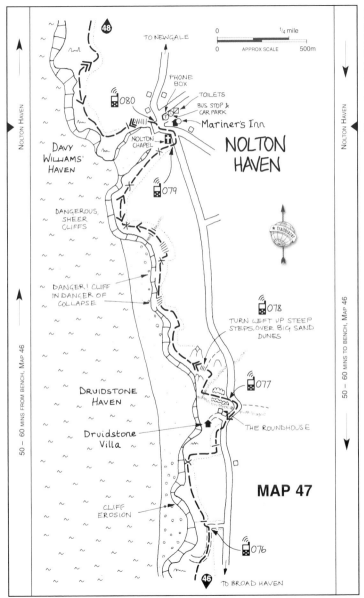

NOLTON HAVEN

NOLTON HAVEN

48

TO NEWGALE

0   ¼ mile

0   500m
APPROX SCALE

PHONE
BOX

080

TOILETS

BUS STOP &
CAR PARK

Mariner's Inn

NOLTON CHAPEL

NOLTON HAVEN

DAVY WILLIAMS' HAVEN

079

DANGEROUS, SHEER CLIFFS

DANGER! CLIFF IN DANGER OF COLLAPSE

078

TURN LEFT UP STEEP STEPS, OVER BIG SAND DUNES

077

DRUIDSTONE HAVEN

THE ROUNDHOUSE

Druidstone Villa

MAP 47

CLIFF EROSION

076

50 – 60 MINS FROM BENCH, MAP 46

50 – 60 MINS TO BENCH, MAP 46

46   TO BROAD HAVEN

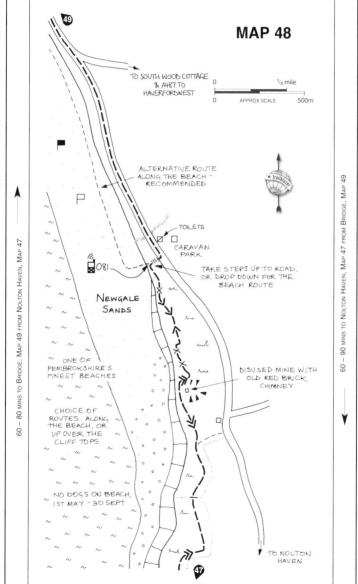

MAP 48

TO SOUTH WOOD COTTAGE
& A487 TO
HAVERFORDWEST

0   1/4 mile

0   APPROX SCALE   500m

ALTERNATIVE ROUTE
ALONG THE BEACH –
RECOMMENDED

★ trailblazer

TOILETS

CARAVAN
PARK

081

TAKE STEPS UP TO ROAD,
OR DROP DOWN FOR THE
BEACH ROUTE

NEWGALE
SANDS

ONE OF
PEMBROKESHIRE'S
FINEST BEACHES

DISUSED MINE WITH
OLD RED BRICK
CHIMNEY

CHOICE OF
ROUTES ALONG
THE BEACH, OR
UP OVER THE
CLIFF TOPS

NO DOGS ON BEACH,
1ST MAY – 30 SEPT.

TO NOLTON
HAVEN

49

47

60 – 80 MINS TO BRIDGE, MAP 49 FROM NOLTON HAVEN, MAP 47

60 – 90 MINS TO NOLTON HAVEN, MAP 47 FROM BRIDGE, MAP 49

ROUTE GUIDE AND MAPS

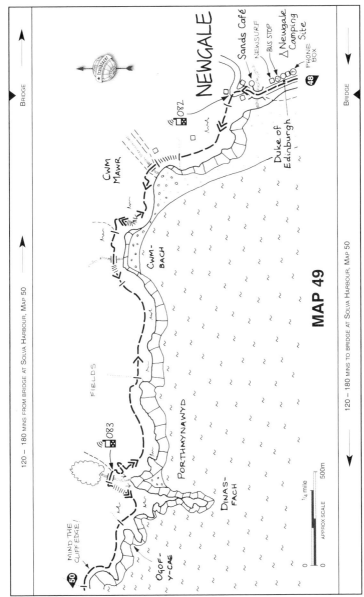

NEWGALE

Sands Café

NEWSURF

BUS STOP

△ Newgale Camping Site

PHONE BOX

48

082

Duke of Edinburgh

CWM MAWR

CWM-BACH

083

FIELDS

PORTHMYNAWYD

DINAS-FACH

MIND THE CLIFF EDGE!

50

OGOF-Y-CAE

MAP 49

120 – 180 MINS FROM BRIDGE AT SOLVA HARBOUR, MAP 50

120 – 180 MINS TO BRIDGE AT SOLVA HARBOUR, MAP 50

BRIDGE

BRIDGE

¼ mile

APPROX SCALE

0   500m

Trailblazer

(cont'd from p156) For a substantial but pretty standard meal try the **Duke of Edinburgh** (☎ 01437-720586; food daily noon-3pm & 6-9pm), the rather tatty pub on the front. The pub itself is open daily all day from noon, earlier in summer.

The smarter **Sands Café** (☎ 01437-729222; daily July/Aug 8.30am-8pm, rest of year daily 9.30am-5pm) has a variety of snacks, sandwiches and all-day breakfasts; it's the blue building on the corner across the bridge.

NEWGALE TO CAERFAI BAY (FOR ST DAVID'S)   MAPS 49-52

These **nine miles** (**14km, 3¹/₂-4¹/₂hrs**) begin with some very strenuous terrain just north of Newgale but become somewhat less arduous once past Solva.

From Newgale the path climbs up a very steep hillside and then drops all the way down the other side into **Cwm Mawr**, a small, deep valley. The path then continues over some more tough cliffs eventually settling down somewhat following a high cliff top before dropping into another small valley and passing the rocky promontory of **Dinas-Fach**.

The scenery is quite magnificent along this stretch and at **Dinas-Fawr** you can take the short detour to the end of the headland for great views along the coast. Ahead you can see the southern tip of Ramsey Island (see box p163) while back the way you came are the high cliffs that you have just come over and the sweeping sands at Newgale. Add 15 to 20 minutes to your time if you choose to explore the Dinas-Fawr headland.

Follow the line of the cliffs all the way to Solva Harbour and the beautiful village of **Solva**.

SOLVA (SOLFACH)   [see map p162]
Solva is probably the prettiest village on the coast path. It is worth keeping a couple of hours spare to stop for lunch here or, even better, to spend the night.

The lower village is a line of painted houses tucked below the steep hillside that leads to the little harbour. The claustrophobic nature of this part is due to its situation. It sits in an old **glacial meltwater channel** formed some 10,000 years ago at the end of the last ice age. Melting ice sent torrents of water towards the sea carving out deep gorges. There are many examples of this in Pembrokeshire, often with a small bay or cove at the end, but the one at Solva is one of the finest. In fact there are two here: the second, the southern one, is crossed on the way to the village along the main coast path.

Next to the harbour there are some of the well-preserved **lime kilns** which can be seen at many of the coves and inlets along the coast.

Services
The prettiest part of the village is **Lower Solva** which has most of the eating places as well as a **phone box** and some public **toilets**. There's no tourist office, though the village does boast its own website which is very useful: ⌨ www.solva.net. The **Puffin Shuttle bus** (No 400) stops on Main St, as does Richards Brothers/Summerdale's No 411 service; see pp44-7 for details.

Upper Solva, meanwhile, has the **post office** and a small **shop** all in one; Mon 9am-5pm, Tue-Sat 9am-noon.

Where to stay
Campers should continue past the village along the coast path for another mile where there is cheap camping at *Naw Ffynnon*

(Opposite) Top: Looking east across the entrance to Lower Solva harbour.
Bottom: St Justinian's lifeboat station (see p173).

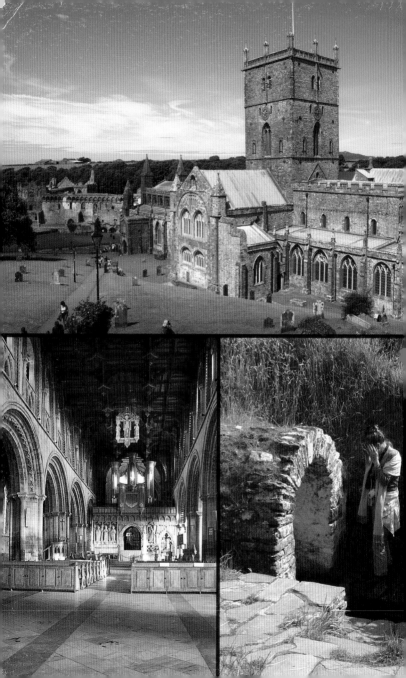

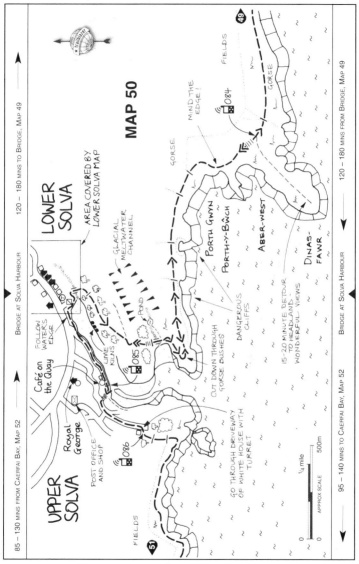

MAP 50

85 – 130 MINS FROM CAERFAI BAY, MAP 52

BRIDGE AT SOLVA HARBOUR

120 – 180 MINS TO BRIDGE, MAP 49

LOWER SOLVA

AREA COVERED BY LOWER SOLVA MAP

GLACIAL MELTWATER CHANNEL

FOLLOW WATER'S EDGE

Café on the Quay

Royal George

POST OFFICE AND SHOP

UPPER SOLVA

085

086

LIME KILNS

POND

CUT DOWN THROUGH GORSE BUSHES

DANGEROUS CLIFFS

GO THROUGH DRIVEWAY OF WHITE HOUSE WITH TURRET

FIELDS

51

PORTH GWYN
PORTH-Y-BÂCH

ABER-WEST

DINAS-FAWR

15-20 MINUTE DETOUR TO HEADLAND – WONDERFUL VIEWS

GORSE

GORSE

MIND THE EDGE!

084

FIELDS

49

120 – 180 MINS FROM BRIDGE, MAP 49

BRIDGE AT SOLVA HARBOUR

95 – 140 MINS TO CAERFAI BAY, MAP 52

¼ mile

500m

APPROX SCALE

0

0

(Opposite) St David's Cathedral (see p166). The patron saint of Wales was born at St Non's where the spring and well (**bottom right**) have attracted pilgrims for centuries. (Photos © Bryn Thomas). **Bottom left**: Cathedral interior. (Photo © Henry Stedman).

ROUTE GUIDE AND MAPS

Campsite (see Map 51, p164; ☎ 01437-721809; Easter-Sep). It is set back from the coast so there is a short detour to reach it from the coast path. The rate for a tent plus two people is £9, and with a car £10. Bookings are recommended in the school summer holidays.

In **Lower Solva** there is B&B at *Gamlyn* (☎ 01437-721542; 17 Y Gribin; 1S/1T/1D) which is just off Main St by the river. The double room is en suite but the others share a bathroom. B&B is from £29 per person.

Felingog (☎ 01437-720076, 🖳 jono@solva.co.uk; 2S/4D, shared facilities) has views straight down the harbour – if you ring but don't get an answer try calling *35* (see Where to eat). Doubles cost £55-60 for two sharing and the singles are £30 per night.

A little further up the street at No 10, *Williams' Accommodation* (☎ 01437-729000, 🖳 www.williamsofsolva.com; 4D/basement studio sleeping two) is a smart Georgian house with large rooms and period furniture including 'superking-sized' beds. All this doesn't come cheap, however, with rooms starting at £37.50/pp for double occupancy and £60 single occupancy.

In **Upper Solva** (Map 50, p161) the *Royal George* (☎ 01437-720002; 13 High St; 1T/2D/1F) offers en suite B&B for £35/pp.

Where to eat and drink

In **Lower Solva** *Harbour Inn* (☎ 01437-720013, 🖳 www.harbourinnsolva.com; food daily noon-2.30pm & 6-9pm) is where its name suggests. It's a lovely spot with tables out by the river and standard bar food as well as some great local seafood and a carvery Sunday lunch. If requested in

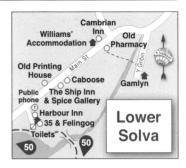

Lower Solva

advance they are able to provide packed lunches; they can also fill flasks and provide hot drinks to take away. The owners are also happy to advise on local walks.

Next door, and actually the first place you come to in the village, is *35* (☎ 01437-729236; daily 11am-5pm; extended hours in the summer months), a smart café serving sandwiches and simple meals as well as great smoothies.

The *Old Printing House* (☎ 01437-721603; Feb-Oct, daily all day) has a smart restaurant in the 'olde worlde' vein. They do good home-cooked food and are very proud of their herbal teas. All the food is guaranteed to be of local origin.

Virtually opposite is *The Ship Inn* (☎ 01437-721247; Sun-Thur noon-11pm, Fri & Sat noon-midnight, winter Mon-Wed from 4pm); the *Spice Gallery* (daily 5.30-11pm), an authentic Indian restaurant that also offers a takeaway service, is accessed through the pub.

Nearby, *Caboose* (☎ 01437-720503, 🖳 www.cabooseinsolva.co.uk; daily 10.30am-4.30pm, 11 Main St) is a colourful place serving a wide range of gluten-free cakes and pastries. They also have some crafts and local products.

❏ **Important note – walking times**
Unless otherwise specified, **all times in this book refer only to the time spent walking**. You will need to add 20-30% to allow for rests, photography, checking the map, drinking water etc. When planning the day's hike count on 5-7 hours' actual walking.

A little further along the street is *The Old Pharmacy* (☎ 01437-720005; 🖳 www.theoldpharmacy.co.uk; 5 Main St; daily 5.30pm to late; Apr-Oct Mon-Fri noon-2.30pm, daily in school summer holidays). A blackboard outside crows about its recommendations in every *Good Food Guide* since 1999; these are deserved and it serves some great local seafood dishes including crab and lobster as well as some tasty vegetarian options. Up by the bridge is the *Cambrian Inn* (☎ 01437-721210; food served daily 8am-10pm) with good food and on Sundays they serve some excellent roast lamb and beef, both sourced locally. It's often very popular so it's worth booking in advance, especially during holiday periods and for Sunday lunch.

In **Upper Solva** (see Map 50, p161) there's some great – and cheaper – food at the *Royal George* (see Where to stay; food served daily noon-3pm & 6-9pm), which boasts a number of fine ales, a great outdoor seating space and some excellent-value fish dishes.

Café on the Quay (☎ 01437-721725) has a small, sunny upper deck overlooking the harbour where you can enjoy their freshly prepared snacks, home-made cakes and Italian coffees. The café is generally open daily 10am-5pm but may close earlier if the weather is bad or may stay open longer, weather and tide permitting. Crabbers of all ages are catered for.

From Solva the rest of this stage is quite straightforward, following the obvious path along the cliff edge. The cliffs become less high but no less spectacular as you approach **Caerbwdi Bay** passing through slopes of bracken, around a low headland to **Caerfai Bay**. Take care of the low but precipitous cliffs immediately to the left.

❏ Ramsey Island

Ramsey Island is the most northerly of the Pembrokeshire Islands and is another important wildlife reserve managed by the RSPB (see p60). It is a vital seal-breeding area. The fluffy, white and grey seal pups can be seen in late summer and autumn on the rocky beaches around the island. Like the other islands further south there are thousands of seabirds breeding on the cliffs including puffins and manx shearwaters. There is also a herd of red deer on the island; see p66. In Ramsey Sound you can take a boat ride over 'The Bitches', an unusual phenomenon where the confluence of two currents creates churning rapids in the middle of the sea.

Thousand Islands Expeditions (☎ 01437-721721, 🖳 www.thousandislands.co.uk; Apr-Oct daily 8.30am-6pm), Cross Sq, St Davids, on the approach road to the cathedral, offer a number of boat trips from exploration of the sea caves in a jet boat to fishing for mackerel and pollack. They also land on the island and run wildlife excursions; prices start from £15, with discounts for RSPB members. Book in advance by phone.

Voyages of Discovery (☎ 01437-721911, freephone 0800-854367, 🖳 www.ramseyisland.co.uk; 1 High St, St Davids; Mar-Jul & Sep-Oct daily 9am-5pm, Jul-Aug daily 8am-8pm, Nov-Mar Mon-Fri 9am-5pm) offer trips around the island for £24, or a longer voyage to North Bishop Island to view the puffin colonies and watch the shearwaters migrating.

Alternatively you can take their North Coast Explorer around the northern shores of Pembrokeshire – it's a great way to explore many of the coves and beaches that are inaccessible when walking on the coast path. They also run a popular whale and dolphin watch. Departures are from St Justinian's (see Map 54, p173).

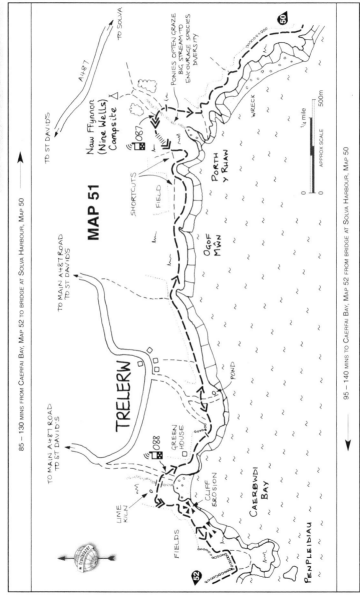

85 – 130 MINS FROM CAERFAI BAY, MAP 52 TO BRIDGE AT SOLVA HARBOUR, MAP 50

95 – 140 MINS TO CAERFAI BAY, MAP 52 FROM BRIDGE AT SOLVA HARBOUR, MAP 50

MAP 51

TO SOLVA

A487

TO ST DAVIDS

Naw Ffynnon (Nine Wells) Campsite

087

PONIES OFTEN GRAZE BIG STREAM TO ENCOURAGE SPECIES DIVERSITY

50

WRECK

PORTH Y RHAW

SHORTCUTS

FIELD

OGOF MÔN

TO MAIN A487 ROAD TO ST DAVIDS

TRELERW

TO MAIN A487 ROAD TO ST DAVIDS

POND

GREEN HOUSE

088

LIME KILN

CLIFF EROSION

CAERBWDI BAY

FIELDS

PENPLEIDIAU

52

¼ mile

APPROX SCALE

500m

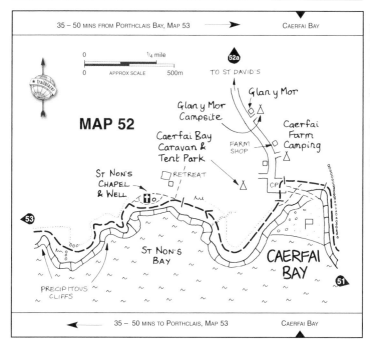

35 – 50 MINS FROM PORTHCLAIS BAY, MAP 53 → CAERFAI BAY

MAP 52

TO ST DAVID'S

Glan y Mor
Campsite

Glan y Mor

Caerfai Bay
Caravan &
Tent Park

FARM
SHOP

Caerfai
Farm
Camping

St Non's
CHAPEL
& WELL

RETREAT

St Non's
Bay

CAERFAI
BAY

PRECIPITOUS
CLIFFS

35 – 50 MINS TO PORTHCLAIS, MAP 53 CAERFAI BAY

CAERFAI BAY MAP 52

This is the best access point for St David's, only a mile from the coast path. If you need money, more food or new socks St David's is your last chance before Fishguard, 40 miles (64km) away; it's a highlight of the walk and a worthwhile diversion in any case.

Campers are spoilt for choice at Caerfai Bay. The biggest of the three campsites is *Caerfai Bay Caravan and Tent Park* (☎ 01437-720274, 🖥 www.caerfai bay.co.uk; Mar-mid Nov). It has a camping ground with toilets, showers and a launderette. Rates are £10-14 for a tent, two people and a car or £4.50 per person for walkers; for the best views ask for pitches G3, H1 or H10.

On the other side of the lane, and a little further up the hill, is *Caerfai Farm*

(☎ 01437-720548, 🖥 www.cawscaerfai.co .uk) with its own **campsite** (late May to end Sep; £6.50/pp, walkers without vehicles £4/pp; rate includes shower/toilet facilities; they also have laundry facilities) as well as a **farm shop** (summer school holidays daily 9am-6pm; May-Jul limited hours) selling their organic products including delicious cheeses such as Caerfai Cheddar, Caerphilly and Caerphilly with leek and garlic, as well as a limited stock of other foods.

A little further on *Glan y Mor Campsite* (☎ 01437-721788, 🖥 www.glan-y-mor.co.uk) has tent pitches from £12 for two people plus £4 per additional person. They also have a **bar** open daily noon to late in the main season.

ST DAVID'S (TYDDEWI)
MAP 52a, p169

St David's is the smallest city in Britain, qualifying for this grand status thanks to its wonderful cathedral; to come here and not visit **St David's Cathedral** (see box below) is like going to Paris and not going to the Eiffel Tower.

To call St David's a city seems to paint an unfair picture of the place. It is really somewhere between a big village and a small town with a definite lazy air pervading the sleepy lanes. In the quieter months the croaking of the ravens in the trees in Cross Sq can sometimes be the only sign of

---

❏ St David and the cathedral

St David was one of a number of Celtic saints from the 6th century and is now the patron saint of Wales. He was born at St Non's (a village named after his mother), where the chapel and the holy well (see Map 52, p165) can be seen just off the coast path to the south of the city. As a missionary his influence was such that the city which now bears his name became an important pilgrimage site and still is to this day.

The cathedral was built on the site of St David's monastery and you can still see a casket in Holy Trinity Chapel which is purported to contain the bones of both St Justinian and St David himself. The cathedral has had a turbulent history. During the 10th and 11th centuries the Vikings regularly raided it and even killed two of the serving bishops in 999 and again in 1080.

The present-day cathedral came into being in 1181 but was all but destroyed by parliamentary soldiers in 1648. Over the years it has been restored to more than its former glory with the 12th-century nave the oldest part of the building. The fantastic 16th-century Irish oak ceiling is testament to the earthquake of 1247 which caused the western wall of the nave to lean outwards.

Entrance to the cathedral (🖳 www.stdavidscathedral.org.uk) is gained via **Porth y Twr**, the 14th-century gateway which sits at the top of the steps above the cathedral. The current bells of the cathedral, which were hung in the 1930s, are somewhat surprisingly found here, because it was feared the cathedral tower could collapse with the weight if they were hung there.

One of the original medieval bells can still be seen in the permanent **exhibition** (Mon-Sat 8.30am-5.30pm, Sun 12.45-5.30pm; £1), also in the gateway, while through another of the gateway's doors is the **Lapidarium**, housing a number of stone treasures including another example of a ring-cross stone, similar to the one that stands in the wall by the National Trust office at Martin's Haven (see p143).

Round the back of the cathedral are the remains of the **Bishop's Palace** (☎ 01437-720517; Apr-Oct daily 9am-5pm, Nov-Mar Mon-Sat 9.30am 4pm, Sun 11am-4pm; £3 adults, £2.60 concessions). Largely constructed by Bishop Henry de Gower (1328-47), the palace, with its arcaded parapets, state rooms and an impressive Great Hall complete with intact wheel window, speaks eloquently of the wealth and luxury that the early bishops enjoyed – a far cry, it must be said, from the frugal lifestyle of St David himself!

It is well worth trying to catch the atmospheric sound of the bells ringing out across the dell. The local bellringers practise their pealing on Wednesdays and Fridays between 7.45 and 9pm. For something even more moving try getting a ticket for the Cathedral Festival of Classical Music (see p26) which is held at the end of May and beginning of June each year. The acoustics of the building make for an unforgettable concert.

Guided tours (🖳 cathedraltours@yahoo.co.uk; £4 donation requested) are available.

life. Summer is a different matter as hundreds come to this remote pilgrimage site.

You can book a **boat trip** around the RSPB reserve of Ramsey Island or take a trip to see whales and dolphins with Voyages of Discovery or with Thousand Islands Expeditions, who actually land on the island. For more information on Ramsey Island and boat trips there see box p163.

Services

As mentioned before, once past St David's you won't find another shop or bank until Fishguard (40 miles, 64km away) so think carefully about what you will need for the next few days.

Oriel y Parc, the **National Park Visitor and Education Centre** (☎ 01437-720392, 🖳 www.orielyparc.co.uk; Easter-Oct daily 9.30am-5.30pm, Nov-Easter daily 10am-4.30pm) is also home to the **tourist information centre**, an **art gallery** exhibiting world-class and local artwork (exhibitions change) and works by Graham Sutherland. There is also a kidszone, a **shop** selling local crafts and books and a *café*. There are also public **toilets** and **phone boxes**. If you are coming up the lane from Caerfai Bay you will see the rather impressive glass-fronted TIC on the left where the lane joins the main road entering St David's.

Cross Sq is the hub of the city. There are a number of **banks** around Cross Sq including HSBC and Lloyds, both of which boast cashpoints, and a **chemist** for any blister problems. The **post office** (☎ 01437-720283; Mon-Fri 9am-5.30pm, Sat 9am-1pm), which is in a **shop** (Mon-Sat 6.45am-5.30pm, Sun 6.45am-12.30pm), and main

supermarket, CK's Foodstore (Mon-Sat 7am-10pm, Sun 10am-4pm) meanwhile, are on New St, just a short walk away.

For **internet access**, visit The Bench (see p170) on the High St, which is pricey (£1 for 20 mins, £2.75 per hour) but the connection is fast. The tourist office also offers internet facilities and it's slightly cheaper too at £1 for 30 mins.

Just off Cross Sq, a good place to replace any holey socks or buy any camping equipment is **TYF** (☎ 01437-721611, 🖳 www.tyf.com, 1 High St, Mon-Sat 9am-5.30pm, Sun 10am-4pm). This is also the place to go for an adrenaline rush since they run sessions on a variety of outdoor activities from surfing (see box p154) and canoeing to climbing and coasteering (see box below).

On the other side of the road, **Belmont House** (☎ 01437 720264, 🖳 www.belmonthouseshop.co.uk; daily 10am-5pm, longer in the main season) is a second decent outdoor shop selling a range of useful equipment including Coleman fuel.

Ma Sime's Surf Hut (☎ 01437-720433, 🖳 www.masimes.co.uk; 28 High St; daily 10am-5.30pm) rents out wetsuits and surfboards and can arrange surfing lessons if you fancy a break from walking. Lessons lasting two and a half hours cost £30.

Transport

St David's is well served in terms of **buses** as it is on the route for the Puffin Shuttle, Strumble Shuttle and Celtic Coaster bus services. Richards Bros/Summerdale's No 411 also stops here. There are stops on New St, Goat St and at Grove Car Park and City Hall. For further information see the public transport map and table on pp44-7.

❏ Coasteering

Coasteering is a real hands-on approach to exploring the Pembrokeshire coastline but is not a sport that everyone will be familiar with. It involves traversing sheer sea cliffs by scrambling, climbing, jumping off ledges into the churning sea and getting very wet. It makes quite a change from simply walking along the cliff tops and certainly provides more of an adrenaline rush. For guidance on how to do it properly **TYF** (see above), who claim to have invented this fast-growing sport, offer day courses around the cliffs of the St David's peninsula.

For a **taxi** try Frank (☎ 01437-721731), Tony (☎ 01437-720931), or Bob (☎ 01437-720987).

Where to stay

Thanks to the city's fame as a popular tourist and pilgrimage site St David's is full of places to stay.

Just off the High St on Anchor Drive is *The Waterings* (☎ 01437-720876, 🖳 www .waterings.co.uk; 2D/4F, all en suite), which charges £37.50-40 per person. Two of the family rooms sleep three people and the other two sleep four. Several of the rooms also have a sitting area.

For a place with more character the friendly little *Pen Albro* (☎ 01437-721865, 1S/1T/1D; shared facilities), 18 Goat St, offers very comfortable beds for just £25 per person and a hearty breakfast to boot. It's also just a short stagger away from one of the best pubs in town.

On the High St try either *Bryn Awel* (☎ 01437-720082, 🖳 www.brynawel-bb.co .uk; 2D), which has en suite – if slightly cramped – rooms from £32.50/pp for two sharing, or the smart *Coach House* (☎ 01437-720632, 🖳 coach_house15@yahoo .co.uk; 1T or D/1F, all with private facilities), at No 15, which charges £25 for room only; breakfast is not served. They also boast a delightful little cottage (1D, en suite) round the back which two people can stay in for £60 but it can sleep up to four (£120).

Alternatively *Grove Hotel* (☎ 01437-720341, 🖳 www.grovestdavids.co.uk; 2T/4D/one suite, all en suite) charges £90-95 (single occupancy £65).

On Cross Sq *The Square Gallery B&B* (☎ 01437-720333; 1S or T/1D, both en suite) charges from £40 per person. Rooms contain works of art by the proprietor.

More beds can be found along Nun St: at No 7, *Glendower Guesthouse* (☎ 01437-721650; 4D/4T or F, all en suite) which has B&B from £25-35 per person (£25-55 single occupancy); while further down the road, at No 43, is *Alandale Guesthouse* (☎ 01437-720404, 🖳 www.stdavids.co.uk/guesthouse/ alandale.htm; 1S/3D/1T) which has en suite rooms from £36 per person; *Y-Glennydd Hotel* (☎ 01437-720576, 🖳 www.yglenny

dd.co.uk; 2S/1T/5D/2F, all en suite), at No 51, has rooms from £32.50 per person, or £37.50 for a single; and *Y-Gorlan* (☎ 01437-720837, 🖳 www.stdavids.co.uk/gorlan; 1S/2D/1T/1F, all en suite), at No 77, charges £32.50-37.50/pp for two sharing, the single costs £35-40.

Sitting all on its own in a quiet location south-west of the city on the lane to Porthclais, the smart *Ramsey House* (☎ 01437-720321, 🖳 www.ramseyhouse.co .uk; Lower Moor; 3D/3T, all with private facilities) offers B&B from £45 per person (single occupancy £60-90).

If money is no obstacle and you fancy the height of luxury consider *Warpool Court Hotel* (☎ 01437-720300, 🖳 www .warpoolcourthotel.com; 3S/16D or T/3F), off Goat St. The cheapest single room will set you back around £95 whilst doubles go for £140 and up, with discounts if you're staying for more than one night.

For a touch of class at a more affordable price go to Cross Sq where the grand *Old Cross Hotel* (☎ 01437-720387, 🖳 www.old crosshotel.co.uk; 2S/7T/6D/1F, all en suite) has rooms from £70 to £110 (£40-65 for a single).

Where to eat and drink

There are all sorts of places to eat in St David's, although many of them can be a bit on the expensive side. For something a bit different dine at *The Refectory* (☎ 01437-721760; daily Easter-Sep 10am-5pm, Jul-Sep also 5.30-8.30pm, Oct-Easter daily winter 11am-4pm) inside the cathedral. The interior of St Mary's Hall has been refurbished and modernised to provide a bright airy space in which to have a hot drink or snack, although it also serves good-value, full evening meals (around £12 for a main course and glass of wine) during the summer.

Pebbles Yard Espresso Bar (☎ 01437-720122; daily 9am-5.30pm), also on The Square, is an atmospheric, cosy place serving coffee and cakes as well as sandwiches and smoothies. It's above a gallery and gift shop.

On the same street, *Jones Café* (☎ 01437-721001; summer Mon-Sat 8am-

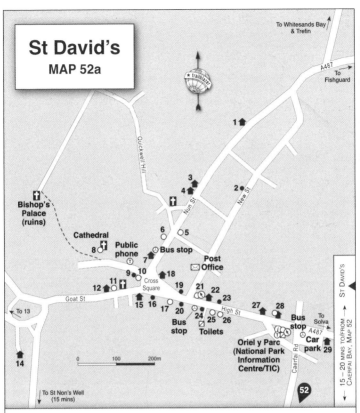

St David's
MAP 52a

To Whitesands Bay & Trefin

A487 To Fishguard

Bishop's Palace (ruins)

Cathedral

Quickwell Hill

Nun St

New St

1

3
4

2

Public phone

6
5

8

Bus stop

Post Office

7
9 10
18

Cross Square

11
12

Goat St

15 16
17 20
19
21 22
23

High St

27 28

Bus stop
Toilets

Bus stop

24 25 26

To Solva
A487

Car park
29

Caerfai Rd

Oriel y Parc (National Park Information Centre/TIC)

52

To 13

To St Non's Well (15 mins)

To Whitesands Bay

14

0   100   200m

ST DAVID'S

15 — 20 MINS TO/FROM CAERFAI BAY, MAP 52

Where to stay
1 Y-Gorlan
3 Y Glennydd Hotel
4 Alandale Guesthouse
7 Glendower Guesthouse
12 Pen Albro
13 Ramsey House
14 Warpool Court Hotel
15 The Square Gallery B&B
18 Old Cross Hotel
22 Coach House
27 Bryn Awel
28 Grove Hotel
29 The Waterings

Where to eat
5 Morgan's Restaurant
6 The Sampler

8 The Refectory (in Cathedral)
10 Pebbles Yard Espresso Bar
11 Farmers Arms
17 Dyfed Café
21 The Bench
25 Jones' Café
26 Cwtch
28 Orchard Restaurant

Other
2 CK's Foodstore
9 Thousand Island Expeditions
16 Chemist
19 TYF; Voyages of Discovery
20 Belmont House Outdoor Shop
23 Food & Wine Delicatessen
24 Ma Sime's Surf Hut

5pm, Sun 9am-5pm, Tue-Sun 6pm to late; winter hours may vary) serves a full Welsh breakfast (£5.25-6.50; vegetarian breakfast £5.50) and in the evening becomes a reasonably priced unlicensed restaurant where you can bring your own alcohol.

Further up the road is *Cwtch* (☎ 01437-720491; daily 6-9.30pm, Nov-Easter Tue-Sun 6-9pm), a place that might be short of vowels (the name means 'snug', 'cosy' or 'to hug' in Welsh) but is not short of some delicious meals, including pork belly and Trealy Farm sausages with Welsh black pudding, or wild sea trout with cockle cake and marsh samphire. They charge £23 for two courses, £28 for three.

At the top of the street virtually opposite the tourist office, Grove Hotel (see Where to stay) offers a selection of bar meals and nibbles as well as finer fare in their *Orchard Restaurant* (daily noon-3pm & 6-9pm), where the menu changes regularly.

The long-established *Morgan's Restaurant* (☎ 01437-720508, 🖳 www .morgans-restaurant.co.uk; Apr-Oct Wed-Mon 6.30-9pm, Nov-Mar Thur-Mon but check in advance; 20 Nun St) changes the menu according to the season. Their duo of new season Pembrokeshire lamb (£17.95) is extremely tasty.

For good pub grub head down Goat St to one of the best pubs in town, the *Farmers Arms* (food served daily noon-2.30pm & 6-9pm), which often serves a fine fish chowder and has a small beer garden overlooking the cathedral in which to enjoy their range of real ales.

A lovely little coffee shop is *The Sampler* (☎ 01437-720757, 🖳 www.sam plertearoom.co.uk; 17 Nun St; Mar-Oct, Mon-Thur 10.30am-5pm plus some weekends) with friendly service and an open fire. They serve home-made cakes (Welsh cakes are only 75p), as well as filling jacket potatoes and toasties, both from £4.70.

Fish and chips to take away can be found at *Dyfed Café* (☎ 01437-720250; Mon-Sat noon-8pm, summer Sun noon-8pm), opposite TYF outdoor shop.

No summary of the St David's food scene would be complete, however, without mentioning *The Bench* (☎ 01437-721778, 🖳 www.bench-bar.co.uk; summer daily 9am-9pm, rest of year Mon-Sat 9am-9pm, Sun 9am-4pm; lunch served daily noon-3pm), a wonderfully friendly and busy café-cum-restaurant.

Open during the day for snacks including some delicious paninis, pizzas, pasta, hot drinks and their award-winning ice cream, after 6pm they serve some surprisingly sophisticated meals; in the summer they specialise in fish, such as crab and laverbread cakes (£9.95), and in the winter months game including a delicious pheasant casserole (£11.95). Their apple and rhubarb crumble is the perfect way to round off any meal.

CAERFAI BAY TO WHITESANDS BAY   MAPS 52-55

This is a wonderful part of the coast. It is **8½ miles (14km, 3-4hrs)**, all of them beautiful, to yet another of Pembrokeshire's fantastic sandy beaches at Whitesands Bay. As the path ventures further west the scenery gets progressively wilder with a real sense of isolation out on the windswept headlands by Ramsey Sound.

From Caerfai Bay the path follows steep vegetated slopes to **St Non's Bay**, named after St David's mother. Here, just off the coast path, you can see the remains of **St Non's Chapel**, the birthplace of the patron saint and the **Holy Healing Well**. More low cliffs lead to the beautiful little harbour of **Porthclais** where you can see more fine examples of some lime kilns. At the wild and lonely **Porthlysgi Bay** a footpath heads north to the campsite at Pen-cnwc.

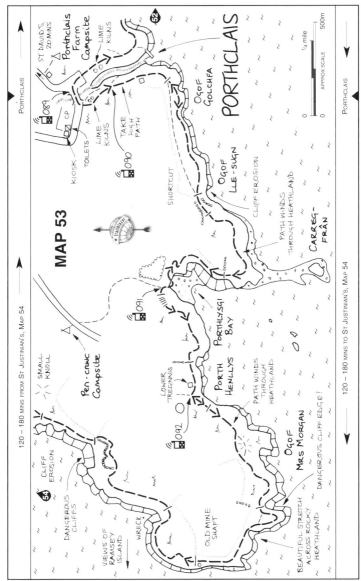

PORTHCLAIS   MAP 53, p171

This lonely stretch of wild coast is dotted with a number of coves and small bays with little in the way of accommodation. However, there are a few farms that offer camping and one or two B&Bs.

The Celtic Coaster **bus** (No 403) stops at Porthclais Harbour; see pp44-7 for details.

At Porthclais there is a seasonal National Trust **kiosk** that also sells ice creams, drinks and snacks and there are **toilets**.

There is a **campsite** at *Porthclais Farm* (☎ 01437-720256, 🖳 www.porth clais-farm-campsite.co.uk; Easter to end Oct; from £6 per adult) just up the road,

heading east from the inlet. You can also reach the campsite by cutting away from the coast path at various points before Porthclais Harbour and crossing into one of the camping fields. There's also a path that remains high above the harbour and curls round to access the site.

At **Porthlysgi Bay** you can leave the coast path and by heading north for half a mile on the public footpath reach *Pen-cnwc Campsite* (☎ 01437-720523, 🖳 www.flo ronpencnwc.co.uk; Apr-Sep) charging £5-6 per adult. The site has all the standard facilities. Advance booking is essential in July and August.

Staying on the coast path the terrain becomes progressively more barren and wild. Rocky knolls decorate the headland around the tiny cove of **Ogof Mrs Morgan** and low but precipitous cliffs form a twisting savage coastline. Above Ramsey Sound there are fine views over to Ramsey Island. Keep an eye out for seals on the shoreline and schools of dolphins and porpoises further out.

Once past the lifeboat station at **St Justinian's** take extra care along the level cliff top as the narrow path brushes the edge without warning on a number of occasions.

ST JUSTINIAN'S   MAP 54

There is a summer ferry to Ramsey Island (see box p163) and inland there's **camping** along the lane towards St David's at *Rhosson Ganol* (☎ 01437-720361; Apr-Oct), which charges from £5.50 per person.

The site has shower and toilet facilities.

The **Celtic Coaster** (No 403) bus stops by the car park; see public transport map and table on pp44-7 for details.

PORTHSELAU   MAP 54

At Porthselau Beach, at the southern end of Whitesands Bay, *Pencarnan Farm Caravan & Camping Park* (☎ 01437-720580, 🖳 www.pembrokeshire-camp ing.co.uk; Mar to early Jan) has a wonderful location overlooking the bay. They

charge £8-15 per person but only take bookings of a week or more during summer school holidays. They have a shower/toilet block as well as a **shop** (open daily all day) in the summer school holidays selling basic groceries and camping equipment.

Moving on around the headland the sands of **Whitesands Bay** come into view with the small rocky hills of **Carn Llidi** (see Map 56, p176; where there's a small Neolithic burial chamber) and Carn Perfedd behind.

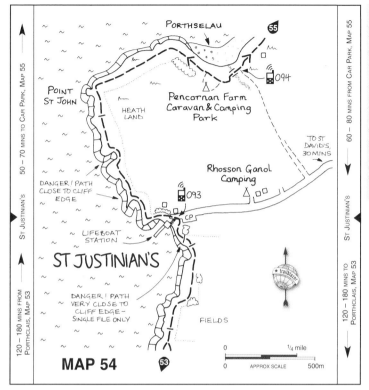

MAP 54

WHITESANDS BAY (PORTH MAWR)
MAP 55, p175

At the car park by Whitesands Bay there is a **phone box**, public **toilets** and a **drinking-water tap** but little else. The Celtic Coaster **bus** (No 403) stops by the beach; see pp44-7 for details.

With the closure of the only remaining B&B, *St David's Youth Hostel* (☎ 0845-371 9141, ✉ StDavids@yha.org.uk; Apr-Oct), which despite the name is not in St David's but here above Whitesands Bay, is the only accommodation in the area. It's in an old farmhouse in a great spot below the craggy hill called Carn Llidi. Accommodation is in the superbly renovated cowshed – which is a lot more salubrious than it sounds! – with 30 beds at £11.95

for members. The hostel is self-catering only; it has a small **shop** at the reception desk. To reach the hostel follow the lane up from the car park, turn left by the campsite, bear right then left to Upper Porthmawr and follow the footpath around the hillside.

Whitesands Beach Campsite (☎ 01437-721472; Mar-Oct) is on the left as you walk up from the car park. They charge £5 per person. The site has showers and toilet facilities.

The only place to get **food** is the large *café* (daily 10am-5pm, lunch served noon-2pm) in the surf shop at the top of Whitesands Bay car park; paninis and burgers cost from £4.25.

WHITESANDS BAY TO TREFIN   MAPS 55-60

ROUTE GUIDE AND MAPS

Once again the rugged coastline of the St David's peninsula makes this a wonderful but tough **11 miles (18km, 5-6hrs)**.

From the car park the path climbs up above cliffs and back down to the
sandy bay at **Porthmelgan**. For those staying at the youth hostel there is a
more direct route from the hostel that avoids having to return to the car park
(see Map 55).

From Porthmelgan the path crosses beautiful slopes of heather to the craggy **St David's Head** jutting into the Atlantic. The path can be rather indistinct
in places, crossing rocky heathland to some old fields enclosed by stone walls,
though as long as you keep the sea roughly to your left you can't go too far
wrong. The route takes a sharp right at **Penllechwen Head** and skirts the pretty coves and bays that make up the coastline until it reaches **Carn Penberry**
hill. This small hill is one of several igneous intrusions that crop up on this section of the coastline. Unfortunately, it's also one of the few that you can't walk
around; thus for the walker the only way past this obstacle is to climb over its
shoulder.

About two miles (3km) from Carn Penberry the path drops down into a
small gorge the other side of which there is a sign and footpath leading to *Celtic
Camping* (☎ 01348-837405, 🖳 www.celtic-camping.co.uk; Apr-Oct), Pwll
Caerog Farm, 500 metres from the coast path. They also have a barn with hostel-
type accommodation; bedding is provided and there are showers and kitchen
facilities; the rate is £12 per person. However, this is primarily for groups. The
campsite pitches are from £12 for a two-man tent (from £6 for a one-man tent).

At the beach of **Abereiddy** you can see the remains of the old quarrymen's
houses, destroyed by floods in the 1920s (see box below). As you climb up
above the bay you will see **The Blue Lagoon**, a flooded quarry, to the left.

❏ A lost industry

A number of ruins can be seen around Abereiddy and Porthgain, evidence of a once-
thriving industry. From around 1840 until the 1930s slate, brick and stone were quar-
ried on the cliff tops between the two villages where the old slag-heaps and evidence
of the tramway, which carried the slate from the quarry at Abereiddy to the harbour
at Porthgain, can still be seen. At Porthgain you can also see the restored brickworks
by the tiny harbour.

Look out too for the flooded slate quarry known as 'The Blue Lagoon' as you
climb up onto the cliffs above Abereiddy and the ruins of the quarrymen's houses by
Abereiddy Bay. The sad remains of these houses which were built in the 1840s are
testament to the great storm of January 14, 1938, when the swell of the sea severely
damaged five of the homes. The storm damage and an ensuing typhoid epidemic
effectively brought the local slate quarry industry to an end.

Yet even to this day the product of the quarry can be seen in Porthgain. One of
the boats carrying slate from Porthgain sank in Ramsey Sound. About 100 years later
the boat was found on the seabed and the slate was recovered to re-roof the houses of
Porthgain.

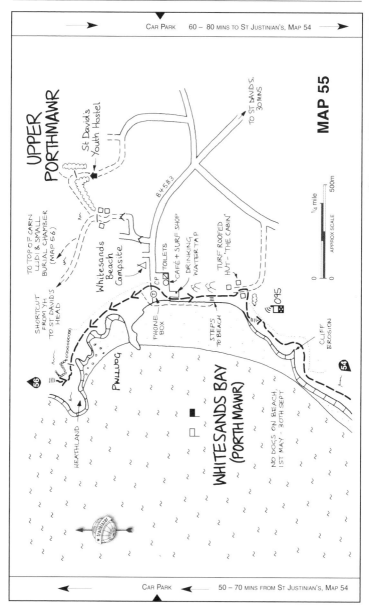

CAR PARK   60 – 80 MINS TO ST JUSTINIAN'S, MAP 54

MAP 55

UPPER PORTHMAWR

St David's Youth Hostel

B4583

TO ST DAVID'S, 30 MINS

¼ mile

APPROX SCALE

0   500m

TO TOP OF CARN LLIDI & SMALL BURIAL CHAMBER (MAP 56)

Whitesands Beach Campsite

CP

TOILETS

CAFÉ + SURF SHOP

DRINKING WATER TAP

TURF ROOFED HUT – "THE CABIN"

SHORTCUT FROM YH TO ST DAVID'S HEAD

56

HEATHLAND

Porthmawr

PHONE BOX

STEPS TO BEACH

CLIFF EROSION

54

WHITESANDS BAY (PORTH MAWR)

NO DOGS ON BEACH, 1ST MAY - 30TH SEPT

095

CAR PARK   50 – 70 MINS FROM ST JUSTINIAN'S, MAP 54

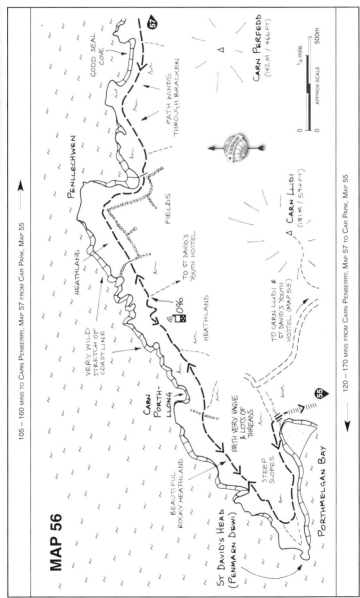

MAP 56

105 – 160 MINS TO CARN PENBERRY, MAP 57 FROM CAR PARK, MAP 55

120 – 170 MINS FROM CARN PENBERRY, MAP 57 TO CAR PARK, MAP 55

GOOD SEAL COVE

PATH WINDS THROUGH BRACKEN

CARN PERFEDD
(142M / 466FT)

PENLLECHWEN

FIELDS

HEATHLAND

TO ST DAVID'S YOUTH HOSTEL

HEATHLAND

CARN LUDI
(181M / 594FT)

VERY WILD STRETCH OF COASTLINE

CARN PORTH-LLONG

TO CARN LUDI & ST DAVID'S YOUTH HOSTEL (MAP 55)

PATH VERY VAGUE & LOTS OF THREADS

STEEP SLOPES

BEAUTIFUL ROCKY HEATHLAND

ST DAVID'S HEAD (PENMAEN DEWI)

PORTHMELGAN BAY

0 500m
0 ¼ mile
APPROX SCALE

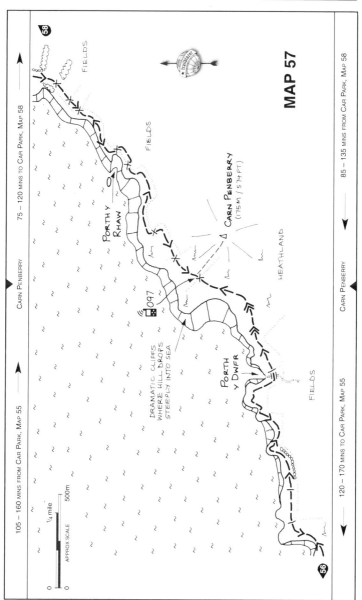

MAP 57

105 – 160 MINS FROM CAR PARK, MAP 55

75 – 120 MINS TO CAR PARK, MAP 58

85 – 135 MINS FROM CAR PARK, MAP 58

120 – 170 MINS TO CAR PARK, MAP 55

CARN PENBERRY

CARN PENBERRY

58

56

FIELDS

FIELDS

FIELDS

FIELDS

PORTH Y RHAW

CARN PENBERRY
(175M / 574FT)

HEATHLAND

DRAMATIC CLIFFS
WHERE HILL DROPS
STEEPLY INTO SEA

PORTH Y DWFR

1097

1/4 mile

500m

APPROX SCALE

0

0

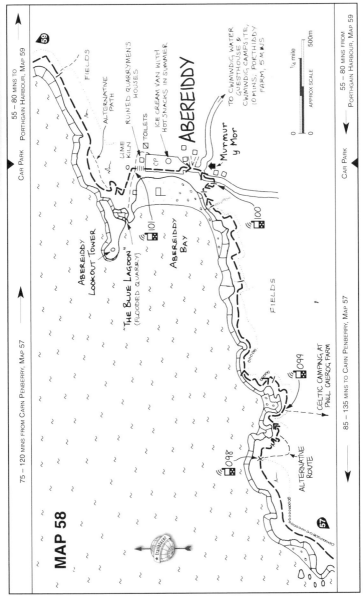

MAP 58

FIELDS

ALTERNATIVE PATH

RUINED QUARRYMEN'S HOUSES

LIME KILN

TOILETS

ICE CREAM VAN WITH HOT SNACKS IN SUMMER

ABEREIDDY

CP

TO CWMWDIG WATER (GUESTHOUSE & CWMWDIG CAMPSITE, 10 MINS; PORTHIDDY FARM, 5 MINS)

Murmur y Mor

ABEREIDDY LOOKOUT TOWER

"THE BLUE LAGOON" (FLOODED QUARRY)

101

ABEREIDDY BAY

100

FIELDS

099

CELTIC CAMPING AT PWLL CAEROG FARM

098

ALTERNATIVE ROUTE

57

0   ¼ mile
APPROX SCALE
0   500m

ABEREIDDY   MAP 58

Don't expect to find much at this hamlet. In the summer there is usually an ice-cream van in the beach car park selling **drinks and hot snacks**, as well as ice creams. At the far end of the car park is a public **toilet**.

The **Strumble Shuttle** bus (summer only) stops in the car park; see public transport map and table, pp44-7 for details.

Celtic Camping (see p174), one mile back along the coast path, offers camping and bunkbarn accommodation.

Open Easter to early October only, *Murmur y Mor Guest House* (☎ 01348-831670; 1D/1T, all with private facilities) has beds from £30 per person.

A mile up the hill from the bay is *Cwmwdig Water Guesthouse* (☎ 01348-831434, 🖳 www.cwmwdigwater.co.uk; 1T/2D/1F) which has B&B in converted farmhouse barns from £30 per person or £35 in an en suite room (some of the rooms

are en suite and the others have private facilities). If requested in advance they will serve a walker's supper (such as soup and baguette) for anyone who doesn't have a car.

Next door, *Cwmwdig Campsite* (also known as *Camping and Caravanning Club at St David's*; ☎ 01348-831376 before 8pm, 🖳 www.thefriendlyclub.co.uk; Apr-Sep) is run by the Camping and Caravanning Club of Great Britain. Each of the 40 pitches costs from £6.60 to £7.49 per person plus a £6.46 pitch fee for non-members. It's always advisable to book in advance.

To get to Cwmwdig from the coast path climb up the lane for about five minutes. Just past Porthiddy Farm take the public footpath on the right. This takes you up to the guesthouse, a big peach-coloured building by the road junction, and the campsite.

The path follows a nice level cliff top around the beautiful beach of **Traeth-Llywn** and past a few coves to arrive at some old quarry buildings, slate slag heaps and evidence of the old mine tramway on the cliffs above the village of **Porthgain**.

PORTHGAIN   MAP 59, p181

This is an unusual little place with a great pub, a modern café and an explosion of art galleries. Up on the hill is a disused stone quarry that hints at the stone industry of the 19th century. The tiny harbour was used to export stone for building projects elsewhere. Nowadays the village is home to tourists and artists, whose work can often be seen in **Harbour Lights Gallery**. The **Strumble Shuttle** (No 404) bus stops by The Sloop Inn; see pp45-6 for details.

The Sloop Inn (☎ 01348-831449, 🖳 www.sloop.co.uk) is one of the best pubs on the whole trail. Easily spotted on the far side as you drop down into the village, it usually has a trail of smoke coming from the chimney. It is a lovely rustic old inn dating from 1743. In the past it was, no doubt, a popular haunt for the quarrymen but is now a regular stop-off for coast-path walkers.

The inn does good **food** daily (breakfast 9.30-11am, lunch noon-2.30pm, school summer holidays limited menu 3-5pm, evening meals 6-9.30pm) and the bar is open daily 9.30am-11pm. All in all, an essential stop on the coast path.

Decent competition for The Sloop is provided by *The Shed Wine Bar & Bistro* (☎ 01348-831518, 🖳 www.theshedporthgain.co.uk; summer daily 10.30am-4.30pm & 6.30-9pm, winter Wed-Mon 10.30am-4.30pm but hours may vary, Fri, Sat & Sun eves; booking essential for the evening at any time of the year), which has won various awards – and deservedly so, as this family-run establishment not only cook the fish, they catch their crab and lobster from their own boat! All the fish is locally caught; on Monday they serve great fish and chips for around £8.50 whilst the rest of the week the dishes are dependent on

ROUTE GUIDE AND MAPS

what's caught but expect delicious seafood and shellfish, with main courses from £18.95. The bouillabaisse at £21.95 is pricey but worth treating yourself with.

Accommodation in Porthgain is thin on the ground. *Ynys Barry* (☎ 01348-831180, 🖥 www.ynysbarry.com; 3D/1T) is a series of holiday cottages, let on a minimum three-night basis, a week in the school summer holidays, and twin or double-room en suite lodges that can be rented for one

night for £60 (no reduction for single occupancy). During the school summer holiday rooms in the lodges are only let for a minimum of two nights.

Breakfast is not offered, other than fruit and cereal bars, but as you can have breakfast at The Sloop Inn that's not a problem. Because of the shortage of accommodation in the area if the owners are not busy they are prepared to pick walkers up if they want to stay here for a second night.

From Porthgain the path follows gentle cliffs to the little bay of **Aber Draw**. This is the first of the access routes to Trefin, climbing up the steep road ahead, but if you're not staying at Caerhafod Lodge (see below), a better idea is to continue along the coast path until you see the signpost for the youth hostel; this is near the cliffs at Trwyn Llwyd. The footpath here is the best way into **Trefin**.

TREFIN   MAP 60, p183

Trefin (pronounced 'Tre-feen', like 'ravine') is a quiet little village sitting on top of a windswept hill. It feels as if you have stepped back in time when you first set foot in the place and is worth visiting either for a quick pint or an overnight stop.

Services

The **post office**, which has rather irregular opening times, is not very obvious. It's the small pebble-dashed bungalow on the left as you enter the village by the steep road from the coast. Be warned that there is no shop in the village.

Both the Strumble Shuttle (No 404) and Richards Brothers No 413 **bus** services (Mon-Sat only) call in en route between St David's and Fishguard; for further details see the public transport map and table, see pp44-7.

Where to stay

Prendergast Caravan Park (☎ 01348-831368, 🖥 www.prendergastcaravanpark .co.uk; Apr-Sep) has a small sheltered **campsite** suitable for six to ten tents; for this reason it is best to book in advance during the school summer holidays. The site

has a toilet and shower block as well as laundry facilities. Rates are £8-9 per night for two adults.

The former YHA hostel has reopened as *The Old School Hostel* (☎ 01348-831800, 🖥 www.theoldschoolhostel.co .uk). Arty and quirky, it has six rooms accommodating up to 25 people in various formations; dorm-style accommodation starts at £11 if you're walking, cycling or using public transport. They can also arrange doubles and twins (£14-18/pp), or single rooms (£18-28). Family rooms sleeping up to five are £42.

Breakfast (with as much organic and locally sourced produce as possible; their porridge is recommended) is available for £5 as are packed lunches (if possible request these in advance). They have a self-catering kitchen, a drying room and they also offer towel hire and free **internet access**.

Caerhafod Lodge (Map 59; ☎ 01348-837859, 🖥 www.caerhafod.co.uk; open all year) is a wonderful, friendly hostel with five en suite dormitories and a self-catering kitchen. It sleeps 23 people; £15 per person. From the point where the coast path joins the road before Trefin, follow the road uphill in the St David's direction; the hostel

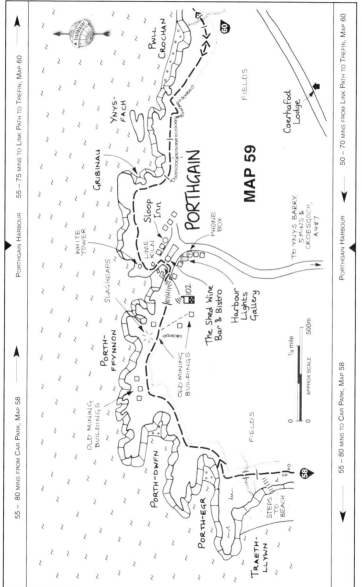

is about half a mile up the road on the left.

In the centre of the village there is B&B at *Hampton House* (☎ 01348-837701, 🖳 viv.kay@virgin.net; 1S/1T/1D) with rooms from £30 per person. The double has private facilities but the other rooms share.

Bryngarw Guest House (☎ 01348-831211, 🖳 www.bryngarwguesthouse.co .uk; Abercastle Rd; Feb-Oct; 4D/2T, all en suite) is on the edge of the village. B&B starts at £37.50 per person, with a £12.50 surcharge for single occupancy. Full-board prices including a four-course supper start at £60/pp.

Where to eat and drink
The *Ship Inn* (☎ 01348-831445; food daily noon-3pm & 6-9pm) is the last place for a pint before Goodwick 19 miles (30km) away. The food's only average, but it's filling.

TREFIN TO PWLL DERI   MAPS 60-63

These 9¹/₂ **miles (15km, 3¹/₂-4¹/₂hrs)** begin by following a beautiful line of snaking cliffs to the hamlet of **Abercastle** sitting at the end of yet another pretty cove. There are no facilities for the walker though the **Strumble Shuttle** (No 404) bus does stop here; see pp44-6 for details.

Just before Abercastle you should keep an eye out for the stones of **Carreg Sampson** marking the site of a neolithic burial chamber, or *cromlech*, dating back 5000 years. It is only a short detour from the coast path and is the most impressive cromlech on the path. Look out for the signpost just before the coast path drops down the steps to the cove.

From Abercastle the path climbs up through cliff-top fields and past the bay at **Pwllstrodur**. If you want to stop for a dip in the sea the beaches at **Abermawr** and **Aber-Bach** are nice enough but it's much better to wait until you get to Pwllcrochan.

Pwllcrochan is a fantastic location for a swim; well sheltered with a backdrop of sheer cliffs. It's all the more interesting because the only way to get to it is by climbing down a rope hanging over a short section of cliff. It's not quite as dangerous as it sounds but you should be careful as you climb down. (Note, this is not an official part of the route, nor is it recommended by the park authorities. As such, the author and publisher accept no responsibility for potential accidents.) Since climbing over cliffs isn't everybody's cup of tea the beach is usually pretty quiet. Look out for the path leading to the rope at the southern end of the bay.

After a swim it's back to the hard grind. The path climbs relentlessly uphill to gain the long ridge leading to Pwll Deri. This rugged ridge of heather and rocky bluffs provides great views of the Pembrokeshire countryside to the east but even more outstanding are the 100-metre (300ft) cliffs, covered in bracken and scrub, which plunge down into the sea. It all culminates in the wonderful circle of cliffs around **Pwll Deri**. If the weather's good, it's worth sitting down on top of the ridge to take in the view.

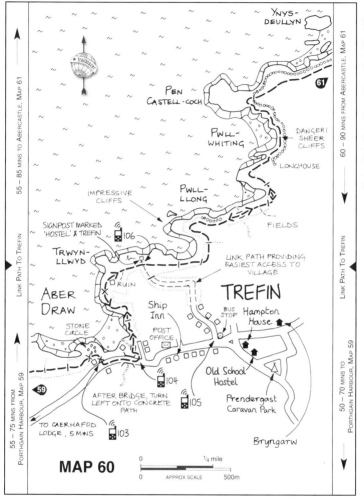

ROUTE GUIDE AND MAPS

YNYS-DEULLYN

61

PEN CASTELL-COCH

PWLL-WHITING

DANGER! SHEER CLIFFS

LONGHOUSE

PWLL-LLONG

FIELDS

IMPRESSIVE CLIFFS

SIGNPOST MARKED 'HOSTEL' & TREFIN ▥106

TRWYN-LLWYD

LINK PATH PROVIDING EASIEST ACCESS TO VILLAGE

RUIN

ABER DRAW

TREFIN

Ship Inn

BUS STOP

Hampton House

STONE CIRCLE

POST OFFICE ✉

59

▥104

AFTER BRIDGE, TURN LEFT ONTO CONCRETE PATH

▥105

Old School Hostel

Prendergast Caravan Park

TO CAERHAFOD LODGE, 5 MINS ▥103

Bryngarw

MAP 60

0 .... ¼ mile

0 .... 500m
APPROX SCALE

trailblazer

60 – 90 MINS FROM ABERCASTLE, MAP 61

LINK PATH TO TREFIN

50 – 70 MINS TO PORTHGAIN HARBOUR, MAP 59

55 – 85 MINS TO ABERCASTLE, MAP 61

LINK PATH TO TREFIN

55 – 75 MINS FROM PORTHGAIN HARBOUR, MAP 59

❏ **Important note – walking times**
Unless otherwise specified, **all times in this book refer only to the time spent walking**. You will need to add 20-30% to allow for rests, photography, checking the map, drinking water etc. When planning the day's hike count on 5-7 hours' actual walking.

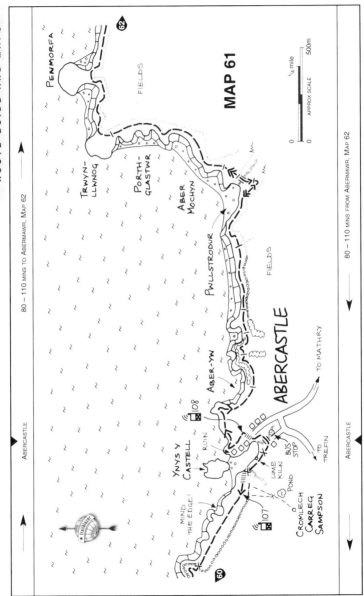

MAP 61

80 – 110 MINS TO ABERMAWR, MAP 62

80 – 110 MINS FROM ABERMAWR, MAP 62

ABERCASTLE

ABERCASTLE

PENMORFA

FIELDS

TRWYN-LLWNOG

PORTH-GLASTWR

ABER MOCHYN

PWLLSTRODUR

FIELDS

ABER-YN

ABERCASTLE

TO MATHRY

108

YNYS Y CASTELL

RUIN

MIND THE EDGE!

BUS STOP

TO TREFIN

LIME KILN

POND

CROMLECH CARREG SAMPSON

107

0   1/4 mile

APPROX SCALE

0   500m

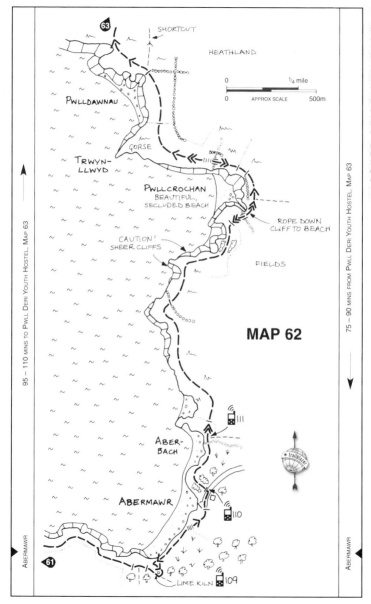

63

SHORTCUT

HEATHLAND

0   1/4 mile

0   APPROX SCALE   500m

PWLLDAWNAU

GORSE

TRWYN-
LLWYD

PWLLCROCHAN
BEAUTIFUL,
SECLUDED BEACH

ROPE DOWN
CLIFF TO BEACH

CAUTION!
SHEER CLIFFS

FIELDS

MAP 62

ABER-
BACH

ABERMAWR

110

61

LIME KILN   109

95 – 110 MINS TO PWLL DERI YOUTH HOSTEL, MAP 63

75 – 90 MINS FROM PWLL DERI YOUTH HOSTEL, MAP 63

ABERMAWR

ABERMAWR

trailblazer

ROUTE GUIDE AND MAPS

PWLL DERI   **MAP 63**

Directly above the cliffs at Pwll Deri is *Pwll Deri Youth Hostel* (☎ 0845-371 9536; Apr-Oct, 29 beds). It is surely one of the most impressive locations for a youth hostel, sitting precariously 125 metres (410ft) above the sea. It can be found just off the lane that skirts the cliff tops. After a hard day's walk, sitting in the conservatory with your dinner admiring the sun setting over the sea is a great way to chill out. On a clear day you can see southern Ireland. The hostel is self-catering only and charges £9.95 each for YHA members.

PWLL DERI TO FISHGUARD   MAPS 63-68

The coast along these **10½ miles (17km, 4-5hrs)** is wild and in places rough going. The cliffs are less sheer and sometimes relatively low but they are rugged and hide countless rocky coves and bays.

The path begins by crossing through wild country of rocky hillocks, grass and heather, passing a barren headland with fine views all around. Parts of the trail here can be boggy when the weather is bad. Just past a narrow cleft in the cliffs the path comes to the car park at **Strumble Head** (Map 64) where the white lighthouse can be seen on the island just off the headland. The **Strumble Shuttle bus** (No 404) stops at the car park; see pp44-6 for details.

The path continues through heathland and bracken to **Porthsychan Bay**, three miles (5km) further north, where a footpath heads inland for *Fferm Tresinwen* (☎ 01348-891238) where there is **camping** for a pittance (just £2 per night for one and £4 per night for two people and a tent). Alternatively follow the road inland from Strumble Head for about a mile. At **Carreg Wastad Point** make sure you take the quick detour to the top of the heathery hill to see the stone commemorating the last invasion of Britain (see box below).

Around the bay of **Aber-Felin** the path passes through some pretty woodland before winding its way up and over rough hillocks with the cliffs becoming less severe, eventually tapering to gentle heathery slopes at **Penanglas**. Here the path swings southwards through a number of old fields before joining the residential road, New Hill.

As the road starts to descend more steeply, a zig-zagging path drops down onto Quay Rd which leads into the centre of **Goodwick**.

❏ **The last invasion of Britain**

On 22 February 1797 four French sailing vessels, led by the American Colonel Tate, anchored off Carreg Wastad Head, west of Fishguard. This was the beginning of the last invasion of Britain, a somewhat half-hearted and short-lived affair. The 1400 or so Frenchmen occupied the stretch of coast around Strumble Head for a grand total of two days. The story goes that they got so drunk on stolen beer that the locals soon overpowered them, and they finally surrendered on the sands of Goodwick on 24 February 1797.

The hero of the whole affair was one Jemima Nicholas who, to this day, is something of a local folk hero. Armed with her pitchfork she single-handedly rounded up 12 Frenchmen and is now honoured by having a local ale named after her. A memorial stone to the last invasion stands at Carreg Wastad Point (see Map 65).

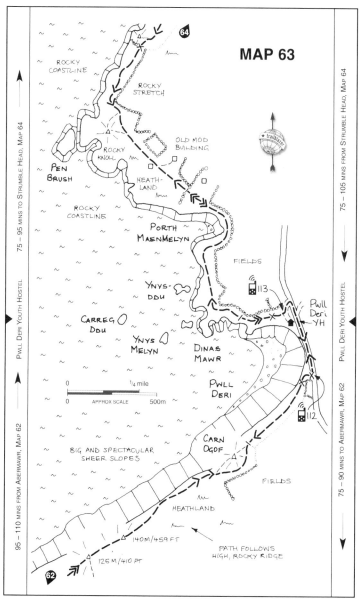

MAP 63

ROCKY
COASTLINE

ROCKY
STRETCH

OLD MOD
BUILDING

ROCKY
KNOLL

PEN
BRUSH

HEATH-
LAND

ROCKY
COASTLINE

PORTH
MAENMELYN

FIELDS

YNYS-
DDU

113

CARREG
DDU

YNYS
MELYN

DINAS
MAWR

PWLL
DERI

Pwll
Deri
YH

0   ¼ mile

0   APPROX SCALE   500m

CARN
OGOF

112

BIG AND SPECTACULAR
SHEER SLOPES

FIELDS

HEATHLAND

△ 140M/459 FT

PATH FOLLOWS
HIGH, ROCKY RIDGE

△ 125 M/410 PT

62

75 – 95 MINS TO STRUMBLE HEAD, MAP 64

PWLL DERI YOUTH HOSTEL

95 – 110 MINS FROM ABERMAWR, MAP 62

75 – 105 MINS FROM STRUMBLE HEAD, MAP 64

PWLL DERI YOUTH HOSTEL

75 – 90 MINS TO ABERMAWR, MAP 62

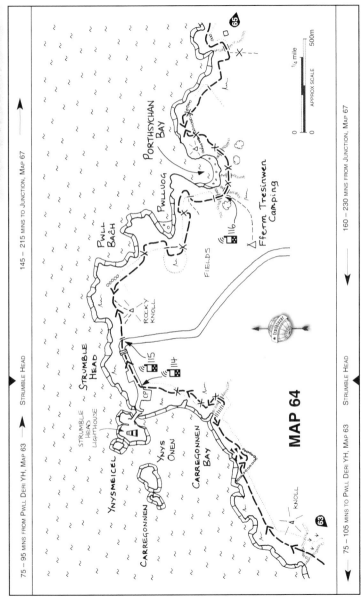

ROUTE GUIDE AND MAPS

75 – 95 MINS FROM PWLL DERI YH, MAP 63 ——→ STRUMBLE HEAD

145 – 215 MINS TO JUNCTION, MAP 67

160 – 230 MINS FROM JUNCTION, MAP 67

75 – 105 MINS TO PWLL DERI YH, MAP 63   STRUMBLE HEAD

MAP 64

¼ mile

APPROX SCALE

0   500m

PORTHSYCHAN BAY

PWLLUOG

Fferm Tresinwen Camping

116

FIELDS

PWLL BACH

ROCKY KNOLL

115   114

STRUMBLE HEAD

STRUMBLE HEAD LIGHTHOUSE

YNYSMEICEL

YNYS ONEN

CARREGONNEN BAY

CARREGONNEN

KNOLL

65

63

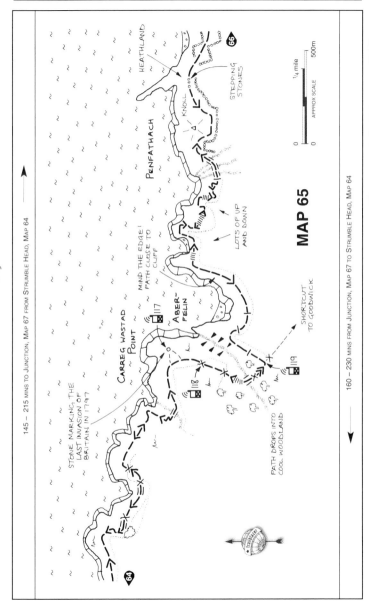

145 – 215 MINS TO JUNCTION, MAP 67 FROM STRUMBLE HEAD, MAP 64

160 – 230 MINS FROM JUNCTION, MAP 67 TO STRUMBLE HEAD, MAP 64

MAP 65

HEATHLAND

66

STEPPING STONES

PENFATHACH

KNOLL

LOTS OF UP AND DOWN

MIND THE EDGE! PATH CLOSE TO CLIFF

117

ABER-FELIN

SHORTCUT TO GOODWICK

118

119

PATH DROPS INTO COOL WOODLAND

CARREG WASTAD POINT

STONE MARKING THE LAST INVASION OF BRITAIN IN 1797

64

¼ mile

500m

0

0

APPROX SCALE

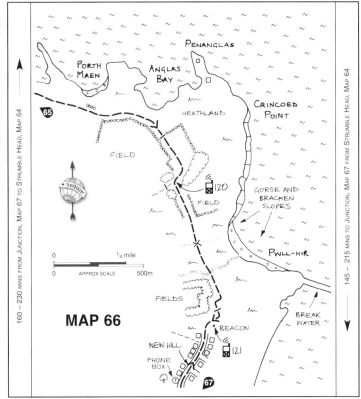

MAP 66

GOODWICK (WDIG)   MAP 67

Goodwick is often considered to be an extension of Fishguard but it's really a separate town. Its main claim to fame is its role as a ferry port, shipping holidaymakers to and from Ireland. It may be somewhat overshadowed by its bigger twin but it does have plenty of eating places and accommodation, most notably the very grand Fishguard Bay Hotel, originally built for passengers when the ferry route to Ireland opened in 1906.

Since then it has been used to house the film crew of *Moby Dick* which was filmed in Lower Fishguard, and, later, the men who constructed one of the Milford Haven oil refineries.

Services

The **tourist information centre** (☎ 01348-872037,   ⌨ fishguardharbour.tic@pembrokeshire.gov.uk; Apr-Oct daily 9.30am-5pm, to 6pm in the school summer holidays, Nov-Mar daily 10am-4pm) is in the **Ocean Lab Centre** (daily 10am-5pm) on Fishguard Rd. There is also an **internet café** (£2 for 30 minutes), though internet access is free in the library in Fishguard (see p192).

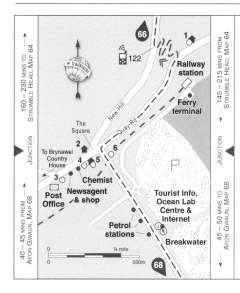

Goodwick
(Wdig)

MAP 67

Where to stay
1 Fishguard Bay Hotel
2 Glendower Hotel
5 Hope & Anchor

Where to eat
1 Fishguard Bay Hotel
3 No 10 Café
4 Farmhouse Kitchen
5 Hope & Anchor
6 Gary's Takeaway

As you come into the town centre you will see a **chemist** next to a small **shop and newsagent**.

A little further on is the **post office** (☎ 01348-872842; Mon, Tue, Thur, Fri 9am-5.30pm, Wed & Sat to 1pm) which is in a **shop** (Mon-Fri 7.30am-6pm, Sat 7.30am-7.30pm Sun 7.30am-1pm).

Transport
The **Strumble Shuttle** (No 404) bus stops in The Square; the No 410 town service also runs from The Square to Fishguard; the No 413 runs between Fishguard and St David's. Fishguard **train station** is actually here in Goodwick, by the ferry terminal. The train service is timed to coincide with the arrival of the ferry. See the public transport map and table, pp44-7.

Goodwick is where the **ferry** leaves for Ireland. Adventurous sorts could take a day-trip over to sample the Guinness. The catamaran takes less than two hours to Rosslare while the ferry takes under four hours. Passenger-only fares start from £25 on the ferry. Contact Stenaline Ferries (see box p42) for further details.

Where to stay
In the centre of town *Glendower Hotel* (☎ 01348-872873, 🖳 glendowerhotel@hotmail.com; 3S/1D/6T/1F, all en suite) charges £39 for a single, doubles/twins are £34.50/pp for two sharing. Also by The Square is *The Hope & Anchor Inn* (☎ 01348-872314; 🖳 www.hopeandanchorinn.co.uk; 4D/1F sleeping four, all en suite) with very smart rooms with flat-screen TVs; they charge from £70 per room, £55 single occupancy for walkers.

On top of the hill, about half a mile from town, is the very welcoming *Brynawel Country House* (☎ 01348-874155, 🖳 lloyd@westwalesmail.co.uk; 2T or D/1F, all with private facilities). They will provide a pick-up/drop-off service for walkers who are booked to stay with them so you can even base yourself here for several days while tackling the entire northern section of the coast path: contact them for details. What's more, if you are coming by car, they will keep your car in a safe place for the duration of your stay. The rate is £30-32 per person for B&B; single occupancy costs £40 but rates are negotiable for stays of longer than one night. They are able to provide packed lunches if requested in advance.

For complete pampered luxury (though at a price), *Fishguard Bay Hotel* (☎ 01348-873571, 🖳 www.fishguardbay hotel.co.uk; 10S/27T/14D/4D or F/four suites, all en suite) is a grandiose building set in woodland at the end of Quay Rd. Built over a century ago when a room would set you back five shillings, these days B&B starts at £62.50 for a single (£75-80 for single occcupancy) or £90-100 (the exact tariff depending on whether you've got a sea view) in a double. A suite costs £150. They also have dinner, bed & breakfast rates. Make sure you wipe your hiking boots before you enter.

Where to eat and drink
On the corner of The Square is the *Hope and Anchor* (see Where to stay; food served daily 11.30am-3.30pm & 6-11pm) with basic but good value and tasty fare.

Next door is the *Farmhouse Kitchen* (Tue-Sat 7-10pm) where the menu is constantly changing. They do a good three-course menu for £13.95 (£18.50 on Fri and Sat evening). Continuing past these, near the post office is the *No 10 Café*, offering sandwiches and simple snacks. *Gary's Takeaway* (☎ 01348-873616; daily 5-10.30pm) serves fish and chips.

At the other end of the spectrum is the restaurant (daily 7-8.45pm) at *Fishguard Bay Hotel* (see Where to stay), which is open to non-residents. The bar menu is served Mon-Sat noon-1.45pm & daily 6.30-8.45pm. On Sundays lunch (noon-1.45pm) is served in both the bar and the restaurant.

Once past the information centre the coast path follows the tarmac path known as **Marine Walk**, though it is now signposted Pembrokeshire Coast Path. This effectively bypasses much of the residential part of Fishguard. Arriving at Slade, a small lane lined with pretty cottages, you have a choice: left and down to continue along the route to Lower Fishguard (see p194), where the Afon Gwaun drains the Cwm Gwaun valley and the Preseli Hills; or up and right to bring you into the centre of the main part of **Fishguard**, which sits on high ground above Fishguard Harbour.

FISHGUARD (ABERGWAUN)
Fishguard is a surprisingly amenable place. It is big enough to provide everything you need and small enough to maintain a quiet charm. This is the capital of 'Last Invasion Country' (see box p186); the peace treaty was signed at the Royal Oak Inn on Market Sq.

Services
Market Sq is the hub of the town. The **tourist information centre** (☎ 01437-776636, 🖳 fishguard.tic@pembrokeshire .gov.uk; Easter-Oct Mon-Fri 9.30am-5pm, Sat 10am-4pm, school summer holidays Sun 10am-4pm; Nov-Easter Mon-Sat 10am-4pm) is in the Town Hall on Market Square. They have two computer terminals and offer free **internet access** for 15 minutes but if you want longer or to be able to print out (a charge is made for this) it is best to go up to the library (☎ 01437-776638; Mon, Tue, Wed & Fri 9.30am-5.30pm, Thur 9.30am-6.30pm, Sat Apr-Sep 9.30am-5pm Oct-Mar 9-30am-1pm), also in the Town Hall, which has six terminals.

There is a **supermarket** on High St. The **post office** (Mon-Fri 9am-5.30pm, Sat to 12.30pm) is on West St. **Glan y Mor Art Gallery** (☎ 01348-874787; Mon/Tue/Thur/ Fri 10am-5pm, Wed 10am-1.30pm, Sat 10am-4pm; Jan-Mar please check in advance), West St, sells affordable Welsh art and crafts created by locals as well as jewellery and is worth a browse.

If you're searching for supplies on a Saturday the fortnightly **farmers' market** (Apr-Oct 9am-2pm) is well-worth visiting; it's held in the town hall.

Transport

Buses leave from Market Sq. Richards' No 410 town service goes to Goodwick as does the No 413; the No 412 stops at Dinas and Newport en route to Cardigan. Fishguard is on both the Strumble Shuttle (No 404) and the Poppit Rocket (No 405) services.

Fishguard **train station** is not actually here but in Goodwick (see p191). See the public transport map and table, pp44-7, for full details.

Where to stay

Campers should continue another two miles (3km) to *Fishguard Bay Caravan & Camping Park* (see p194).

In town, budget travellers will appreciate *Hamilton Backpackers Lodge* (☎ 01348-874797, 🖳 www.hamiltonbackpackers.co.uk; 23 Hamilton St; 1D/2F), which has an en suite double and two rooms sleeping four – one with four beds and the other with a double and bunk beds. It's a rough-and-ready place, run by a friendly guy who keeps them ticking over in a very informal way, and is open all year. It's a useful stop if you arrive late in the day since there is no curfew. However, booking in advance is recommended especially in the peak season. Rates are from £16 for a bed, with a simple make-it-yourself breakfast of tea and toast.

On Main St is the smart Georgian *Manor Town House Hotel* (☎ 01348-873260, 🖳 www.manortownhouse.com; 1S/1T/3D/1F, all en suite) which has B&B accommodation from £40 to £47.50 per person for two sharing (the single costs from £50) and some cracking views over the harbour below.

Cartref Hotel (☎ 01348-872430, 🖳 www.cartrefhotel.co.uk; 15-19 High St; 4S/2T/2D/2F, all en suite) has rooms from £68 for two sharing, from £37 for a single. On Market Sq *Abergwaun Hotel* (☎ 01348-874716; 2S/4T/4D/2F, all en suite) charges from £20 per person plus £4.95 for breakfast.

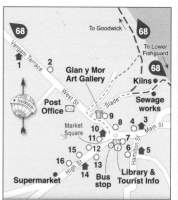

Fishguard (Abergwaun)

Where to stay
1 Inglewood
3 Manor Town House Hotel
5 Hamilton Backpackers Lodge
10 Abergwaun Hotel
14 Cartref Hotel

Where to eat
2 The China Chef
4 Bar 5
6 Dragon House Chinese Restaurant
7 Fish & Chips
8 Royal Oak Inn
9 Celf
11 Bakery/takeaway
12 Navy Tavern
13 Orange Tree Deli & Coffee Shop
15 Taj Mahal
16 Ship & Anchor

Inglewood (☎ 01348-873475; 2D/1T), at No 13 Vergam Terrace, offers B&B from £25-30 per person. One double is en suite and the other rooms share a bathroom. Further along is *Tara Hotel* (Map 68; ☎ 01348-872777, 🖳 www.tara-hotel.co.uk; 1S/2T/ 2D/2F, all with private facilities) charging from £27.50 per person for two sharing a double/twin (single occupancy £35), £30 for the single.

Where to eat and drink

Probably the most popular place – and justifiably so – is the *Royal Oak Inn* (☎ 01348-

872514; food daily noon-2.30pm & 6-9pm, bar open daily 10.30am-midnight), a rustic pub on Market Sq with an extensive menu of hearty home-cooked food. On Tuesdays, your dining will be accompanied by the sound of folk music during their popular 'Folk at the Oak' evening – it's an open session so feel free to join in.

For something cheap but filling try the *Ship and Anchor* (Mon-Sat 11am-3pm & 5.30-8.30pm, Sun noon-3pm only, closed evenings). It's the big pink building on High St and does bacon and onion baguettes for £2.95 as well as more substantial meals. Close by is *Taj Mahal* (☎ 01348-874593; 22 High St; daily 5pm to midnight) for typical Indian dishes. You can get a take-away until midnight.

Nearby is *Navy Tavern* (food served daily noon-3pm, Sun-Tue & Thur/Fri 7-9pm) which does a decent afternoon tea that you can eat in their peaceful back garden, while opposite is *Orange Tree Deli and Coffee Shop* (☎ 01348-875500; Mon-Sat 9am-3pm) selling snacks and baguettes from £2.

Bar 5 (☎ 01348-875050; closed Jan-Mar; Thur & Sat 6-11pm, Fri & Sun 11am-11pm), on Main St, is thriving in an old Georgian townhouse. A large establishment with restaurants on three floors, a bar and an outside terrace overlooking the old town below, Bar 5's décor is contemporary and chic, though the food, much of which is locally produced, reared or caught, remains reasonably priced.

The first place you come to on the way into town is *Celf* (☎ 01348-873867; Mon 10am-4pm, Tue-Sat 10am-4.30pm), a smart café-cum-gallery (West Wales Art Centre) at 16 West St that has a small but regularly changing menu of fine lunches starting at around £8.95 but sandwiches and soups start at £4.95. They also open for dinner on some Fridays and Saturdays (6.30-10pm); booking required, contact them for details.

Opposite Hamilton Backpackers is *Dragon House Chinese Restaurant* (Wed-Mon 5-11pm) for takeaway Chinese food, and another Chinese, *The China Chef* (daily 5.30-11pm), on Vergam Terrace. There is a **fish and chip** place on Main St and a cheap and cheerful **bakery-cum-takeaway** on the main square next to the Abergwaun where you can also eat in.

FISHGUARD TO NEWPORT
MAPS 68-72

It's **11 miles (18km, 4¹/₂-5hrs)** if you follow the entire coast path via the peninsula known as Dinas Island. Cheats, or those in a hurry, can take the shortcut marked on Map 70, bringing the distance down to nine miles (14km, 3¹/₂-4hrs).

The pretty fishing village of **Lower Fishguard** with its colourful houses lining the quay below the hillside and boats bobbing in the harbour contrasts greatly with the bustling main town on top of the hill. Lower Fishguard was the setting for Dylan Thomas's *Under Milk Wood* and was also used in the 1956 film *Moby Dick*. The *Ship Inn* (☎ 01348-874033; summer daily noon-11pm; winter Mon from 5pm) is a good place for a pint though they don't do food.

From the top of the steep climb up the main road the path passes through gorse bushes to the remains of the 220-year-old **Fishguard Fort**.

Another mile and a half (2km) and the path brings you directly into *Fishguard Bay Caravan & Camping Park* (Map 69; ☎ 01348-811415, 🖳 www.fishguardbay.com; Mar-Nov) where a pitch for one person costs £9 (£13 for two). Campers have access to a launderette, a small shop and microwave ovens as well as shower/toilet facilities. The path continues along the edge of steep, high cliffs all the way to the tiny sheltered beach of **Aber-Bach** and, around 30 minutes later, the minuscule settlement of Pwllgwaelod.

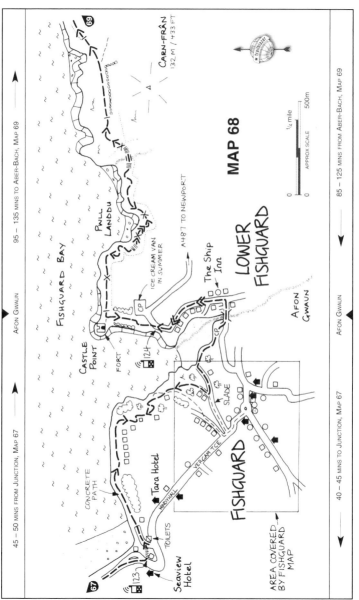

69

CARN-FRÂN
132 M / 433 FT

95 – 135 MINS TO ABER-BACH, MAP 69

FISHGUARD BAY

PWLL LANDDU

ICE CREAM VAN
IN SUMMER

A+87 TO NEWPORT

The Ship Inn

CP

124

CASTLE
POINT

FORT

LOWER
FISHGUARD

AFON GWAUN

AFON GWAUN

MAP 68

0   APPROX SCALE   500m
0   ¼ mile

85 – 125 MINS FROM ABER-BACH, MAP 69

ROUTE GUIDE AND MAPS

45 – 50 MINS FROM JUNCTION, MAP 67

CONCRETE
PATH

Tara Hotel

TOILETS

Seaview
Hotel

123

67

SLADE

FISHGUARD

VERGAM TCE

HIGH ST

40 – 45 MINS TO JUNCTION, MAP 67

AREA COVERED
BY FISHGUARD
MAP

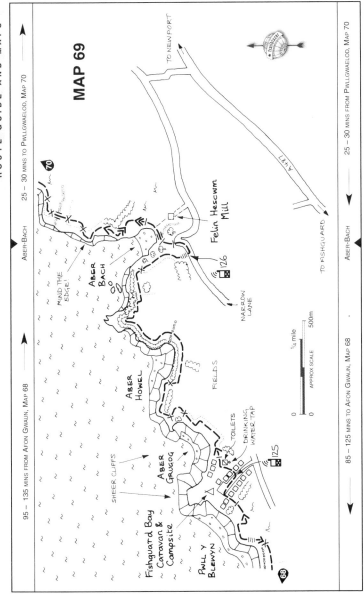

MAP 69

95 – 135 MINS FROM AFON GWAUN, MAP 68

ABER-BACH

25 – 30 MINS TO PWLLGWAELOD, MAP 70

85 – 125 MINS TO AFON GWAUN, MAP 68

ABER-BACH

25 – 30 MINS FROM PWLLGWAELOD, MAP 70

TO NEWPORT

TO FISHGUARD

A487

Felin Hescwm Mill

NARROW LANE

ABER BACH

MIND THE EDGE!

ABER HOWEL

FIELDS

SHEER CLIFFS

ABER GRUGOG

TOILETS

DRINKING WATER TAP

Fishguard Bay Caravan & Campsite

PWLL Y BLEWYN

126

125

70

68

¼ mile

APPROX SCALE

500m

0

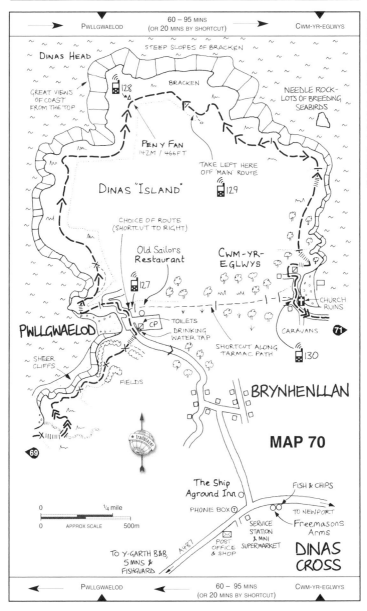

▼ PWLLGWAELOD 60 – 95 MINS (OR 20 MINS BY SHORTCUT) CWM-YR-EGLWYS ▼

~ DINAS HEAD ~

STEEP SLOPES OF BRACKEN

128

BRACKEN

GREAT VIEWS OF COAST FROM THE TOP

NEEDLE ROCK- LOTS OF BREEDING SEABIRDS

PEN Y FAN
142M / 466FT

TAKE LEFT HERE OFF MAIN ROUTE

129

DINAS "ISLAND"

CHOICE OF ROUTE (SHORTCUT TO RIGHT)

CWM-YR-EGLWYS

Old Sailors Restaurant

127

CHURCH RUINS

PWLLGWAELOD

CP TOILETS

DRINKING WATER TAP

CARAVANS 71 ▶

SHORTCUT ALONG TARMAC PATH

130

SHEER CLIFFS

FIELDS

BRYNHENLLAN

MAP 70

69

X

★ trailblazer

0 1/4 mile
0 APPROX SCALE 500m

The Ship Aground Inn

PHONE BOX (T)

FISH & CHIPS

TO NEWPORT

Freemasons Arms

A487

POST OFFICE & SHOP

SERVICE STATION & MINI SUPERMARKET

DINAS CROSS

TO Y-GARTH B&B, 5 MINS & FISHGUARD

◀ PWLLGWAELOD ◀ 60 – 95 MINS (OR 20 MINS BY SHORTCUT) CWM-YR-EGLWYS ▲

PWLLGWAELOD   MAP 70, p197

There is a **drinking-water tap** next to the public **toilets** in the car park. In the summer the **Poppit Rocket** stops in the car park before heading to Dinas Cross; see pp44-7 for details. There's nowhere to stay here

but *The Old Sailors Restaurant* (☎ 01348-811491; Apr-Oct daily 11am-11pm, Oct-Apr Thur-Tue 11am-6pm, booking advisable Fri and Sat lunch) has tasty lobster and crab lunches.

DINAS CROSS   MAP 70, p197

Dinas Cross is a short detour from the coast path. It can be reached by walking up the lane from Pwllgwaelod through Brynhenllan to the main road and turning right (20 mins from the coast path). Here there is a service station with a mini **supermarket**, **post office** and an **off-licence**.

The Poppit Rocket, Strumble Shuttle and Richards/Acorn's No 412 (Cardigan to Haverfordwest) **bus** services stop here; see pp44-7 for details.

There is also a **fish and chip shop** (Tue-Sat noon-2pm & 5-9pm. Next door is the *Freemasons Arms* (☎ 01348-811243;

daily noon-11pm; food daily noon-2pm & 5.30-9pm) where you can treat yourself to a pint. They serve standard pub fare.

Along the lane between Brynhenllan and Dinas you will find good pub grub at the *Ship Aground Inn* (☎ 01348-811261; bar open daily 11am-11pm, food daily noon-3pm & 6.45-9pm).

A short walk back towards Fishguard along the A487 is *Y Garth B&B* (☎ 01348-811777, 🖳 www.y-garth.co.uk; 2D/1D or T, all with private facilities), with rooms going for £40/pp; single occupancy of a room £40-50.

At Pwllgwaelod you must decide if you want to include the peninsula of **Dinas Island** in your walk. If the answer is no follow the well-made straight path through the valley to Cwm-yr-eglwys.

If the answer is yes take the easy-to-follow path which climbs steadily through heather and bracken all the way to the 142-metre (466ft) Pen y Fan, the summit of **Dinas Head**. Look out for breeding seabirds on Needle Rock.

The path continues around the peninsula above high slopes of bracken before passing through bushes and trees to emerge at **Cwm-yr-eglwys** (Church Valley) named after the church which lies in ruins by the beach. With everything squeezed into such a narrow valley the effect is claustrophobic so it is a relief to escape by walking up the steep lane out of the village. There are some public toilets here.

After ten minutes or so of lung-busting ascent the path can be found sneaking between high hedges on the left next to a house. The path is well hidden by hedges and trees until you reach cliffs above the cove at **Fforest**. The cliffs along the next section are sheer and in places overhanging. The path can be very close to the edge so watch your step.

The next cove is a real beauty. The turn-off to Tycanol campsite (see p200) is just before the boathouse here. The unspoilt nature of the area makes it quite a rarity. Unlike most of these coves there is no road, nor are there any houses – just woodland, a marsh and a stony beach. From here the path continues along the edge of precipitous cliffs to **Parrog**, and the edge of Newport town where it briefly crosses the shingle, mud and sand on the seafront.

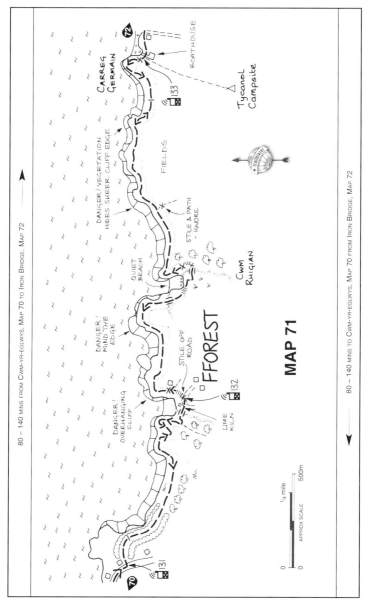

80 – 140 MINS FROM CWM-YR-EGLWYS, MAP 70 TO IRON BRIDGE, MAP 72

80 – 140 MINS TO CWM-YR-EGLWYS, MAP 70 FROM IRON BRIDGE, MAP 72

72

CARREG GERMAIN

BOATHOUSE

133

Tycanol Campsite

DANGER / VEGETATION HIDES SHEER CLIFF EDGE

FIELDS

STILE & PATH - IGNORE

QUIET BEACH

CWM RHIGIAN

DANGER / MIND THE EDGE

FFOREST

STILE OFF ROAD

132

LIME KILN

DANGER / OVERHANGING CLIFF

MAP 71

131

70

¼ mile

500m

APPROX SCALE

ROUTE GUIDE AND MAPS

PARROG   MAP 72

The Poppit Rocket **bus** (No 405) stops at the car park.

Ty Canol Campsite (Map 71; ☎ 01239-820264, ☐ www.tycanolfarm.co.uk; open all year) is 200 yards from the coast path. Turn inland just before the boat house by Carreg Germain. Camping costs £10 per person but there is also a great **room** sleeping four – more like a rudimentary, rustic apartment and completely charming – in the loft of their barn, for which they charge just £15 per person. However, they do not mix people so it is only suitable for families/groups of up to four people. Toilet and shower facilities are downstairs. *Morawelon Coffee Shop* (☎ 01239-

820565; daily 9am-4.30pm, Thur-Sat 4.30-9.15pm; closed Nov) does a variety of snacks and light lunches, serves innovative mains in the evening and has a sun-trap of a garden out the back as well as good views over Newport Beach from the front. There is also a cosy atmosphere if you just fancy a drink. You can't miss it; it's on the seafront near the yacht club. Call in, even if you're not stopping in the village. They also offer **camping** (Mar-Oct; contact details as above) in a basic but beautifully situated site immediately behind the café. Tent pitches cost £5 per person. If the coffee shop is closed knock on the door if you want to camp here.

Where the path passes the salt marsh and some woodland there are two lanes, both of which provide access to the centre of **Newport**. The first leads up to the national park information centre, while the second takes you to the youth hostel.

NEWPORT (TREFDRAETH)   MAP 72

Rising behind Newport are the Preseli Hills (see pp203-5). The hill directly behind the town is Carn Ingli rising to 337 metres (1105ft). From the top you can see the mountains of Snowdonia on a clear day.

The town itself is small and friendly. The **Norman castle** and **church** at the top were built along with the original town in the 12th century when the Norman invader Robert Martin chose the spot beside the Newport estuary to set up home. Unfortunately the castle is privately owned so visitors must content themselves with a view from the outside.

On Lower St Mary St is a carreg, or burial chamber, one of many that can be found in this part of Wales. **Carreg Coetan** is typical, consisting of several standing stones surmounted by a capstone, and is perhaps of greater interest for its location, in an unassuming residential corner of Newport surrounded by bungalows.

In terms of facilities, Newport is a surprisingly well-equipped little town. Almost everything you could possibly need can be found in the compact centre. It's the perfect place to stay before the tough final leg of the journey to St Dogmaels.

Services

The **National Park Information Centre** (☎ 01239-820912, ☐ NewportTIC@pem brokeshirecoast.org.uk; Easter-Oct Mon-Sat 10am-1pm & 1.45-5.30pm, also in summer Sun 10am-1.15pm; Nov-Easter Mon & Fri 10.30am-3pm, Tue-Thur & Sat 10.30am-1pm) is also the **tourist information centre**. **Internet access** is available: £1 for 30 mins/£2 for an hour. There is also internet access at the **library** (Mon 2-5pm, Wed 10am-1pm, Fri 10am-noon & 2-5pm).

The **post office** (☎ 01239-820200; Mon-Fri 9am-5.30pm, Sat 9am-1pm) is on the corner of Long St and the main road, Bridge St. The **bank** on Bridge St has a cashpoint. The best place for provisions is Spar **supermarket** (daily 8am-10pm) on Market St. Alternatively Newport Garage's **mini-market** is on Bridge St.

Dirty socks can be washed at the **launderette** (daily 9am-9pm; dryers 50p for 10 mins), and there's a **chemist** (☎ 01239-820239; Mon-Fri 9am-5.30pm, Sat 9am-1pm) on Market St.

Transport

The Poppit Rocket **bus** (No 405) and the

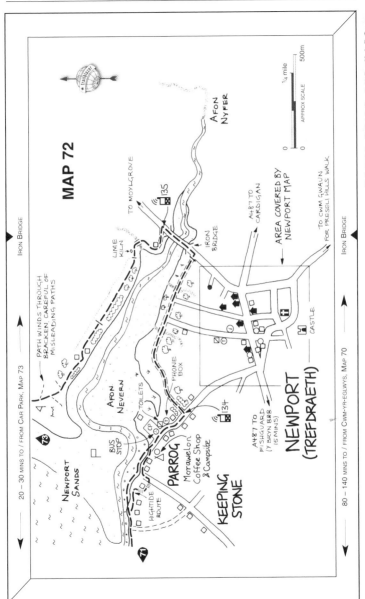

MAP 72

IRON BRIDGE

20 – 30 MINS TO / FROM CAR PARK, MAP 73

AFON NYFER

TO MOYLGROVE

135

IRON BRIDGE

LIME KILN

A487 TO CARDIGAN

AREA COVERED BY NEWPORT MAP

TO CWM GWAUN FOR PRESELI HILLS WALK

IRON BRIDGE

PATH WINDS THROUGH BRACKEN CAREFUL OF MISLEADING PATHS

AFON NEVERN

TOILETS

PHONE BOX

NEWPORT (TREFDRAETH)

CASTLE

A487 TO FISHGUARD (Y BRYN B&B 5 MINS)

NEWPORT SANDS

BUS STOP

PARROG

Morawelon Coffee Shop & Campsite

KEEPING STONE

HIGHTIDE ROUTE

134

80 – 140 MINS TO / FROM CWM-YR-EGLWYS, MAP 70

APPROX SCALE

0   ¼ mile

0   500m

Strumble Shuttle (No 404) stop by Castle Hotel. Richards/Acorn's No 412 service also stops in Newport; for details see the public transport map and table, pp44-7.

Where to stay

Newport Youth Hostel (☎ 0845-371 9543, ☐ newport@yha.org.uk; Lower St Mary St) is a converted schoolhouse with 28 beds costing £9.95 for members. The hostel is self-catering only but this is not a problem since there are plenty of places serving food in Newport.

There are some good places to stay along East St. Recommended is *The Golden Lion* (☎ 01239-820321, ☐ www .goldenlionpembrokeshire.co.uk; 7D/3T/ 1F, all en suite) which has modern, well-presented en suite rooms for £75-95 in the pub itself (single occupancy £50), with three more basic double rooms (shared bathroom; £60, or £50 for single occupancy) over the road in the cottage. If requested in advance they will provide a packed lunch (£2-3); they also offer a baggage-transfer service (contact them for details). Dogs are also welcome for a £10 charge.

Further along the road *Llys Meddyg Guest House* (☎ 01239-820008, ☐ www .llysmeddyg.com; 4T or D/1D/3D or F) has en suite rooms starting at around £50-75 per person; single occupancy £85-135. On the same road *Cnapan Country House* (☎ 01239-820575, ☐ www.cnapan .co.uk; 2D/3T, en suite) charges from £40 per person, with a £10 single occupancy supplement. Prices include breakfast.

On Bridge St is another good pub-cum-hotel: *Gwesty'r Castell* (Castle Hotel; ☎ 01239-820742, ☐ www.thecastlehotel newport.com; 3D, T or F) is a pleasant place where the owners are very welcoming and helpful and the en suite rooms very comfortable. They charge £65 for two sharing a room, £75 for three and £80 for four; single occupancy is from £50.

The Globe (☎ 01239-820296; Upper St Mary St; 1D/1T, shared bathroom) has comfortable rooms at £55 for two sharing (£40 for single occupancy); discounts for a stay of more than one night are available, which may come in useful as the landlady

also offers a pick-up or drop-off service (50p per mile) covering the last, lengthy stretch to Cardigan.

To the west of Newport on the road to Dinas Cross is the smart, 4-star *Y Bryn* (☎ 01239-820288; ☐ www.brynbedandbreak fast.co.uk; 2D/2F, all with private facilities), with three rooms overlooking the sea, and the other with views towards the Preseli Hills. Rates are £65-70 per room, or £40-45 single occupancy.

Where to eat and drink

Newport has no shortage of great places to eat. For breakfast or a snack try one of the coffee shops; the first one you come to as you walk towards the town on the coast path is actually in **Parrog** (see p200).

In the centre of the town is *The Canteen* (☎ 01239-820131; Market St; Mon-Sat 10am-8.30pm, Sun noon-4pm; in the winter months they may close early) where dishes are home made and include vegetarian options. From 6pm to 7pm they offer a great-value two-course supper for £12. Just next door is *Y Mochyn Drwg* (☎ 01239-820807, ☐ www.ymochyndrwg.co .uk; summer Tue-Sat 11am-3pm & 7-8.45pm, Sun 12.30-2.30pm; winter hours vary), a smart place serving hake fishcakes for £13.50 and roast meats from £15.95.

Further up Market St, opposite Spar supermarket, *Fronlas Café* (☎ 01239-820351; daily 9am-8pm; winter to 6pm) does breakfasts and afternoon snacks; booking essential in the school summer holidays. Food can be eaten in or taken away. Back down on East St, look out for *The Golden Lion* (see Where to stay; daily noon-2pm & 6.30-9pm), which does very good, hearty food (the menu in both the bar and the restaurant is the same and main dishes cost £9-15) and has friendly bar staff.

Another good choice is the *Royal Oak Inn* (☎ 01239-820632; food served daily 11am-9.30pm), on Bridge St, where they know how to knock up a good curry and have a winning way with fish too. The traditional pub is an unlikely-looking curry house but their extensive Indian menu should be enough to convince you.

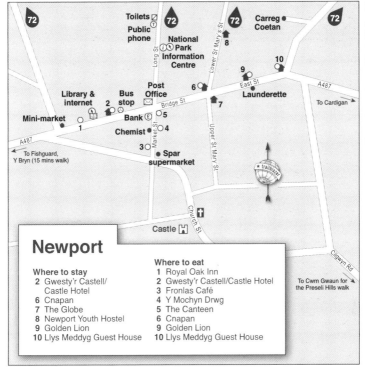

Newport

Where to stay
2 Gwesty'r Castell/
  Castle Hotel
6 Cnapan
7 The Globe
8 Newport Youth Hostel
9 Golden Lion
10 Llys Meddyg Guest House

Where to eat
1 Royal Oak Inn
2 Gwesty'r Castell/Castle Hotel
3 Fronlas Café
4 Y Mochyn Drwg
5 The Canteen
6 Cnapan
9 Golden Lion
10 Llys Meddyg Guest House

Alternatively *Gwesty'r Castell* (see Where to stay; food served daily noon-2pm & 6.30-9pm) has local food, real ales and a roaring log fire. For a straightforward restaurant *Cnapan* (see Where to stay; Wed-Mon 6.30-8.45pm) does high-quality, if slightly expensive, evening meals, with two courses costing £23 and three from £29. *Llys Meddyg* (see Where to stay; daily noon-2pm & 7-9pm) also offers supper in their smart, white-linen-dressed dining room, with mains starting at £16.50. In the summer months their garden restaurant is open daily noon-3pm and 6-9pm.

Walking in the Preseli Hills (Mynydd Preseli) and Cwm Gwaun
The Preseli Hills rise behind Newport, dissected by the deep Cwm Gwaun glacial valley. This little-known area is well worth exploring if you have time to spare as it provides some wonderful secluded walking away from the more popular coast. This is bluestone country. The rock here was transported all the way to Salisbury Plain for the construction of Stonehenge by some miracle of Druidian engineering. There are Iron-Age hill-forts and standing stones dotted all along the crest of the hills with fantastic views over the coastline and the sweep of Cardigan Bay.

The Preseli Hills are divided into three distinct parts. On the northern side is the lowest line of hills reaching 337m (1105ft) on Carningli Common above Newport. The higher Mynedd Preseli to the south reaches a height of 536m (1758ft) at Foel Cwmcerwyn, while the heavily wooded Cwm Gwaun valley separates the two. The circular walk outlined below starts in Newport and takes in the Cwm Gwaun valley before returning over the ridge of the lower hills via the distinctive peak of Carningli.

Safety Do not underestimate these hills. They may be relatively low but they are exposed and the weather can change suddenly as with the rest of Britain's western hills. The ridge is a broad one with few distinctive landmarks and little in the way of signposts and other waymarks, making it very inhospitable in

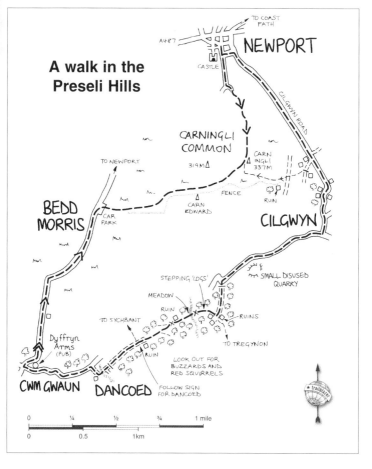

A walk in the Preseli Hills

bad weather. Take the OS Outdoor Leisure Map 35 of North Pembrokeshire (yellow cover) and a compass in case the cloud comes down. Warm waterproof clothing and plenty of food and water for the day are also essential.

A circular walk (see map opposite) This walk is about **11 miles** (17.5km) and takes about **4-6 hours** (please note, the times below are cumulative). From Newport follow the road up Church St with the castle to your right and the church to the left. Continue up Cilgwyn Rd. Stay on the lane following the signs for Cwm Gwaun. The lane now heads downhill to a sharp right-hand corner. Continue up the hill, ignoring the left turn. The lane eventually meets another lane at a T-junction where you should turn right. After passing the tiny disused quarry on your left the road drops down with a fine view of the valley ahead. At the sharp right-hand bend it's time to leave the road and head along the woodland track through the gate to your left (1-1^1/2hrs). This beautiful stretch of path passes through some impressive beech forest where red squirrels and buzzards can frequently be spotted. The path passes a number of ruined houses hinting at a time when the Cwm Gwaun was more heavily populated.

Keep to the path on the edge of the forest, passing fields on your right, eventually reaching the farm at **Dan Coed** (2-2^3/4 hrs) where you have to rejoin the lane. It is a short walk along the road to the eccentric *Dyffryn Arms* (☎ 01348-881305; daily 11am-11pm; 2^1/2-3^1/4 hrs) where you can get beer poured from a jug and passed through a hatch in what is effectively landlady Bessie's living room. It's a good spot to eat your lunch, although the pub itself doesn't do food.

After a break it's time for the steep climb up to the hilltop. Turn right after the pub and climb the hairpin lane, reaching the bleak windswept moor at **Bedd Morris** where there is a car park and fine views of Dinas Head on the coast (3-4hrs). At the car park follow the track through the heather. In bad visibility a compass will be needed. Head directly east until you come to a fence. Follow the fence line, passing the rocks of **Carn Edward** on the right. From the end of the fence head up onto the 337m (1105ft) rocky top of **Carn Ingli** (3^1/2-5hrs), an interesting little hill with views over Newport on an otherwise featureless upland moor. Look out for the hut circles on the ridge leading to the top. To get back to Newport follow the obvious path north down the slopes and join the track which takes you back onto Church Rd (4-6hrs).

NEWPORT TO ST DOGMAELS   MAPS 72-79

There's nothing like leaving the best till last but there's always a catch. This is the toughest section of the entire walk. If you have come all the way from Amroth you will either be feeling fitter than ever or you will be feeling 30 years older and will find these last **16 miles** (26km, 5^1/2-7^1/2 hrs) pretty strenuous.

The cliffs are bigger here, the distances longer, there is nowhere to get any food, nowhere to get any water and only one place to stay until you get to Poppit Sands. These are all ingredients for a tough day, so count on taking at least two to three litres of water with you and more if it's a hot day. That one place to stay is in the village of **Moylgrove** (see p208) near Ceibwr Bay. If you intend to stay there you are well advised to book in advance. Alternatively, you can, of course, walk up to Moylgrove and catch the **Poppit Rocket** (see pp45-7) bus to

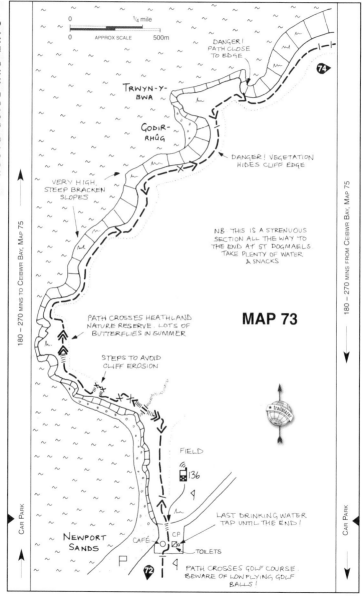

0 ¼ mile
0 500m
APPROX SCALE

DANGER!
PATH CLOSE
TO EDGE

74

TRWYN-Y-BWA

GODIR-RHÛG

DANGER! VEGETATION
HIDES CLIFF EDGE

VERY HIGH,
STEEP BRACKEN
SLOPES

NB THIS IS A STRENUOUS
SECTION ALL THE WAY TO
THE END AT ST DOGMAELS
TAKE PLENTY OF WATER
& SNACKS

180 – 270 MINS TO CEIBWR BAY, MAP 75

180 – 270 MINS FROM CEIBWR BAY, MAP 75

MAP 73

PATH CROSSES HEATHLAND
NATURE RESERVE. LOTS OF
BUTTERFLIES IN SUMMER

STEPS TO AVOID
CLIFF EROSION

trailblazer

FIELD

136

CAR PARK

CAR PARK

LAST DRINKING WATER
TAP UNTIL THE END!

NEWPORT
SANDS

CAFÉ   CP

TOILETS

72

PATH CROSSES GOLF COURSE.
BEWARE OF LOW FLYING GOLF
BALLS!

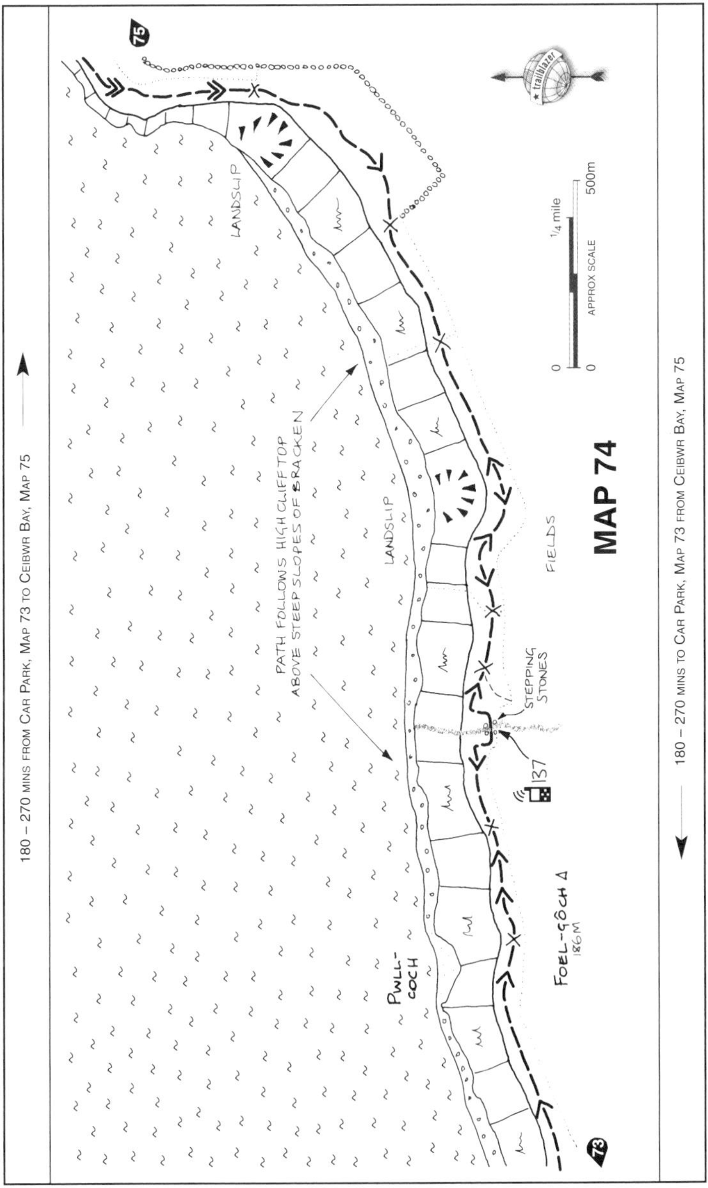

MAP 74

180 – 270 MINS FROM CAR PARK, MAP 73 TO CEIBWR BAY, MAP 75

180 – 270 MINS TO CAR PARK, MAP 73 FROM CEIBWR BAY, MAP 75

LANDSLIP

LANDSLIP

PATH FOLLOWS HIGH CLIFFTOP
ABOVE STEEP SLOPES OF BRACKEN

FIELDS

STEPPING
STONES

137

PWLL-
COCH

FOEL-GÔCH ▲
186M

APPROX SCALE

0   ¼ mile

0   500m

75

73

Cardigan or Newport, then return to Moylgrove the next day in order to complete the walk. This alternative, of course, involves a bit of pre-planning and knowledge of local bus times – but it does neatly divide the walk in two.

After crossing the iron bridge over the **Afon Nyfer** the path follows the northern edge of the estuary, through bushes and bracken and across a golf course to a car park next to **Newport Sands**. Here there is a small seasonal **café**, **toilets** and a **drinking-water tap**, which is the last place to fill up easily but there is a natural spring in Moylgrove (see below) if you find yourself short on the final stretch. The **Poppit Rocket** (No 405) bus (see p47) also stops here.

This is where the hard stuff begins. The path climbs up onto high cliffs, passing through a beautiful heathland nature reserve. In the summer this area is alive with butterflies. The path continues above very high, steep slopes of bracken and around some spectacular bays sheltered by terrifying barren cliffs, climbing steadily higher and higher to reach 150 metres (492ft) where the hill of **Foel-Gôch** plunges into the sea.

Once past a couple of huge old **landslips**, which are no doubt still vulnerable to collapse, the path drops down to lower cliffs, eventually arriving at the spectacular formations around the Witch's Cauldron. A great wedge of rock lies just offshore trapping a finger of the sea below the cliffs. The path, rather worryingly, passes very close to the nasty drop down into this pool. Watch your step. Further on is the **Witch's Cauldron** itself, a sea cave where the roof has collapsed. The result is a beautiful cove with a natural bridge making it appear separate from the main body of the sea. A little further on is **Ceibwr Bay** with its shingle beach; a good halfway point for lunch. The village of **Moylgrove** is along the valley road; the only accommodation for miles lies just beyond the village.

MOYLGROVE (TREWYDDEL)
OFF MAP 75

This pretty hamlet lies about half a mile up the lane through the valley from **Ceibwr Bay**. There's a **public toilet** and a natural spring where you can fill water bottles.

The very welcoming *Mount Pleasant B&B* (☎ 01239-881268, 🖥 www.moyle grove.co.uk; 1D/1T) is uphill from the car park in the centre of the village in the direction of Newport. Both rooms are en suite and have adjoining utility rooms with drying facilities. Each has its own entrance ensuring complete privacy. The charge is £65 per room (£40 single occupancy).

In the summer *Pavilion Café* (☎ 01239-881359; Mon-Sat 10.30am-5pm, Sun to 4.30pm), at Penrallt Garden Centre and Nursery (off Map 76), is a good spot to pick up light snacks, tea and coffee. You can reach it by following the track inland from the beach and climbing the path up the steep wooded nose of the hill in front. It sits at 100 metres above sea level so you might want to hide your rucksack in some bushes at the bottom to avoid carrying it. The walk is about two miles and takes some 30 minutes.

The Poppit Rocket **bus** (see p47) stops at the entrance to the car park in Moylgrove.

After skirting around the flanks of **Foel Hendre**, spectacular cliffs come into view. The impressive folding of the rock in these cliffs will have geologists drooling. The path here begins to spasm in a series of excruciating descents and ascents. In places it climbs quite improbably steep slopes.

(Opposite) Top: The path winds its way through bracken and gorse beneath Carn Penberry (see p177). **Bottom**: Seal basking on the shore, Penllechwen. (Photos © Henry Stedman).

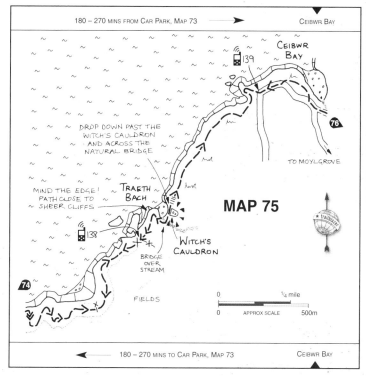

180 – 270 MINS FROM CAR PARK, MAP 73 ➞   CEIBWR BAY

CEIBWR BAY

📱139

DROP DOWN PAST THE
WITCH'S CAULDRON
AND ACROSS THE
NATURAL BRIDGE

🔵76

TO MOYLGROVE

MIND THE EDGE!
PATH CLOSE TO
SHEER CLIFFS

TRAETH
BACH

MAP 75

* trailblazer

📱138

WITCH'S
CAULDRON

BRIDGE
OVER
STREAM

🔵74

FIELDS

0 .... ¼ mile
0 ..... APPROX SCALE 500m

◀ **180 – 270 MINS TO CAR PARK, MAP 73**   CEIBWR BAY

Once above the aforementioned cliffs the path swings to the east reaching the highest point of the entire coast path at 175 metres (574ft). The steep slopes of bracken that sweep down to the sea certainly make you feel a long way up.

Soon the path passes an old **lookout building** and drops down to the broad **Cemaes Head** before heading south to Allt-y-coed Farm and Campsite (see p212) where the track joins a country lane. The lane leads steadily downhill to the lifeboat station and car park at **Poppit Sands**, where there's a plaque commemorating the opening of the path in 1970 by local war correspondent, journalist and broadcaster Wynford Vaughan Thomas.

POPPIT SANDS (DRAETH POPPIT)
MAP 77, p211 & MAP 78, p212
Poppit Sands refers to the scattering of houses that stretch from Allt-y-coed Farm all the way down the lane to the car park and the RNLI lifeboat station next to Poppit Sands itself, an enormous beach that fills the mouth of the Afon Teifi estuary. There's a **phone** by the car park and a seasonal **café**. *(cont'd on p212)*

(Opposite) Top: The lighthouse off Strumble Head (see p188). **Middle**: Carreg Sampson (see p182). **Bottom**: Impressive rock striations at Cemaes Head. (Photo © Henry Stedman).

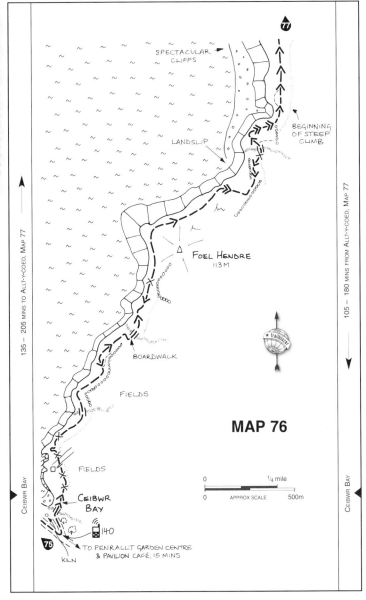

SPECTACULAR CLIFFS

BEGINNING OF STEEP CLIMB

LANDSLIP

△ FOEL HENDRE
113M

135 – 205 MINS TO ALLT-Y-COED, MAP 77

105 – 180 MINS FROM ALLT-Y-COED, MAP 77

BOARDWALK

FIELDS

MAP 76

FIELDS

CEIBWR BAY

CEIBWR BAY

CEIBWR
BAY

0   1/4 mile

0   500m
APPROX SCALE

140

75

KILN

TO PENRALLT GARDEN CENTRE
& PAVILION CAFÉ, 15 MINS

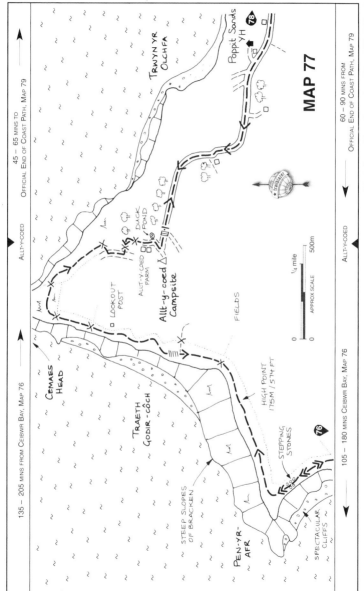

MAP 77

45 – 65 MINS TO
OFFICIAL END OF COAST PATH, MAP 79

60 – 90 MINS FROM
OFFICIAL END of COAST PATH, MAP 79

ALLT-Y-COED

ALLT-Y-COED

135 – 205 MINS FROM CEIBWR BAY, MAP 76

105 – 180 MINS CEIBWR BAY, MAP 76

TRWYN YR OLCHFA

Poppit Sands YH

DUCK POND

ALLT-Y-COED FARM

Allt-y-coed Campsite

LOOKOUT POST

CEMAES HEAD

TRAETH GODIR-COCH

FIELDS

HIGH POINT 175M / 574 FT

STEPPING STONES

STEEP SLOPES OF BRACKEN

PEN-YR-AFR

SPECTACULAR CLIFFS

APPROX SCALE
0   1/4 mile
0   500m

ROUTE GUIDE AND MAPS

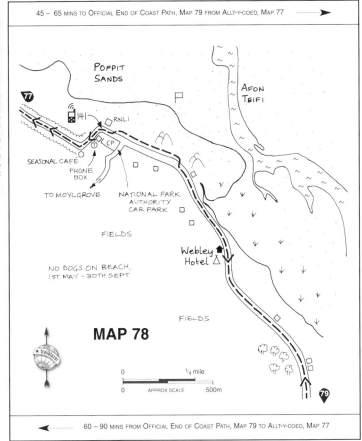

POPPIT
SANDS

AFON
TEIFI

141 RNLI

T CP

SEASONAL CAFÉ
PHONE
BOX

TO MOYLGROVE

NATIONAL PARK
AUTHORITY
CAR PARK

FIELDS

NO DOGS ON BEACH,
1ST MAY - 30TH SEPT

Webley
Hotel

FIELDS

MAP 78

0   ¼ mile
0   APPROX SCALE   500m

79

(cont'd from p209) The Poppit Rocket **bus**
stops at the entrance to the car park and
Richards' No 407 service calls here; see
pp44-7 for details.

The official end of the path is still a
mile and a half (2km) from Poppit Sands.
However, there are plenty of places to stay
along this stretch leaving very little to do
the next morning. The first place you come
to after rounding Cemaes Head is **Allt-y-
coed Farm** (Map 77; ☎ 01239-612673, ▣
www.alltycoed.co .uk). The coast path runs
right through the farmyard, which is listed

on the Ordnance Survey maps as Allt-y-
Goed. Just up the slope past the duck pond
is their **campsite** offering pitches all year
from £5 per person. Facilities are basic at
present but the new owners have plans to
improve these by summer 2010. They also
hope to have round tents which people
without tents can rent. From the farm the
path joins the narrow Poppit Sands Lane.

Half a mile further on is **Poppit Sands
Youth Hostel** (☎ 0845-371 9037, ▣ pop
pit@yha.org.uk; open all year); it overlooks
the Sands and is less than an hour from the

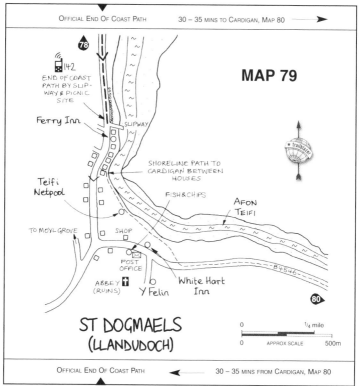

78

📶 142

END OF COAST
PATH BY SLIP-
WAY & PICNIC
SITE

Ferry Inn

SLIPWAY

MAP 79

SHORELINE PATH TO
CARDIGAN BETWEEN
HOUSES

Teifi
Netpool

FISH & CHIPS

AFON
TEIFI

TO MOYLGROVE

SHOP

POST
OFFICE

White Hart
Inn

ABBEY
(RUINS)   Y Felin

B4546

80

ROUTE GUIDE AND MAPS

ST DOGMAELS
(LLANDUDOCH)

0   ¼ mile

0   APPROX SCALE   500m

end of the trail. It is self-catering only, has 34 beds at £9.95 for members and is very popular in the summer.

If you hadn't already noticed you are now in the Welsh-speaking part of Pembrokeshire, but you certainly will if you go to **Webley Hotel** (☎ 01239-612085; 🖳 www.webleyhotel.com; 8D/1F), about half a mile down the road from Poppit Sands. B&B is £75-85 (single occupancy £55-65). Most rooms have private facilities

but some need to share. They also have a field where you can **camp** (£5 per tent per night); there are toilets and running water but no showers. In the **bar** (daily 11am-3pm & 6-11pm, food served daily noon-2.30pm & 6-8.30pm) there's reasonable food, much of it home-cooked and including daily specials; prices start from £4.95. They may close on Mondays and Tuesdays in the winter months.

And so the path continues on to **St Dogmaels**, where the coast path officially ends. Though purists may want to keep on walking to Cardigan to cross the **Afon Teifi** – the river that marks the border between Pembrokeshire and its neighbour, Ceredigion – the official end of the coast path is the unassuming slipway at the northern end of St Dogmaels where there is now a slate Coast Path marker.

ST DOGMAELS (LLANDUDOCH)
MAP 79, p213

St Dogmaels is stretched along a dogleg in the river estuary. The coast path ends at the slipway at the northern limit of the village but the main centre is further south.

Before rushing through on your way to Cardigan it's worth taking a look at the old **abbey ruins** which can be found in the main part of the village. Head down the hill and look behind the **post office** (☎ 01239-612563; Mon, Tue, Thur (8.30am) & Fri 9am-1pm & 2-5.30pm, Wed & Sat 9am-noon).

There is a small convenience **shop** (Mon-Sat 7am-10pm, Sun 8am-8pm) here but Cardigan, on the other side of the river, has far more to offer.

Both the Poppit Rocket (No 405) and Richards' No 407 **bus** services stop here en route to Cardigan; see pp44-7 for details. Alternatively you can phone for a **taxi**: Cardi Cabs (☎ 01239-621399).

Right by the end of the path, *The Ferry Inn* (☎ 01239-615172; food served daily noon-2.30pm & 6-9.30pm, Sun to 9pm; bar open daily 11am-11.30pm) is the perfect spot for a celebratory pint; they have decking overlooking the river. *Teifi Netpool Inn* (☎ 01239-612680; food served Fri-Sun noon-2pm, daily 6-8.30pm; pub open daily all day in the summer, from 4pm in the winter months) is another good place to kick the boots off and congratulate yourself with a pint or two. It has typical pub food and does a good plate of fish and chips.

There is a *fish and chip shop* (Tue-Thur noon-2pm & 5-8.30pm, Fri & Sat to 9.30pm) next to the post office and a little further down the hill is another good pub, *White Hart Inn* (☎ 01239-612099; food served daily noon-10pm except Tuesday) with decent pub grub. Down the road opposite is *Y Felin* (☎ 01239-613999; Mon-Sat 10am-5pm) where you can visit one of the last working water mills left in Wales and which produces traditional stoneground flour. Next door is a **tea room** run by the Coach House.

For more accommodation, shops and transport options, Cardigan, just a little over a mile away, is a better bet than St Dogmaels. To reach it, catch one of the buses (see below) that run between the two or, if you prefer to walk, turn left at the central junction in St Dogmaels to follow the B4546 road down to the bridge across the **Afon Teifi**.

CARDIGAN (ABERTEIFI)   MAP 80

Cardigan is a mile (2km) beyond the end of the coast path. If you are using public transport to get home Cardigan is the place to go. There are also a number of places to spend the night and recover before heading home the next day.

Services

The **tourist information centre** (TIC; ☎ 01239-613230, ✉ cardigantic@ceredigion .gov.uk; summer Mon-Sat 10am-5pm, July & Aug Sun 10am-5pm, winter Mon-Sat 10am-1pm & 2-5pm) is in the Theatr Mwldan building. There are plenty of **banks** and all the **shops** you need along High St as well as the **post office** (Mon-Fri 9am-5.30pm, Sat 9am-12.30pm).

Down Quay St, off High St at the river end, is a Somerfield **supermarket**. The **library**, on the fourth floor of the mini-mall next to the tatty indoor market, has free **internet access**, though you may have to wait a while for a terminal.

Fforest (☎ 01239-623633, 🖥 www.ffo restoutdoor.co.uk) sells outdoor gear and clothing and has a small café (see p216). Fforest also has an activity centre in Cilgerran that leads canoeing, kayaking, sea kayaking, coasteering, and climbing expeditions in the area.

Transport

Cardigan is on a number of bus routes and the all-essential **bus stop** is on Finch Sq.

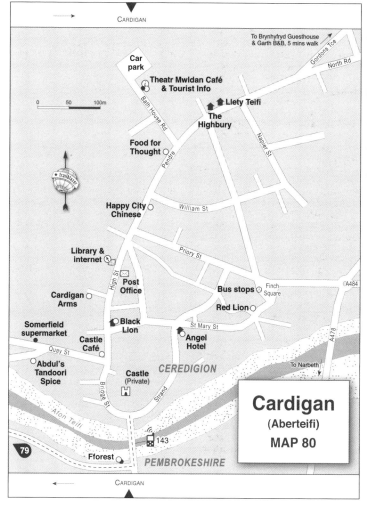

Cardigan (Aberteifi) MAP 80

The Poppit Rocket (No 405) goes from here to St Dogmaels, and ultimately Fishguard, whilst Richards'/Acorn's Bus No 412 goes to Haverfordwest via Newport and Fishguard.

Richards' No 407 goes to St Dogmaels and Poppit Sands; their No 430 goes to Narberth and their Nos 460/461 go to Carmarthen.

If you have left your car at the start of the path take Richards Brothers' service No 412 to Haverfordwest, then Silcox's No 381 to Kilgetty. See the public transport map and table, pp44-7, for details.

Where to stay

A very friendly place to stay is *The Highbury* (☎ 01239-613403, 🖳 www.llety .co.uk; Pendre; 2S/8D). They have comfortable rooms and serve big breakfasts in a sunny conservatory. Prices start from £30 for a single with private bathroom; for a double, all of which are en suite, it's £60-70. The same people run *Llety Teifi* (☎ 01239-615566; 1S/5T/4D, all en suite), the raspberry-coloured boutique-style guesthouse next door on Pendre. Rooms cost £70-80/pp for two sharing or £45-55 for the single or single occupancy.

There are more affordable B&Bs along Gwbert Rd: *Brynhyfryd Guest House* (☎ 01239-612861; 2S/2T/3D) costs from £26 per person in a single room with a shared shower room, or £52 for a twin room with private bathroom or an en suite double; single occupancy of an en suite double is £37.50; and *Garth* (☎ 01239-613085, 🖳 joywakefield@live.co.uk; 1S/2T/2D/1F), which charges from £25/pp. One of the twins and a double share a bathroom but the other rooms are en suite. Both Brynhyfryd and Garth are about five minutes on foot from the town centre.

The *Black Lion* (☎ 01239-612532; 3S/5D/2T/2F, all en suite), on High St, charges £45 for a single, £65 for a double or twin, and £130-160 for a family room (one of which has four single beds).

On St Mary St, *Angel Hotel* (☎ 01239-612561; 1S/5D/2T, all en suite) charges £37.50/pp for B&B or £45/pp for dinner, bed and breakfast.

Where to eat and drink

Just before you cross the bridge to enter Cardigan you'll find *Fforest* (see Services; Mon-Sat 10am-5.30pm), which includes a great little café selling Fairtrade coffee, chocolate muffins, flapjacks and other snacks.

On the far side of the bridge, *Abdul's Tandoori Spice* (☎ 01239-621416; daily noon-2pm & 5-11.30pm) is hidden down Quay St by the river. This is an award-winning restaurant with very friendly waiters and a menu that takes a good half-hour to read. Book your table in advance because it is very small and the locals like it a lot. They do takeaway as well.

The *Black Lion* (see Where to stay; food served daily noon-2.30pm, Mon-Sat 6-9pm) has an extensive menu while *Angel Hotel* (see Where to stay; food served summer daily noon-2pm & 6.30-9pm, winter evenings only) has an extensive menu with daily specials; non-residents are welcome.

For something quick and easy there are a number of takeaway places and coffee shops along High St and Pendre; try *The Castle Café (Caffi'r Castell)* (☎ 01239-621882; daily 8.30am-4pm, Thur-Sat food served 7-10pm, open to midnight), on the corner with Quay St. In the evenings they often have live music or some form of entertainment.

The *Cardigan Arms* (☎ 01239-614969; daily 8am-8pm) is, despite its name, just a café though the menu's cheap and the portions large.

At the old theatre, which also houses the TIC (see p214), you will find *Theatr Mwldan Café* (Mon-Sat 10am-5pm). At the top of town on Pendre is *Food for Thought* (daily) which offers decent coffee and wholesome snacks. Also on Pendre is *Happy City Chinese* (Sun-Thur 5-10.30pm, Fri/Sat 5-11pm).

To let your hair down after the long walk the best place for a drink is the very Welsh *Red Lion* (☎ 01239-612482; Sun-Thur noon-midnight, Fri & Sat noon-2am), tucked behind Finch Sq. The friendly bar staff are only too happy to welcome strangers despite this being very much a locals' hangout. Be prepared for some strong Welsh singing once the beer starts flowing.

APPENDIX: GPS WAYPOINTS

Each GPS waypoint below was taken on the route at the reference number marked on the map as below. This list of GPS waypoints is also available to download from the Trailblazer website – 🖳 www.trailblazer-guides.com.

MAP REF	GPS WAYPOINTS	DESCRIPTION
1b	001	51°41.668' / 04°41.264'	Approach road to Amroth
1b	002	51°41.841' / 04°41.175'	Leave path after gate, join dirt track
2	003	51°43.446' / 04°41.052'	Wiseman's Bridge Inn
3	004	51°43.849' / 04°40.046'	After steps cross straight over 'crossroads'
3	005	51°43.976' / 04°39.300'	Radio mast
5	006	51°39.444' / 04°42.958'	Leave South Beach, walk through dunes
5	007	51°39.396' / 04°43.738'	Turn left off A4139 onto dirt track
5	008	51°39.173' / 04°44.035'	MoD firing range flag
6	009	51°38.824' / 04°45.985'	Junction: left to Manorbier, right Lydstep
6	010	51°38.583' / 04°46.541'	Steps (right/north-west) to Manorbier Youth Hostel
7	011	51°38.532' / 04°46.972'	Turn left (east) off road along high fence
7	012	51°38.479' / 04°47.262'	Turn left (south) past MoD building
8	013	51°38.615' / 04°49.074'	Take high path up steep ridge
9	014	51°38.880' / 04°51.399'	Turn right (north) for higher part of Freshwater East
10	015	51°37.463' / 04°54.084'	Stackpole Quay
11	016	51°37.150' / 04°54.237'	Bottom steps, access Barafundle Bay
11	017	51°37.018' / 04°54.256'	Leave Barafundle Bay, climb steps
11	018	51°36.705' / 04°54.047'	Blowhole on Stackpole Head
11	019	51°36.757' / 04°54.144'	Junction, shortcut across Stackpole Head and main path
11	020	51°36.776' / 04°54.254'	Continue straight on (west) ignoring alternative paths
11	021	51°36.786' / 04°54.510'	Gate above Raming Hole
11	022	51°36.696' / 04°54.878'	Junction by Big Hollow – shortcut across headland
11	023	51°36.594' / 04°55.142'	Junction before gate – shortcut rejoins main path
11/12	024	51°36.451' / 04°55.491'	National Trust Visitor Centre
12	025	51°36.271' / 04°55.433'	MoD firing range flag
12	026	51°35.954' / 04°56.235'	Car park above St Govan's Chapel
13	027	51°36.086' / 04°57.056'	Cross cattle grid and stile to join dirt track
13	028	51°36.317' / 04°57.564'	Go through gate, cross cattle grid, ignore paths left and right
14	029	51°36.717' / 04°59.842'	Car park above the Green Bridge of Wales
16	030	51°39.287' / 05°03.486'	Car park and access to Freshwater West
17	031	51°39.771' / 05°03.775'	Leave Freshwater West through dunes
19	032	51°41.175' / 05°06.379'	Car park above West Angle Bay
19	033	51°41.283' / 05°06.515'	Turn left (east) onto path before house
20	034	51°41.386' / 05°05.901'	Cross gate, join dirt track, continue east
20	035	51°41.375' / 05°05.685'	Leave dirt track, branch left into forest
20	036	51°41.302' / 05°04.701'	Cross dirt track above lifeboat station and rejoin path
20	037	51°41.038' / 05°05.259'	Angle, join road, head south-east
26	038	51°40.753' / 04°55.185'	Branch left, through stile, join track across field and leave Pembroke
25	039	51°40.970' / 04°55.795'	Stepping stones across stream
25/27	040	51°41.101' / 04°56.709'	Through gate, join road, climb to Pembroke Dock
28	041	51°42.983' / 04°56.723'	Turn left at end of bridge and pick up poorly marked path

MAP	REF	GPS WAYPOINTS	DESCRIPTION
28	042	51°42.693' / 04°56.672'	Leave path and join Cambrian Road
29	043	51°42.459' / 04°57.330'	Turn left (west) off Trafalgar Terrace to join Church Road
29	044	51°42.261' / 04°58.317'	Ferry House Inn – take steep lane behind pub
29	045	51°42.209' / 04°58.452'	Leave dirt track, cross gate and head south-west on path
29	046	51°42.138' / 04°59.751'	Gate after bridge over pipelines
30	047	51°42.159' / 05°00.203'	Gate – continue west across fields
30	048	51°42.331' / 05°00.400'	Gate – continue east across fields
30	049	51°42.618' / 05°00.420'	Venn Farm – turn right (north) up road
30	050	51°42.807' / 05°00.477'	Turn left (west) on B4325
31	051	51°42.928' / 05°01.283'	Turn left above boat yard onto Cellar Hill
32	052	51°42.660' / 05°03.217'	Leave Picton Road, join path west
32	053	51°42.445' / 05°04.649'	Go down steps onto beach to cross under pipeline
33	054	51°43.301' / 05°05.703'	Continue straight on – ignore path right beyond stile
33	055	51°43.560' / 05°05.422'	Turn left (north-east), cross stone steps over hedge
34	056	51°43.509' / 05°06.265'	Leave road to cross Sandy Haven Pill
34	057	51°43.511' / 05°06.532'	Turn left (south), off road and up steps
34	058	51°42.777' / 05°07.067'	Turn left (west) off dirt track beyond beacon
35	059	51°42.893' / 05°08.716'	Monk Haven – remain on coast path, ignore broader, better defined path going inland
36	060	51°42.955' / 05°09.511'	Join beach below Musselwick, turn left (north-west) and walk along stony beach
36	061	51°43.189' / 05°10.027'	Cross The Gann on wooden planks
37	062	51°42.214' / 05°09.277'	Dale Point
38	063	51°41.617' / 05°09.726'	Leave dirt track and join path west above Watwick Bay
38	064	51°40.918' / 05°10.486'	St Ann's Lighthouse
38	065	51°41.051' / 05° 10.587'	Leave road, cross gate and join path west
37	066	51°42.489' / 05°11.150'	Junction, above Westdale Bay, with shortcut to Dale avoiding peninsula
39	067	51°43.455' / 05°13.064'	Junction, path north inland to Marloes Sands YH
40	068	51°43.526' / 05°13.871'	Junction, path east inland to Marloes Sands YH
40	069	51°43.987' / 05°14.684'	Gate, join road, turn left (north) to Martin's Haven
41	070	51°44.115' / 05°12.512'	Junction, path inland to Marloes
42	071	51°45.248' / 05°11.120'	Car park and path onto St Brides Haven beach
43	072	51°46.021' / 05°09.940'	Old Lime Kiln above Mill Haven
44	073	51°46.062' / 05°07.126'	Gate, join road and turn left (east)
44	074	51°46.071' / 05°06.999'	Leave road (left), join track north-east
44	075	51°46.107' / 05°06.953'	Car park, path in north corner
47	076	51°48.298' / 05°06.163'	Leave tarmac, continue north on path
47	077	51°48.695' / 05°06.050'	After Druidstone/Roundhouse leave road, branching left (west) onto path
47	078	51°48.764' / 05°06.174'	Junction, turn left (north-west) up steps over steep sand dune
47	079	51°49.472' / 05°06.386'	Join road by Nolton Chapel
47	080	51°49.499' / 05°06.472'	Car park above Davy Williams' Haven
48	081	51°50.688' / 05°07.012'	Take steps (right) up to road or drop down left to Newgale Beach

MAP	REF	GPS WAYPOINTS	DESCRIPTION
49	082	51°51.518' / 05°07.632'	At hairpin bend branch left (north-west) onto steep path
49	083	51°51.885' / 05°09.466'	Ignore broad path right (north) and cross small bridge ahead
50	084	51°51.870' / 05°10.581'	Junction – left (south-west) detour to Dinas Fawr headland
50	085	51°52.323' / 05°11.717'	End of quay, join path
50	086	51°52.332' / 05°11.851'	White house with turret – go through driveway and join path
51	087	51°52.453' / 05°13.029'	Junction – right (north-east) to Nine Wells Campsite
51	088	51°52.452' / 05°14.695'	Cross dirt track above Caerbwdi Bay
53	089	51°52.232' / 05°16.993'	Bridge over stream entering Porthclais
53	090	51°52.182' / 05°16.951'	Junction – take high path (right/south)
53	091	51°51.981' / 05°17.846'	Junction – take right (north) to Pen-cnwc Campsite
53	092	51°51.861' / 05°18.325'	Junction after Lower Treginnis – take left (south-west)
54	093	51°52.733' / 05°18.500'	St Justinian's lifeboat station
54	094	51°53.156' / 05° 18.252'	Junction – take right (south-east) for road to St David's
55	095	51°53.538' / 05°17.740'	Join dirt track briefly – continue north above Whitesands Bay
56	096	51°54.656' / 05°17.621'	Junction – turn right (south-east) to St David's YH
57	097	51°55.018' / 05°15.124'	Junction – right (south-east) to climb Carn Penberry
58	098	51°55.777' / 05°13.515'	Junction – both paths descend to river
58	099	51°55.781' / 05°13.390'	Junction – right (south) for Celtic Camping
58	100	51°56.007' / 05°12.413'	Join road, turn left (north) to Abereiddy
58	101	51°56.242' / 05°12.415'	Junction – left (west) to Blue Lagoon
59	102	51°56.917' / 05°10.899'	Porthgain harbour
60	103	51°56.847' / 05°09.329'	Join road, turn left (east)
60	104	51°56.886' / 05°09.140'	Leave road, turn left (north) onto concrete path
60	105	51°56.943' / 05°08.761'	Trefin – take road heading north for easiest access to coast path
60	106	51°57.151' / 05°09.213'	Junction – right (south-east) to Trefin
61	107	51°57.656' / 05°07.884'	Junction – right (south) to Carreg Sampson
61	108	51°57.608' / 05°07.580'	Climb steps above Abercastle
62	109	51°58.040' / 05°05.152'	Junction – head left (north) around lime kiln
62	110	51°58.345' / 05°04.783'	Leave road, take path left (north-west)
62	111	51°58.448' / 05°04.895'	Leave beach at Aber-Bach, climb 5m then take left (north) fork in path
63	112	52°00.276' / 05°04.188'	Join road, turn left (north) to Pwll Deri YH
63	113	52°00.443' / 05°04.335'	Leave road, join path west
64	114	52°01.735' / 05°04.226'	Car park by Strumble Head Lighthouse
64	115	52°01.804' / 05°04.001'	At hairpin leave road and join path east
64	116	52°01.496' / 05°03.274'	Junction – right (south-west) to Fferm Tresinwen Camping
65	117	52°01.410' / 05°01.439'	Carreg Wastad Point
65	118	52°01.359' / 05°01.485'	Cross stile take left path (south-west) ignoring other trails
65	119	52°01.251' / 05°01.441'	Junction – left (north-east) on coast path, right (south-east) shortcut to Goodwick
66	120	52°01.170' / 04°59.523'	Junction – take left (south) for coast path

MAP	REF	GPS WAYPOINTS	DESCRIPTION
66	121	52°00.837' / 04°59.345'	Beacon above Goodwick
67	122	52°00.484' / 04°59.553'	Leave road, turn left (east) through gap in stone wall onto dirt path
68	123	51°59.941' / 04°59.290'	Before hairpin take steps on left (east)
68	124	51°59.918' / 04°58.196'	Leave road and join path to Castle Point (north)
69	125	52°00.365' / 04°56.391'	Fishguard Bay Caravan and Campsite, turn left (north-east) for coast path
69	126	52°00.509' / 04°55.272'	Join road, turn left (east), leave road at hairpin 80m later
70	127	52°01.313' / 04°54.557'	Junction by Old Sailors Restaurant for shortcut avoiding Dinas Head (right)
70	128	52°01.972' / 04°54.538'	Pen y Fan trig point
70	129	52°01.899' / 04°54.080'	Junction – take lower, left path (easterly)
70	130	52°01.417' / 04°53.271'	Cwm-yr-Eglwys and junction with shortcut avoiding Dinas Head
71	131	52°01.300' / 04°53.469'	Leave road, left (east) and join path
71	132	52°01.124' / 04°52.737'	Join dirt track briefly on hairpin, leave at stile and climb steps
71	133	52°01.331' / 04°51.062'	Junction at boathouse – right (south-west) to Tycanol Campsite
72	134	52°01.203' / 04°50.393'	Leave road left (north-east) and join dirt track
72	135	52°01.248' / 04°49.463'	Leave road after bridge over Afon Nyfer and join dirt track left (west)
73	136	52°01.756' / 04°50.239'	Cap park Newport Sands, take path north
74	137	52°03.308' / 04°48.389'	Stepping stones across stream
75	138	52°04.217' / 04°46.355'	Junction – take left (north-east) for coast path
75	139	52°04.638' / 04°45.850'	Join road briefly, turn left (east) towards Ceibwr Bay
76	140	52°04.566' / 04°45.535'	Leave dirt track and branch left (north) for bridge over stream at Ceibwr Bay
78	141	52°06.264' / 04°41.964'	RNLI at Poppit Sands
79	142	52°05.351' / 04°40.935'	Slate marker at St Dogmaels marking end of coast path
80	143	52°04.838' / 04°39.651'	Bridge over Afon Teifi, separating Pembrokeshire and Ceredigion

INDEX

TRAILBLAZER GUIDES – TITLE LIST

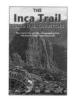

www.trailblazer-guides.com

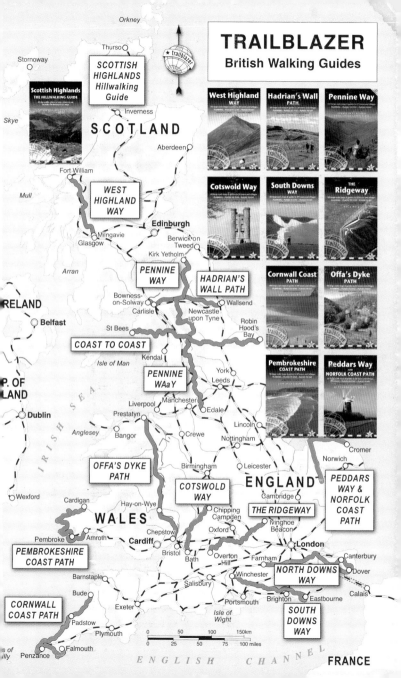

TRAILBLAZER
British Walking Guides

Orkney

Thurso

SCOTTISH HIGHLANDS Hillwalking Guide

Scottish Highlands
THE HILLWALKING GUIDE

Stornoway

Skye

Inverness

SCOTLAND

Aberdeen

Fort William

Mull

WEST HIGHLAND WAY

Milngavie
Glasgow
Edinburgh
Berwick-on-Tweed
Kirk Yetholm

Arran

PENNINE WAY

HADRIAN'S WALL PATH

Bowness-on-Solway
Carlisle
Wallsend
Newcastle upon Tyne

RELAND

Belfast

St Bees

COAST TO COAST

Robin Hood's Bay

Kendal

P. OF LAND

Isle of Man

PENNINE WAaY

York
Leeds

Dublin

Liverpool
Manchester
Prestatyn
Edale

Anglesey

Bangor
Crewe
Lincoln

Nottingham

Cromer

Norwich

OFFA'S DYKE PATH

Birmingham
Leicester

ENGLAND

Cambridge

PEDDARS WAY & NORFOLK COAST PATH

Wexford

Cardigan

COTSWOLD WAY

Hay-on-Wye
Chipping Campden

THE RIDGEWAY

WALES

Chepstow
Oxford
Ivinghoe Beacon

Pembroke
Amroth
Cardiff
Bristol
Bath

London

PEMBROKESHIRE COAST PATH

Barnstaple
Overton Hill
Farnham
Canterbury

Bude
Salisbury
Winchester

NORTH DOWNS WAY

Dover
Calais

CORNWALL COAST PATH

Exeter
Portsmouth
Brighton
Eastbourne

Padstow
Isle of Wight

SOUTH DOWNS WAY

s of illy
Penzance
Falmouth
Plymouth

West Highland WAY

Hadrian's Wall PATH

Pennine Way

Cotswold Way

South Downs WAY

THE Ridgeway

Cornwall Coast PATH

Offa's Dyke PATH

Pembrokeshire COAST PATH

Peddars Way and NORFOLK COAST PATH

| 0 | 50 | 100 | 150km |
| 0 | 25 | 50 | 75 | 100 miles |

ENGLISH CHANNEL

FRANCE

Pembrokeshire Coast Path   AMROTH – CARDIGAN